Claiming Identity in the Study of Religion

Culture on the Edge
Series Editor: Steven W. Ramey, University of Alabama

Culture on the Edge is devoted to studies – both monographs and collections of essays – that explore how social formation involves a series of strategies that present identity as static and uniform. Volumes in this series study identity formation as a series of interconnected historical practices, revealing ways that the image of stable selves and groups conceals the precarious and shifting nature of cultures.

Forthcoming:
Codes of Conduct: Code Switching and the Everyday Performance of Identity
Edited by K. Merinda Simmons and Monica R. Miller

The Problem of Nostalgia in the Study of Identity: Towards a Dynamic Theory of People and Place
Edited by Vaia Touna

Claiming Identity in the Study of Religion

Social and Rhetorical Techniques Examined

Edited by
Monica R. Miller

eQuinox

SHEFFIELD UK   BRISTOL CT

Published by Equinox Publishing Ltd.

UK: Office 415, The Workstation, 15 Paternoster Row, Sheffield,
        South Yorkshire S1 2BX
USA: ISD, 70 Enterprise Drive, Bristol, CT 06010

www.equinoxpub.com

First published 2015

British Library Cataloguing-in-Publication Data
A catalogue record for this book is available from the British Library.

ISBN-13 978 1 78179 071 7 (hardback)
        978 1 78179 074 8 (paperback)

Library of Congress Cataloging-in-Publication Data
Claiming identity in the study of religion: social and rhetorical
techniques examined / edited by Monica R. Miller.
    pages cm. – (Culture on the edge)
Includes bibliographical references and index.
ISBN 978-1-78179-071-7 (hb) – ISBN 978-1-78179-074-8 (pb)
1. Identification (Religion) 2. Identity (Psychology)–Religious aspects.
I. Miller, Monica R., 1981-editor.
BL53.C56 2015
200.7–dc23
                    2015010618

Typeset by S.J.I. Services, New Delhi
Printed and bound by Lightning Source Inc. (La Vergne, TN), Lightning
Source UK Ltd. (Milton Keynes), Lightning Source AU Pty. (Scoresby,
Victoria)

Contents

    The Serpent's Gift   97
    Russell T. McCutcheon

Topic IV: Costs of Conceptual Colonialism

7. Conceptual Colonialism: How Descriptions Carry
    Explanations   118
    Craig Martin

8. "It's a Lie. There's No Truth in It! It's a Sin!": The
    Costs of Saving Others from Themselves   124
    Russell T. McCutcheon

Topic V: Cost-Benefit Analysis

9. Authorizing Identifications, Disciplining Techniques:
    The Affinities of Public Advocacy   162
    Steven W. Ramey

10. Affinities, Benefits, and Costs: The ABCs of Good
    Scholars Gone Public   169
    Russell T. McCutcheon

Topic VI: Limiting Engagements

11. What's New Is Old Again: The Αναπαλαίωση of Tradition   191
    Vaia Touna

12. The Resiliency of Conceptual Anachronisms: On the
    Limits of "the West" and "Religion"   200
    Russell T. McCutcheon

    Afterword
    Accidental Favorites: The Implicit in the Study of
    Religion   223
    Steven W. Ramey

    Index   239

Acknowledgments

I am deeply grateful *to* and *for* the scholarly community and scintillating intellectual energy of the Culture on the Edge international collaborative. This project would not be possible without their collective efforts. In particular, I'm indebted to the formative role that Russell T. McCutcheon has played in the initial evolution of this group, and for the ways he continues to push and refine my own thinking and scholarly trajectory around topics involving identity and identification – especially in the academic study of religion.

All of my thanks to Equinox Press for housing the *Culture on the Edge* book series giving life to this volume, as well as the press's continued commitment to publishing thought-provoking and boundary-pressing scholarship in the academic study of religion. A debt of gratitude is owed to Janet Joyce and Valerie Hall at Equinox Press for their sustained attention to and continuous support of every dimension of this project. Their enthusiasm and conscientious diligence throughout the process contributed much to the advancement and completion of this book.

Much appreciation to the presses that provided permission to reprint McCutcheon's articles in this project and again to Russell for allowing us to use this collection of work as data for the identification of and further engagement with social and rhetorical techniques that often make certain claims to identity possible.

To everyone involved in the project on the publishing end, your support and energy has made this project enjoyable. My deepest thanks to Christopher M. Driscoll for reading and providing feedback on various iterations of the Introduction and my own chapter in this volume – your sharp and always well-considered insight continues to challenge me to think in new ways.

Finally, I am greatly indebted to my colleagues at Lehigh University in Religion Studies and Africana Studies, for providing space, resources, and collegial support as this project unfolded. I hope that *Claiming Identity in the Study of Religion* contributes to critical and *edgy* conversations, much needed, in the academic study of religion today.

Sources

Topic I: Claiming Identity

McCutcheon, Russell T. 2010. "Will Your Cognitive Anchor Hold in the Storms of Culture?" *Journal of the American Academy of Religion* 78(4): 1182–93. Reprinted by permission of Oxford University Press.

Topic II: Behind the "Ahistorical"

McCutcheon, Russell T. 1993. "The Melancholy Empire Builder: The Life and Works of Mircea Eliade," a revised version of the essay published under the title "The Myth of the Apolitical Scholar: The Life and Works of Mircea Eliade," *Queen's Quarterly* 100(3): 642–63. Reprinted by permission of Queen's University, Kingston, Ontario.

Topic III: Theoretical and Methodological Cake

McCutcheon, Russell T. 2008. "A Gift with Diminished Returns: On Jeff Kripal's *The Serpent's Gift*," a revised version of the essay published under the title "A Gift With Diminished Returns: Review Essay," *Journal of the American Academy of Religion* 76(3): 748–65. Reprinted by permission of Oxford University Press.

Topic IV: Costs of Conceptual Colonialism

McCutcheon, Russell T. 2006. "'It's a Lie. There's No Truth in It! It's a Sin!': The Costs of Saving Others from Themselves," a revised version of the essay published under the title "'It's a Lie. There's No Truth in It! It's a Sin!': On the Limits of the Humanistic Study of Religion and the Costs of Saving Others from Themselves," *Journal of the American Academy of Religion* 74(3): 720–50. Reprinted by permission of Oxford University Press.

Topic V: Cost-Benefit Analysis
McCutcheon, Russell T. 2005. "Affinities, Benefits, and Costs: The ABCs of Good Scholars Gone Public," *Method & Theory in The Study of Religion* 17(1): 27–43. Reprinted by permission of Brill.

Topic VI: Limiting Engagements
McCutcheon, Russell T. 2006. "The Resiliency of Conceptual Anachronisms: On the Limits of 'the West' and 'Religion,'" *Religion* 36(3): 154–65. Reprinted by permission of Taylor & Francis.

Introduction

Culture, Religion, and the Fabrication of Identities

Monica R. Miller

> It is a common error to attribute this irreducibility of difference
> to the influence of "culture," or more precisely to the exclu-
> sive relationship each individual is supposed to have with "his"
> culture. – Jean-François Bayart (2005: 9)

The above epigraph taken from social theorist Jean-François Bayart's
The Illusion of Cultural Identity (2005) poignantly illuminates a common thought-structure regarding the manner in which categories such
as "culture," or here we might even add "religion," have often been
treated, approached, and theorized as concrete entities, *real* concepts,
and self-evident constructs that alone are often thought to signify and
illumine material experiences and tangible things.

Within the study of religion, there is a certain sort of academic
"culture" of attributing the irreducibility of difference to the influence
and meaning of "religion" as a separate and stand-alone entity unto
itself – often assumedly divorced from identity and cultural affinity. Theorist Russell T. McCutcheon (and others) have responded to
this tendency within the field to cast religion/the sacred/etc. as sui
generis – that is, of its own sort, irreducible, through careful criticisms meant to dislodge the social and political weight of what we
call religion from the academic study of religion. The jury remains
out on how many, and to what degree, such "caretaking" postures
will move towards critical perspectives (McCutcheon 2001; 2003).
Even among many who work to correct for this caretaking, another
kind of caretaking has emerged couched often in cultural terms. This

volume addresses the ongoing concern for the development of a critical and analytical posture for the study of religion, as much as it presses forward with an effort to outline – through example – ongoing challenges and possibilities for the implementation of such a critical methodology through exploration of social and rhetorical techniques widely used in the field today in particular and broader publics more generally. An example of the complexity associated with such a task is in order.

A "Culture" of Influence in Religious Studies: Or, Studying the Influence of Culture

Penumala Pratap Kumar's *Methods and Theories in the Study of Religions: Perspectives from the Study of Hinduism and Other Indian Religions* (2005) sets about to offer a text attentive to the cultural specificity and social insularity of "Indian" and "Hindu" cultural forms treated by scholars of religion as religions, historically. The author's goal involves offering a text that will prove foundational for the cultivation of an "Indian" religious studies discourse, relatively free from the colonial trappings of religious studies discourses dominant in the West. Kumar's text is emblematic of many scholars of religion who, on the one hand, have begun to wrestle with critical perspectives for religious studies, but on the other hand, remain indebted to a paradigm that responds to the irreducibility of difference through various appeals to "culture." Worth quoting and analyzing in succession, Kumar writes:

> Just as we go into a supermarket and find items classified on the shelves according to similarities in properties (e.g., milk products, meat, hardware, books, stationery, and so on), there are concepts that social scientists and historians use to classify data that are considered religious as opposed to non-religious or secular data. Of course, what exactly is religious or not may differ from society to society or culture to culture (2005: x).

Here, immediately a binary stands out. In the first instance, a critical position on those things called religions or religious casts them as arbitrary, categories of like kind, etc. Such a shift and focus on categories of difference is helpful, as much critical scholarship has suggested. Then, Kumar grounds such a relative appraisal with a norm undergirded by society or culture, as in: these things are different precisely because differences exist from "culture to culture." Is not "culture" and are not "cultures" equally arbitrarily constituted? Kumar follows up with:

> That is why, J.Z. Smith talks about religion as scholar's imaginative construct rather than a concrete social or material object. Religion, therefore, is an object of scholar's imagination, and as an analytical concept it depends on what data is incorporated into it. What is incorporated into it depends on the religious tradition/s or cultures that are included in that data (2005: x).

Again, a binary emerges where a critical shift is met with a kind of doubling down on a sui generis assumption that every culture is somehow distinct and of its own type – even though those things called "religions" and/or "religious" are understood as contingent, arbitrary and of the scholar's imagination. But what of our cultural imagination? Are not traditions and "culture" just as relative as the seemingly "religious" data superficially emerging from them?

Pressing home the focus of his text in tandem with its theoretical orientation, Kumar concludes that "All of these acts of classification has a specific western colonial agenda and hence had social and political implications in such classifications...in this book, I make some effort to mainly bring a local perspective from Hinduism and other Indian religions' point of view" (2005: xii). Of course, Kumar is indeed correct to suggest and remind readers of the Western and Eurocentric treatment of religious classifications historically. To wit, underscoring such connections is and remains important work from (and for) any critical perspective. But correcting for one historically assumed connection between culture and religion by recasting such connections in an assumed distinct and understudied cultural context, a "local perspective," runs the risk of reinforcing the very sorts of arrangements absconded from.

Kumar is not alone in this tendency, that perhaps could be thought of as a kind of "have your cake and eat it, too" critical position, critical caretaking as it were. In the field of religious studies, even in expanding to new geographies and topographies of method and theory in useful ways, there remains an often tacit connection between escape from the sui generis and reliance on cultural affinity. What often results is a doubling down on a sui generis thought structure and academic classificatory arrangement through an appeal to "culture." This tendency amounts to shifting from one sort of irreducibility to another. Scholars concerned that they do not call religion its own thing still run the risk of reinforcing this similar position through a turn to cultural experience or identity – seemingly distinct in their own right, though not so distinct when distinction-making propensities are taken into account.

Bayart demonstrates how ideas such as "identity," "culture," and "community" for example are *not* timeless and trans-historical, but, rather, arbitrary, sometimes ambiguous, and in the last instance, manufactured from a certain kind of *social imaginaire* (2005). This *imaginaire* is witnessed in Kumar's reliance on something distinctively "Hindu" or "Indian" that will *surely* shape religious studies scholarship if only given the chance. Such reframing is politically understandable, but analytically questionable as it results in and ultimately produces a fabrication of identities in which politics, among all cultures, manipulate and signify upon for social interests, means and ends. Following Bayart, this volume seeks to give attention to various strategies of identification rather than a simple shift in *identity* (e.g., from Western to Eastern). These strategies of identification are always, at once, universal *and* local, trans-historical *and* historically contingent. Participation within and among sectors of society feed off the economy of symbolic practices – that is, feelings, moods, motivations, and experiences don't precede such involvement; rather, involvement within the *social* and political *imaginaire* produce cultural meanings, establish and ascribe value to signs, etc., among social actors within such a system. Bayart offers a compelling and provocative take on the interpretation and transposition of arbitrary – and, most often, ambivalent – imaginative practices among social actors. From one context and recasting to another, Bayart theoretically demonstrates the manner in which emergent cultural and symbolic productions come to be.

Reified notions of culture – what Bayart refers to as *culturalism* (2005) – are often at the root of systems of violence and war, for example, as well as the icons and indices used to chart violence and the meanings attached to violence. Take for instance an image of a person wearing a cross around their neck – first-order interpretation might suggest that such a social actor is expressing or paying homage to his or her beliefs or ascribed religiosity. However, a second-order approach might suggest that such cross wearing and bearing might in fact *signify* something wholly different – such as making a fashion statement or wearing an heirloom passed down from a family member in tribute to family or a lover, rather than God or creed. For another weighty example, take the Nazi Swastika. In the wake of a series of deeply troubling historical circumstances, that sign became (and currently stands as) a symbol for hatred in much of the world. In yet other social and cultural places and times, the same (or similar) sign carries a very different valence, with very distinct symbolic meaning (if any). Culturalism gives such icons fixed, rigid meanings. But how do such meanings take shape, exactly? And, more important still, how might scholars begin to respond to such rigidity?

Bayart offers insight. He advocates for a social scientific study of the above described *social imaginaire* wherein he begins from the assumption that culture – like religion – does not contain within it an essence, a core, a unified identity or culture unto itself that unfolds or logically precedes a cohesive political identity. Rather, identities, such as the political or religious, are constructs bound within and among history itself. What come to be known and named as cultural representations (e.g., "Hindu") are more often than not used for all sorts of strategic political purposes, manipulations, and the reification of *difference*. When scholars double down on the distinctiveness of their data or the cultural or social hermeneutics they use to interpret and analyze data, they're making a political gesture rooted in a demand for distinctiveness and protection (of one type or another). This propensity and, to push the religious studies example as well as the academic interest in classification, such a reliance on culture are emblematic of what might be called (with intentional clumsiness) *sui generis-ness*.

As the formative work of the great mythologist Roland Barthes has so aptly demonstrated, the metalanguage of *myth* is often turned into a self-evident language about *itself* to the extent that the constellation of signs, often turned into and constituted as signifiers (images), becomes masked thus occluding analyses of the processes involved in such constitutions, as such (1972). Like those approaching culture and society from culturalist perspectives and interpretations, Barthes attempted to rescue myth from being understood as natural, fixed, unconditional, and timeless by placing such discourse within the economy of language and the contingency of history. Barthes was not as much interested in *substituting* myth as he was keen on deconstructing and demystifying it and the assumed cultural knowledge needed for such understanding. Following the efforts of Barthes as much as the theoretical insights of Bayart, this volume works to confront a rather rigid, not often examined presumption about culture within the field of religious studies.

Whether operative in societies or academic discourses, the *imaginaire* comes to inhabit and then strategically produce the *illusion* of *shared* culture, community, meaning, and experiences that become projected onto and treated as tangible and palpable realities. For instance, take a suspected criminal on trial who is cross-examined in a way that strategically attempts to *identify* that such a crime stemmed from some kind of interiorized and natural (read: biological) proclivity for crime and violence. "The accused is a gangster, a thug." Thought of in this way, criminality or deviance, as such, becomes deployed and treated as an *essence*, a dormant virus of sorts residing within a social actor, awaiting activation; thus, making "crime" appear to be rooted in human nature, some sort of Augustinian state of fallenness or sin. Or, supposing the reverse, the defense of a suspected criminal can take shape as an apologia that says the person in question has just simply gone astray: "Billy was really a good kid, even on the honor roll." Either way, *contingency* and *context* are often ignored and omitted from such descriptions and accounts. Like these examples, a certain type of "natural reason" has guided much of what constitutes the academic study of religion where an *alibi* of non-contingent essences has come to serve as proxy for the study of signification, presence, moods, motivations, experiences, and feelings. Such things in the field are quite often treated in self-evident and a priori ways. We know though, as Barthes so eloquently argued, "language is never innocent" (1977). The economy of myth – culture, identity, religion and so on – and the context of its emergence is quite often hidden from purview through social and rhetorical techniques that help to maintain and camouflage the processes of its production. Indeed, think for a moment of the difficulty one might find at an attempt to dislodge the swastika from its historical Nazi appropriation so that it might be worn as a crucifix around the necks of fashion-forward Westerners. Can we even *imagine* such a possibility today, or ever? Take for instance claims to experiences that are linguistically "indescribable," or the assumption that something is (intellectually) "deep" because one repetitively says it is so, or how something like globalization is treated as a naturally occurring phenomenon rather than the political strategy that it in fact is.

The study of the processes and practices that come to constitute the *imaginaire* of such manufacturing necessitate a methodological turn towards the *constitution* of social actors and their symbolic constructions rather than studying the imaginary construction of the symbolic activity itself. Necessitated is a shift in theoretical as well as methodological posture. Such a shift does not suggest that any particular data set (chosen by a scholar) is "right" or "wrong," but that there might just be more (and less) useful ways of approaching, handling, bracketing, and analyzing data. Hence, in this volume, we turn to what thinkers such as Bayart and Judith Butler, among others, refer to as *subjectivation* – the *production* of subjectivities and the strategies of identification they produce – in a number of attempts to hold together meanings and signification of problems that are anything but new. Our volume applies this methodological approach across a number of seemingly distinct data sets and domains of inquiry, flattening the impact of "identities" in order to foreground such cultural, social, and even academic "identities" as constructed constellations of "operational acts of identification" made possible through and by a host of strategic manipulations.

The Logic and Performance behind *Identification*: What We Identify When We *Identify*

In further outlining the parameters of culturalism in practice, Bayart notes that "we identify ourselves less with respect to membership in a community or a culture than with respect to the communities and cultures with which we have relations" (2005: 95). It is a commonly assumed and tightly held supposition that what we as social actors find of use, of interest, meaningful, and so on, somehow emerges from within, and over and against *membership* in a specific community of belonging and orientation, rather than from those spaces by which we as subjects have durable associations and links – those spaces by which we're able to procure recognition and various forms of capital – those things that assist in conferring and bestowing status and value. For instance, it might be as likely that scholars picking up Kumar's book will assume his membership as "Indian" or "Hindu" for various reasons, as much as he might also assume the merit of his thesis – that is, why his text matters – as having something to do with similar memberships (whether or not he counts himself amongst those ranks). But wouldn't such assumptions ignore the complexity of the relations held between Kumar and "Western" readers/thinkers, and the intensely porous and yet politically palpable relations through which he or his book finds footing or capital, broadly defined?

Pierre Bourdieu's social theory and his employment of ideas such as habitus, taste, doxa, capital, and practice are helpful in analyzing and understanding how affinities towards a religious group or an approach to defining religion, for example, create a powerful illusion of cohesion and identity while often obscuring the very operational acts and "invisible" dimensions that fuel our tastes, preferences, interests, and proclivities (1992). Demonstrating this illusion of cohesiveness, Kumar's *Methods and Theories in the Study of Religions* does not elaborate a distinctly "Hindu" religious studies approach, but uses distinctions in the crafting of relations meant to bring about such a specific approach or community of approach. What is exposed through an application of Bayart's shift in orientation is that such projects (as religious studies texts, etc.) have something to do with identity. These texts don't so much exemplify cultural (and especially not "religious") identities, but function to hide a tacit awareness that, in fact, "there is no such thing as identity, only operational acts of identification."

Bayart is not alone in his suggestion. Here, we turn to the historic and groundbreaking work of Butler who in texts such as *Gender Trouble* (1990) and *Bodies That Matter* (1993) helped to expose the manner in which identities, those principally sexed and gendered in particular, are simultaneously created and subverted. Rather than beginning from the presupposition of identity as self-evident, Butler vociferously argued for categories such as sex and gender to be viewed and understood as neither disinterested nor neutral, nor a constitutive part of human identity. Having her finger on something much more complex, Butler established such domains as surfaces upon which culture acts. Much like identity, there is no preexisting "thing" that precedes that which is being *identified*. Instead, that "thing" (often assumed as ultimately *there*) becomes produced in and through a variety of techniques and operational acts through the stratagem of the performative. On this point, she writes, "There is no gender identity behind the expressions of gender" but rather, "identity is performatively constituted by the very 'expressions' that are said to be its results" (Butler 1990: 25). Here, we can see how "identifying" something *as* male or female, Hindu or Western, religious or irreligious, and so on doesn't as much point towards what *is* and *isn't*. Such "operational acts" and performativities say something about the identifiers' own social interests in classifying certain things and social arrangements in particular sorts of ways. For if that thing we call identity is constituted in and through the performative, then attention towards citational acts of rhetoric and naming become all the more important. Are not "rituals," for example, as much as articles, textbooks, symposia, etc., nothing more than performances that are highly repeated as well as regulated?

What gets named when we refer to something *as* religion, or race/ethnicity, or gender and sexuality? More often than not we scholars often get sucked in by and hyper-focused on the "object" we assume we're studying – as if the object is *real*, and *there*, and ripe for analyses, interrogation, and debate. This tendency unfolds as much amongst scholars blind to Eurocentric or colonial cultural infiltrations of discourse and politics as among those fed up with such infiltrations who respond through attempts to establish "Hindu" discourses of religious studies (Kumar 2005) or who constitute "religion" as the purview of a distinctly "Western" cultural imagination (Dubuisson 2003). We know all too well from the work of Ferdinand de Saussure among a host of others that the very thing we call "signs" are not "things" of their own making (Saussure et al. 1983). Rather, such words and forms, etc. rely upon the arbitrary and relational aspects of the very parts (signifier + signified) that make signs legible. A stop sign, for instance, has no intrinsic quality out of which we know that the sign is telling us to "STOP!" Indeed, social agreement is necessary to wed the arbitrary colors and patterns of a stop sign to the sense we have that the sign is *telling* us to stop. Similarly, and for a more focused example of such a process, something like a "black" identity is an arbitrary designation. No one person or group of people is in fact *designated* by the very term. Cultural agreeability – witnessed and exemplified in the "culturalism" denoted by Bayart – allows for a masking and concealing of the competing interests and consensus-building that ultimately determine what such a term will come to signify and be represented by. What's more, if signs are indeed as arbitrary as we're suggesting, and contingent upon the relationality between a signified and signifier, then above all, the domain of meaning, of signification, is ultimately predicated on *difference* as such – on the very oppositions that make something like meaning possible. That is, a stop sign relies not only on an understanding of stopping, but of starting or going. Difference (going) undergirds the sameness (stopping) imposed onto a stop sign. Again in like manner, the arbitrariness of a "black" identity (or any other identity) is undergirded and in a sense "hidden" through its opposite, "white" or "non-black," "Hindu" or "Western/Non-Hindu."

Culture, more generally, functions in a similar capacity. Cultural affinities as well as the treating of cultures as distinct are imaginatively made possible by a "culture" sign (e.g., a stop sign; or "Hindu"), the cultural *imaginaire*. Such acts of identification involve the marking of certain relationships of proximity and distinction, making possible the presumption of a certain sort of *cultural* meaning and *meaning for* the idea of culture. This tendency to turn to culture in response to "religion," or "identity" more generally, seems to be an expression of the "common error" of attributing the irreducibility of difference to the influence of "culture." This volume wrestles with this tendency and tries to chart out a schema of critical response so that it might be offset or at least acknowledged.

The Book You Hold: *Identifying* Social and Rhetorical Techniques, *Capitalizing* on Identification

As with any text, "operational acts of identification" help to constitute the book you hold. Its "identity" emerges from Culture on the Edge, "an international collaborative research group interrogating the contradiction between the historicity of identity, which is always fluid over place and time, and common scholarly assertions of a static and ahistorical origin for an identity community (whether religious, national, ethnic, etc.) against which cultural change can be measured."[1] Members of the collective are trained in a wide range of fields, methods, and disciplines ranging from philosophy to literature, anthropology, and religious studies, along with a variety of perspectives on identity among a host of specialties in area studies. In this sense, readers are encouraged to take as a model Culture on the Edge's disciplinary heterogeneity along with its instances of methodological and theoretical homogeneity for application in a wide array of academic fields.

Through dialogue and collaboration, members of Culture on the Edge came to envision a volume that would talk back to itself, in a sense, engaging past essays and attempts at a critical methodology with shorter commentaries applying the theoretical and methodological moves made in the essays towards or in a new avenue of inquiry, data set, or intellectual domain. The result of their efforts you hold now, as a series of essays and corresponding vignettes meant to demonstrate the methodological applicability of a critical perspective on the field of religion studies in particular, and studies in social and cultural identity across fields.

[1] http://edge.ua.edu/ (accessed July 30, 2014).

We have brought together six previously published essays by scholar of religion Russell T. McCutcheon, and wed them to shorter original introductions that demonstrate the applicability of the methodological nuances employed by McCutcheon across an assortment of topics which work to not simply outline what is happening in the McCutcheon pieces but more importantly identify social and rhetorical techniques at work in claiming identities across disparate sets of data. The goal of the volume is to present and test the methodological applicability of a critical perspective on various domains of data, including itself. The results come together in a way that simultaneously speaks to the challenges of such methodological applicability while outlining the features of such an approach in ways that theoretically mark this work as one possible model – the book's "identity" emerging as a kind of highbrow "how-to" manual for scholars interested in polishing and focusing with a critical lens their treatment of topics related to cultural and disciplinary identity, both within and outside of the academic study of religion.

For context, McCutcheon has spent the majority of his career, thus far, dislodging and untethering the category of religion from a sui generis fixed, trans-historical, universal object towards a realization that what comes to be identified and understood *as* religion doesn't as much define the thing unto itself, but rather, points towards and is indicative of larger processes of social, cultural, historical, and political interests, situations, and circumstances. Following in the historical trajectory of thinkers such as Jonathan Z. Smith and Bruce Lincoln to name two, McCutcheon's work throughout the years has not only provided a new and more critical way to understand and theorize religion, but has, in many ways, demythologized the manner in which the field has come to be articulated and seen – providing new language and a new approach for examining the social formations and processes that make talk of religion possible. His work has come to represent and demonstrate for scholars that it is indeed possible to study this thing we call religion in a way that need not replicate worn-out conceptions of the past, but rather, examine more acutely what is named, classified, and identified when something is called "religion." What's more, McCutcheon's scholarship has provided invaluable resources wherein the analyst can more acutely see that social interests, curiosities, and political management are never disconnected from what comes to be called religion (or not) – that claims to identity are always at stake (e.g., the sacred vs the profane).

Each of McCutcheon's essays is introduced in an essay written by a different member of Culture on the Edge on the topic, beginning with discrete rhetorical strategies and social techniques of identification that often make possible claims to and for identity as something stable and identifiable. In the introductory essays, readers won't as much encounter an urge or impulse to "identify" the "what is *really* going on" in the McCutcheon essays as much as they will meet up with scholars who, in a variety of ways, are attempting to *identify* what types of strategies make certain identities, positionalities, arguments, opinions, and affinities possible, certain, and stable. These contributions highlight the *how* of how such identifying works – sometimes it takes shape under talk of authenticity, or exclusivity; at other times, human interests and curiosities become obscured within and under discourse of sacred, profane, properness, and so on. In this sense, one will encounter, strongly, a deconstructive bent and logic of practice invested in disassembling, breaking apart, so that the parts can be understood in relation to the making and manufacturing of the whole by showing how similar strategies of identification are at work in the everyday mundane world around us. As such, the introductions don't as much offer or rehash "the point" or "main theme" of the larger essay under review, but rather, discursively perform *identification* at work by *identifying* and thus breaking down the assumed coherence and stability within systems of thought that are otherwise assumed to be truth, certainty, and meaning – in a self-evident sort of way. The introductions only mildly introduce or explain the essays under study and instead draw the reader's attention to social techniques unearthed by McCutcheon's critical approach. They use a variety of data to highlight the function of such practices and rhetorical strategies of identity, and apply anew the methods used initially by McCutcheon to demonstrate their wider applicability across a variety of domains.

The six McCutcheon essays have been included because they speak to the range of critical methodological nuances at the disposal of scholars and provide running commentary as to the competing interests shaping scholarly operational acts of identification as much as their cultural counterparts, and for their balanced attention to McCutcheon's own interests in tandem with the interests of those McCutcheon engages in the essays.

Topic I presents McCutcheon's discussion of Ann Taves' *Religious Experience Reconsidered* (2009) along with K. Merinda Simmons' application of McCutcheon's methodology to a discussion of Reza Aslan's *Zealot: The Life and Times of Jesus of Nazareth* (2013). Taken together, this first section suggests that new approaches to scholarship do not necessarily mean solutions to old issues of reliance and ordering based on assumptions about identity and data. Rather, Simmons calls attention away from assumptions of exceptionalism born from the plastic nature of the sui generis and, instead, shifts our focus towards the context and interests of such manufacturing.

In Topic II, Leslie Dorrough Smith looks to the social and cultural weight of sites like Gettysburg Cemetery and its historical context to suggest that behind every "American" claim to exception – or other sorts of exceptionalisms as discussed in McCutcheon's "The Melancholy Empire Builder: The Life and Works of Mircea Eliade" that challenges Eliade's turn to the sacred – a certain type of historical arrangement is relied upon.

In Topic III, Monica R. Miller looks to past and contemporary cultural conversations over the "N-word" – who can say it, why, and when has a lot to do with various groups wanting to outline who can say what and when, so that certain groups retain an option to have it both ways. Such tendencies are as much present in scholarship, not necessarily where a contentious word like "nigger" is concerned, but in other arenas. In this instance, the introduction helps to site and cite some of the more palpable implications of McCutcheon's critique of Jeffrey Kripal's *The Serpent's Gift: Gnostic Reflections on the Study of Religion* (2007) in "A Gift with Diminished Returns: On Jeff Kripal's *The Serpent's Gift*."

In Topic IV, Craig Martin discusses the American documentary *Outrage* (2009) which suggests that the Republican party has a large number of closeted homosexuals who, in their concern to remain in the closet, often vote against legislation that would support gay rights. Looking to McCutcheon's "'It's a Lie. There's No Truth in

It! It's a Sin!': The Costs of Saving Others from Themselves," that critiques Robert Orsi's *Between Heaven and Earth: The Religious Worlds People Make and the Scholars Who Study Them* (2005) on the grounds of smuggling the foreign contraband of explanations and descriptions of others. Here, conspiritorial American political theater and the field of religious studies are both held accountable for sleight-of-hand tactics.

In Topic V, Steven W. Ramey looks to the upheaval caused by celebrity Selena Gomez's donning an accessory traditionally ascribed to "Hindu" culture, as introduction to the essay "Affinities, Benefits, and Costs: The ABCs of Good Scholars Gone Public" where McCutcheon critiques Bruce Lincoln for failing to attend to Lincoln's own claims about identity and authority – by *whom* and *how* it is wielded. The end result is a section indicative of the varied discursive structures that constitute authority and disciplines for those communities of affinity regarded as "cultures."

In Topic VI, Vaia Touna looks to a small village in Central Macedonia to introduce McCutcheon's "The Resiliency of Conceptual Anachronisms: On the Limits of 'the West' and 'Religion'" wherein the essay and introduction engage seemingly distinct data sets, to suggest that scholars, and their use of tradition, rely on and make possible various authorizing acts. Tradition is not a thing unto itself, but a notion offered through reification and manipulations of time, and uncritical, unreflexive, anachronistic uses of methodologies inherited from disciplinary silos.

Shifting towards a new paradigm and approach, *Claiming Identity* highlights the manner in which the struggle over "meaning" under the guise of talk of religion, race, gender, sexuality, and so on points towards a recognition that beneath the surface of seemingly innocuous claims in discourse are battles for capital and positions. On the topic of identity as symbolic capital, Bourdieu reminds us that capital is "the product of a struggle in which each agent is both a ruthless competitor and supreme judge" (1992: 136). In this sense, discourses on, say, "marginal" or "oppressed" identities might become more difficult to register as "operational acts" because symbolic capital "is denied capital, recognized as legitimate, that is, misrecognized as capital," and might be the only "form of accumulation [of capital] when economic capital is not recognized" (Bourdieu 1992: 118). Wanting to be sensitive to misrecognition of how these operational acts take the shape of "identities" as well as to the all-too-real social and political situations arising from competing claims to and about marginal and dominant identities alike, the need for a critical methodology applicable across "distinct" claims to identity seems rather timely and useful. *Claiming Identity* addresses the need for a critical methodology, arguing that understanding identity as operational acts helps to guard against the reapplication and recapitulation of the baggage carried along with such ideas, concepts, and claims, without having to (necessarily) throw away the very terms themselves. In no way is this a foolproof method of supposed objectivity on behalf of the analyst – quite the contrary, for we too are strategic observers and claim bearers. Methodologically, then, reflexivity is a vital component for and of a critical approach: the promotion of reflexivity on the part of the analyst, and the need for such a realization within the method itself, so that identifiable strategies and tactics can be *identified* within and *analyzed* across various domains of data. We hope this volume suggests as much.

Moving Forward

Readers will also find a robust Afterword, "Accidental Favorites," written by Steven W. Ramey, which offers final words of guidance that methodological applicability is difficult, daunting, and damn near impossible without reflexive recognition that the work done by scholars often plays favorites within contemporary culture wars. So what to do? As much inspired by the ideas giving purchase to this volume, while at the same time offering more guidance on how such ideas might find fertile methodological soil, "Accidental Favorites" concludes by arguing for an attempt to avoid reifying the many labels (e.g., Hindu/Sikh, black/white, religious/secular) that take such focus in the study of religion historically and today.

Within the study of religion, despite decades of lone voices crying out from the wilderness of an inherited affinity for certain cultural forms giving birth to what we now call religious studies, the conversation on critical methodology has really just begun. Despite many years of scholarship from McCutcheon and others, critical approaches to questions of cultural as much as academic "identities" remain new, and more conversation is certainly on the horizon. This volume is an effort to contribute to those much needed exchanges. A second Equinox volume, *The Problem of Nostalgia in the Study of Identity: Towards a Dynamic Theory of People and Place* is soon to follow. Taken together, and as outgrowths of the Culture on the Edge scholarly collective, these volumes mark one such "new" beginning. Readers are needed. Early adopters are encouraged. Critical engagement begins with *engagement*, which this and the next volume produce and promote. Having just begun to wrestle with the full impact of a shift from identity to "operational acts of identification," the *identity* of a critical methodology is only now coming into operation.

References

Barthes, Roland. 1972. *Mythologies*. New York: Hill and Wang.

Barthes, Roland. 1977. *Writing Degree Zero*. New York: Hill and Wang.

Bayart, Jean-François. 2005. *The Illusion of Cultural Identity*. Chicago: University of Chicago Press.

Bourdieu, Pierre. 1992. *The Logic of Practice*. 1st ed. Stanford: Stanford University Press.

Butler, Judith. 1990. *Gender Trouble: Feminism and the Subversion of Identity*. New York: Routledge.

Butler, Judith. 1993. *Bodies That Matter*. New York: Routledge.

Dubuisson, Daniel. 2003. *The Western Construction of Religion: Myths, Knowledge, and Ideology*. Trans. William Sayers. Baltimore: The Johns Hopkins University Press.

Kumar, Penumala Pratap. 2005. *Methods and Theories in the Study of Religions: Perspectives from the Study of Hinduism and Other Indian Religions*. New Delhi: Black and White.

McCutcheon, Russell T. 2001. *Critics Not Caretakers: Redescribing the Public Study of Religion*. Albany: State University of New York Press.

McCutcheon, Russell T. 2003. *Manufacturing Religion: The Discourse on Sui Generis Religion and the Politics of Nostalgia*. 1st ed. New York: Oxford University Press.

Saussure, Ferdinand de, Albert Riedlinger, Charles Bally, and Albert Sechehaye. 1983. *Course in General Linguistics*. Chicago: Open Court Publishing Company.

Monica R. Miller is Assistant Professor of Religion and Africana Studies at Lehigh University and Director of Women, Gender and Sexuality Studies. Her research considers the intersections of religion in youth culture, popular culture, identity and difference, theory and method in the study of religion, and new black religious movements.

Topic I: Claiming Identity

1. "Well, Isn't That Special?": What We Talk about When We Talk about Identity

K. Merinda Simmons

Something interesting happened in the fallout from the response of both media and academic commentators alike to Reza Aslan's now infamous interview on Fox News about his book *Zealot: The Life and Times of Jesus of Nazareth* (2013). Well two things, actually. First, those engaged in the debate over whether the questions asked of him were indeed fair and balanced went back and forth with the following primary question: Was his "Muslim identity" appropriate for Lauren Green – Fox's religion correspondent – to bring up as having anything to do with the content of his scholarly work? Why is this interesting? Well, because the same logic was shared both by those defending Aslan and those defending Fox. Namely, both sides saw his "identity" as a stable thing that helps us understand the kind of work he does. It's just that they laid claim to different identities – Fox viewers pointing to his Muslim-ness, and Aslan and his defenders directing attention to his status as an academician and the fact that members of his family (including his wife) are Christians. Either way, friends and foes alike cast identity as a thing supposedly held inside "him," which is simply enacted and performed in different ways for different reasons.

The second interesting bit is something else taken for granted – namely, the substance of Aslan's *Zealot*. The book is Aslan's attempt to uncover and recuperate the "real" history of Jesus the man (as opposed, apparently, to Jesus the Christ) as a product of his sociopolitical context. Instead of relying solely on the gospels, the biography utilizes historical documents about Palestine and Rome during the time of Jesus. If one sees identity as a stable, inherent thing, one is able to recuperate a supposedly "true story" that lies beneath the societal game of Telephone that is thought to inevitably distort the facts of the matter. In what follows, I will briefly outline a few examples of how the rhetoric of experience and identity seeps into academic discourse both orally and in print.

Treating "identity" as a thing in itself is, for many, the only appropriate or reasonable approach for responsible scholars. After all, despite the nods made to anti-essentialism and social construction now prevalent in the academy, something called "identity" so often remains at the centre of conversations about equity and oppression, issues whose importance are taken for granted under the umbrella of humanistic good intentions within the North American academy. To suggest, as Jean-François Bayart does, that "There is no such thing as identity, only operational acts of identification" (2005: 92) is, as far as these conversations are concerned, to undermine and dehumanize individual experience. In two of my own primary areas of research – race studies and feminist theory – where the stakes of articulating and chiseling out certain identifications (deemed marginalized) in contradistinction to others (deemed hegemonic or dominant) strike scholars as particularly high, the terms "identity" and "experience" are often treated as signifiers of knowable and inherently meaningful signifieds. When Nancy Hartsock (1983) coined the phrase "feminist standpoint theory," the idea that "the personal is political" (articulated most famously by Carol Hanisch)[1] had already had an intellectual hold on various North American feminist movements for a little over a decade. One's social context and individual experience became popular fodder for theorizing and scholarly exchange, an emphasis that continues to take shape in academic modes of "recuperating" voices thought to be marginalized in one way or another.

Aslan's book certainly draws upon the maneuvers of this kind of archeological scholarship, purporting to unearth a different, more complex (and implicitly more "accurate") Jesus for his readers. The

---

[1] Originally published in *Notes from the Second Year: Women's Liberation* (1970), the brief essay can now be found online: http://www.carolhanisch.org/CHwritings/PIP.html.

problem with so many recuperative efforts is that they take identity to refer to a thing-in-itself that we can locate and uncover. If we take Bayart's idea seriously, however – that what we have come to call "identity" is a series of social *acts* rather than an abiding and inherent quality residing interiorly – then it seems not enough to make a passing nod to the socially constructed nature of gender, race, religion, and so forth, only to then go on to talk casually about "women" or "men," "blackness" and "whiteness," or "Muslim identity," just to name a few easy referents that make regular appearances in academic writing. This scholarly sticking point came to the foreground for me when I began working in a Religious Studies department. Writing and teaching on the topic of "women and religion," I spent a couple of conference cycles in 2010–11 presenting work at the National Women's Studies Association (NWSA) and at the American Academy of Religion (AAR).

That first year in my new departmental context was especially telling as I began teasing out the possibilities and limitations of theorizing categories of identity and experience. When I went to the NWSA, presenting on a panel entitled "Women and Religion," I was eager to pick the brains of feminists who were incorporating studies of religion into their work and see how they were tackling the intersection. I was reading a paper that dealt with some of the issues of category claims and classification politics in "Women and Religion" courses/ syllabi. The other person on the panel (ours was touted as a special session, kept purposefully small for the sake of good discussion on a complex topic) gave a presentation on what she called "heart-centered pedagogy." Her point as I understood it was that yogic practice and ideology can make for better learning environments. Women, she suggested, are particularly suited for this, as our abilities for compassionate touching and empathy provide a safe space for students to express themselves. I was stunned. While eager questions followed up on my fellow panelist's talk, asking her to explain how she uses the technique in other classroom contexts (she had explored it to great success, she said, in prisons), the questions that came my way primarily pressed the point of why it is exactly that I do not give ample attention in my syllabus to "the experiences of real women." I spent some time reading the huge NWSA program book after my panel was over. Every mention of "religion" was advertising scholars who were participants in a particular faith community talking descriptively about women in that faith community. Muslim women convened for a panel discussing the politics of the hijab in various parts of the world. Jewish women organized to discuss strands of Jewish feminism. I found a panel on goddess movements and one critiquing the patriarchy of Christian doctrine. And so on. In this setting of scholars, "religion" referred to something specific and real – and decidedly experiential.

Later that same year at the AAR, I encountered something of an interesting inversion. While scholars at times (certainly not always) talked about "religion" in more nuanced ways – at least giving a nod to calling it a category – "women" referred to an exceedingly specific, often biological, phenomenon. Conversations about "Women and Religion," then, took the shape of focusing on descriptive anthropological accounts on this or that group of women in this or that country performing this or that ritual. The importance or relevance of the topic was taken to be self-evident – such work's motivation was one of awareness-building and a global humanism cast beneath a tent of well-intended liberalism. Between sessions, I made a point of talking with various people about the topic of women and religion vis-à-vis pedagogy. This time, the questions put to me dealt with how to give ample time in the semester to various religious traditions.

I realized that I had developed a very different reading of our feminist mainstay "the personal is political" from many of my colleagues working in fields of identity studies. If what we identify as "the personal" is an invariably political act, then there is no sense privileging this or that experiential claim or participant viewpoint. Rather, we might more productively set about the business of examining how various – often competing – notions of identity ("the personal") appear as political claims and contestations. The so-called personal is *always* political. It is, indeed, a highly politicized claim to talk about a domain of "the personal" in the first place. What's amazing to me is how often it seems like scholars want to be self-referential without being self-reflexive. We want to lay claim to experiential authority or be detached descriptivists when it suits us, all the while pointing to the "scope of our research" to explain our intellectual projects rather than the politics that motivate our studies. McCutcheon's discussion of Ann Taves' *Religious Experience Reconsidered* (2009) – a book wherein Taves attempts to locate religious experiences as/in cognitive processes and demarcate their "special" (as somehow distinct from singularly religious) characteristics – asks us to be wary of such scholarly moves that, even in the name of progressive social and scientific savvy, talk about identity and experience as stable and inherently valuable rather than as products of complex processes of naming.

Lest the above examples appear merely to be anecdotal gripes about a genre of academic performance wherein we are often trotting out very rough drafts of ideas that have not yet been polished, I would suggest the discussions among academics offer telling moments that we might think about when considering how it is that we go about articulating certain claims to one another. After all, if Reza Aslan's few short minutes in a television interview are able to spark such debate, then surely more concentrated and focused speaking moments in academia – like the structured spaces of conferences – might give us a nice case study that can spell out (at least in useful nutshells) the broad trends in studies of religion and identity. For instance, and perhaps most relevant to the Aslan v. Fox discussion, we might ask why some claims to experiential authority are valued and others criticized. At a recent regional AAR meeting, our academic panels coincided with a meeting of a group of Christians of some charismatic or evangelical stripe. Scholars easily poked kind (and occasionally not so kind) fun at the affable group of religious followers (they were our data, after all), only to conduct panels on their own analyses of "authentic" ritual performances or of a "proper" reading of a passage in the Bible. It strikes me that both groups are simply making competing identity claims using the same logic that supposes a way to access a "true interpretation" of something. Or, for another example, how is it that we decide when, like Aslan did, to make heavy note of our scholarly credentials and when to distance ourselves as far as possible from the academy? After all, many engage in the latter when attempting to distinguish the "ivory tower" from the "real world" (and socially conscious PhDs that we are, we certainly don't want to appear aristocratic!). One of the implications of standpoint theory, as

I read it, is that the so-called life of the mind and the "real" life one leads in the everyday are two different spheres.

As such, standpoint theory is thought to offer something of a bridge between the two, allowing a brand of autobiographical scholarship wherein one's self-identification is simultaneously one's running thesis. Along similar lines, it also validates the scholarly endeavors of descriptive ethnographies that are meant to bring to light or recuperate those voices that have been traditionally silenced. In both these overlapping domains, experience and identity are thought to substantiate each other. So, in order to talk about identities of "women," just describe the experiences of a particular group who employ that category and – *ba-da-bing!* – the work is done. The Aslan-Fox interview is a telling moment within discourses surrounding "Muslim identity" that have recently come into the fore in both popular and academic venues, carrying with them a corrective aim of getting the proverbial story right regarding the intersections of Islam and subjectivity. In an understandable backlash to the broad stereotypes that conflate Islam and violence, for example, these discourses hope to present the emphases on peace and equality present in *authentic* forms of Islam. Aslan invokes his experience – namely, his marriage to a Christian – to *correct* the interviewer's own assumptions about Muslim identity (as something that would necessarily stymie Aslan's efforts to write a compelling text about Jesus Christ). The logic at work in both their approaches is the same, however, in that they both discuss identity – marked by this thing called experience – as stable and inherent.

The easy and misleading reading of "the personal is political" is also very present in discourses surrounding the notion of Muslim identity that are specifically focused on the experiences of women who are practitioners of the very Islam that is said by some to oppress them. Saba Mahmood's much-acclaimed *Politics of Piety: The Islamic Revival and the Feminist Subject* (2005) is one good example. The book has become necessary reading for feminists, postcolonialists, and religionists alike, and its paperback reissue in 2012 with a new preface has revived the conversations around it. The much-praised study is an ethnographic study of women's piety movements in Cairo that attempts to complicate so-called Western feminist readings of Islam. In aiming to make us rethink notions like liberalism, postcolonialism, embodiment, and ethics, however, Mahmood relies upon quick sketches of "Islam," "women," and "piety." In so doing, she maintains traditional understandings of what such ideas refer to ("piety," for example, seems largely to refer to moral reform, belief, and ethics). She simply uses the ideas in different contexts than are typically granted them. She thus presents what she considers to be a more productive, better way to read Islamist movements, especially where women are concerned.

McCutcheon's discussion of *Religious Experience Reconsidered* sheds some light on how the seeming progress of such scholarly trends (or, specifically relevant to his discussion, the popular emphasis currently on cognitive science within the academic study of religion) can actually end up relying on and retaining old modes of organizing and classifying:

> So, as with so many who focus on categorical critique but end up merely using new words to name old things – despite the change in name it is not clear that the data has been reconsidered all that much – we still end up finding people the world over who see "religion-like" things as like. The common (common to us, that is) limits of the folk taxon "religion," naming a distinct domain, are reproduced; once again, then, a local and therefore familiar folk discourse has simply been adopted by scholars and uncritically elevated to the analytic level, and then used by them as if it described actual states of affairs in the world that need to be explained.

Mahmood's brand of ethnography casts religiosity as a real and distinguishable *thing* thought to be housed within and performed through personal, private experience. And, as the following critique of *Religious Experience Reconsidered* reminds us, while some groups and people we study would follow and utilize such logic in organizing their daily lives, others do not. The insistence on cultivating a theory of (for Taves) religion or (for Mahmood) piety and embodiment, or "the feminist subject" within the Islamic revival, then, is an attempt at cross-cultural transliteration that forgets about the politics of classification in the first place. The language of locality, however, allows Mahmood's study and so many others like it within postcolonial and

religious studies to attempt to "recuperate" a cultural group thought
to inhabit a marginalized space within its society. In the case of Reza
Aslan's *Zealot*, we are granted the supposed "real story" of Jesus
Christ. How can books like these *not* fly off the shelves?
What such studies provide is the allure of a seeming *way in* – an
awareness of, appreciation for, or even expertise in insider codes
and participant behavior. For McCutcheon, however, "...the role of
the scholar is not to systematize other people's folk knowledge." In
focusing on experience, scholars maintain a reliance on the supposed
thing itself (whether a culture, gender identification, race, or, in the
case of Taves, religion) rather than the act of calling the thing a this
and not a that. This is why McCutcheon calls our attention to the
constructive possibilities of a "theory of deeming" – far more useful,
he argues, than a theory of religion (and/or, for my examples here,
gender and race). To put it another way, when Dana Carvey's church
lady on *Saturday Night Live* asks the rhetorical question "Well, isn't
that special?" we are directed not to the thing she critiques but to the
caricature of judgment and a certain brand of socialization that she
represents. The entire joke is based on a theory of deeming. Its punchline relies on our keeping focus on the person naming rather than the
thing being named. And whether the context is a cable news interview, academic conference, or scholarly text, our attention should rest
not on something deemed special or unique but on those asking us to
consider it to be so.

References

Aslan, Reza. 2013. *Zealot: The Life and Times of Jesus of Nazareth*. New
    York: Random House.
Bayart, Jean-François. 2005. *The Illusion of Cultural Identity*. Chicago:
    University of Chicago Press.
Hartsock, Nancy. 1983. "The Feminist Standpoint: Developing the Ground
    for a Specifically Feminist Historical Materialism." In Sandra Harding
    and Merrill B. Hintikka, eds., *Discovering Reality*, 283–310. Boston:
    Reidel.
Mahmood, Saba. 2005. *Politics of Piety: The Islamic Revival and the
    Feminist Subject*. Princeton: Princeton University Press.

Taves, Ann. 2009. *Religious Experience Reconsidered: A Building-Block Approach to the Study of Religion and Other Special Things*. Princeton: Princeton University Press.

K. Merinda Simmons is Associate Professor in the Department of Religious Studies at the University of Alabama. Her research and writing are primarily concerned with the ways in which authenticity claims appear in theories of gender and race.

2. Will Your Cognitive Anchor Hold in the Storms of Culture?

Russell T. McCutcheon

The publication of Ann Taves' book, *Religious Experience Reconsidered* (2009), provides me with an opportunity to comment on the synthesis of two aspects of our field, one old and the other new. The first is the common practice – at least since the Pietist-affiliated writers appeared on the scene – of using the category "religious experience" to name the supposedly unseen yet uniform causal force behind the diversity of empirical things that scholars of religion study; the second is the more recent application of findings from that collection of disciplines now known as the cognitive sciences – applied, at first, to those behavioral practices classed as ritual but now being used to explain the persistence (i.e., successful transmission) of certain sorts of beliefs (e.g., in gods, ancestors, the afterlife, etc.).[1] Finding these two seemingly contradictory research traditions in the same book – contradictory inasmuch as one is traditionally concerned with demarcating a uniquely private sentiment that defies rational explanation while the other is concerned with approaching our object of study in a rigorously naturalistic manner – is a curious mix and thus something worth considering.[2]

---

[1] Though dated somewhat, perhaps the best single essay overview of this emergent sub-field is still to be found in Geertz 2004.

[2] That Taves is hardly the only cognitively-inclined scholar to bring these two together (e.g., most recently, see McNamara 2009; see also the essays collected in Andresen 2001) needs to be said, of course. For an alternative approach to the category of religious experience, see Martin and McCutcheon 2012.

To make evident, from the outset, what I mean by my essay's title, consider a talk that I attended a couple of years ago in my own Department, given by a former student then pursuing his MA in anthropology, using work already done in the cognitive science of religion (or what practitioners refer to as CSR).[3] His work was concerned with testing the theory, associated first with Pascal Boyer and now with Justin Barrett (e.g., Gregory and Barrett 2009), that certain ideas, if they differ in some small regard, from what is assumed to be a trans-human stock of hardwired, intuitive knowledge, will be more likely to be remembered and thus hold a competitive advantage when it comes time to pass them along to the next generation. (The assumption being, of course, that the persistence and widespread nature of beliefs in beings just like you and I but who are also, for instance, immortal or immaterial, might be explained by means of this theory.) Apart from confirming some of the more recent experimental results that minimally counterintuitive ideas seem no more catchy (to pick up on Dan Sperber's now widely used epidemiological metaphor [1996]) than other sorts of ideas, the student's presentation made evident the difficulty (some might say impossibility) of trying to study a

---

[3] I admit that I am also curious about the number of acronyms that appear in the writings of those who work in this sub-field. Some examples include: TAVS (threat-activation system), HADD (hyperactive agency detection device), VM (vestibular-motor experiences and sensations), and, of course, the widely cited TOM (theory of mind) and MCI (minimally counterintuitive concepts). While effectively distinguishing the initiated from the uninitiated, and thereby assisting to establish in-group/out-group identities, this shorthand seems to lend a degree of scientific complexity and thus legitimacy to this fairly new sub-field. For while any intellectual pursuit has its own technical vocabulary that practitioners repeatedly employ in their work and while all technical vocabularies are the tips of large bodies of organized sets of assumptions that scholars put into practice while carrying out their work (what we might loosely call theories), not every field relies on abbreviations to do such heavy theoretical lifting – though perhaps there are some literary critics who, when speaking to peers whom they assume equally well understand the trouble of assuming that T (i.e., text) is a repository of an AIM (i.e., author's intended meaning), simply roll their eyes and say "AS IF" (i.e., authorial simplification/intentional fallacy).

presumably necessary, universal, and thus pre-social human trait by means of such historically-shifting, cultural constructs as language (e.g., the just used computer-based metaphor "hardwired").[4]

Case in point: consider the minimally counterintuitive statement, "A rock that is sick," that was part of the questionnaire (or what those in the field might call the stimulus) that the presenter had used with his test subjects, in hopes, I presume, that the odd meaning conveyed by such a sentence would be more memorable than the test's more mundane meanings and statements (i.e., those that confirmed the folk epistemology of the test subjects, such as the uncontroversial "A girl that is wise"). What I found most interesting, however, was that the sick rock prompted one of the other students in attendance jokingly to agree that, yes indeed, the rock was cool. For apart from what it identifies as the "old version" of the word (to signify illness), the online Urban Dictionary (http://www.urbandictionary.com) indicates that the word "sick" is now commonly used to signify the following partial list of synonyms: awesome, sweet, nasty, gross, amazing, tight, wicked, vomit, dope, crazy, disgusting, sex, rad, shit, puke, nice, hot, good, gnarly, bad, great, ugly, drunk, fuck, insane, gay, fresh, fly, dirty, badass, ass, mad, chill, etc. My point? Only if we assume what some would regard as a rather conservative or at least very traditional correspondence theory of meaning (i.e., that words gain their meaning by referring, in some sort of stable and direct relationship, with real things and their actual qualities) could we hope, presumably along with those administering the test, for the statement "A rock that is sick" to elicit something like the following chain of premises and inferences in a hypothetical test subject's mind:

1. All empirical items can be divided between organic and inorganic;

---

[4] It is not difficult to imagine the hardware/software metaphor (commonly used today to distinguish biology from culture) sometime soon sounding just as dated to our ears as does Marx's architectural metaphor of base/superstructure. What both sets of metaphors share, of course, is the effort to identify the pre-linguistic and thus abiding real in distinction from the merely linguistic, the epiphenomenal.

2. All organic items can be further subdivided between animate and inanimate;
3. Poorly functioning animate organic items can be termed sick;
4. Only animate organic things can be sick;
5. All rocks are inorganic;
6. Therefore, rocks cannot be sick.

Only by assuming these premises to be intuitive and thus naturally linked could we attribute the memorability of "A rock that is sick" to its supposed counterintuitiveness. But the moment we abandon the correspondence theory of meaning, the moment we view language as a culturally relative and historically dynamic closed system in which each signifier is made meaningful by its arbitrary and infinitely variable relationship to all other signifiers within the system – such as coming to see "sick" as signifying "rad" or "wicked" or possibly associating "sick rock" with a genre of music that is sweet and tight – then the theorist is back to square one, having no idea why the memory of the rock stuck out – if indeed it is even recalled with any more frequency than the other test sentences (which, according to my former student, it is not).[5] In fact, even if the minimally counter-intuitive thesis held, I could easily imagine a test subject whom feminists might once have called "a male chauvinist pig" remembering what researchers no doubt presume to be one of their less memorable, control sentences, "A girl that is wise," for reasons unanticipated by a more politically liberal researcher (because, for our hypothetical chauvinist, female wisdom could very well be considered counterintuitive). The point being that stimuli meant to signify universal traits are, contrary to the apparent hopes of the researcher, deeply embedded in socially variable worlds.

---

[5] Given that some recent studies have not supported the prediction that minimally counterintuitive ideas are more memorable, we now find ourselves at an interesting moment where this new field in the study of religion will be challenged to live up to its scientific billing as being based on testability and falsifiability. Simply put, as elegant as this theory is, how long will people continue to use it despite evidence to the contrary?

If, of course, you have not controlled for the almost infinite malleability of the medium through which you are studying hypothetically trans-cultural universals (and how, precisely, does one control for this?), and, instead, have drawn conclusions about the universal only because you have pursued such experiments within a socially, and thus semantically, homogeneous audience (in which sick means sick!), then your survey results will simply indicate the degree to which a collection of signifiers are consensually used within your test population and will not necessarily tell us anything about a basic feature of pre-social cognition – an experimental design flaw akin to the once common ethnographic practice of drawing conclusions about an entire group after only interviewing its leaders.[6]

The point I wish to press is that one does not have to be a Derridean deconstructionist to ask these sorts of questions – questions concerned with the apparent ease of moving from part to whole, from contingent to necessary, from history to ahistory, from local to universal, and from culture to nature. My concern is that I am not at all sure that scholars of religion applying the findings from cognitive psychology have sufficiently investigated these sorts of questions. And because of this I am somewhat suspicious of the confidence they seem to have when publicizing the findings of their research.

What therefore troubles me about the attempt to find religious experiences in the mind/brain or religion in the genes is the manner in which, despite the sophistication that informs its use, a culturally and historically local nomenclature (i.e., this is religion, that is not religion) is being dehistoricized and thus normalized by being medicalized and thus naturalized. This troubles me because we all know – or at least I thought we did – of the critiques of the category religion as it was once used (I think here of critiques of the notion of sui generis religion). We all know that none of its possible Latin precursors

---

[6] This, of course, amounts to the common critique of IQ and other standardized tests in which information that is culturally and generationally specific to the researcher is assumed to be universally shared among the test subjects. Playing an edition of a trivia board game that is either too old or too young for its players, or using a dated popular cultural reference to illustrate a point while teaching college students illustrates the problem with making such an assumption.

likely meant what we mean by religion today (or at least as we have commonly defined it for the past few hundred years), thus signaling that the category religion, along with its usages, is itself historically variable – like all language. We also ought to know that my casual uses of "we" are something that also needs attention, for it signifies a rather precise, elite group of specialists, whose scholarly traditions originate in that part of the world commonly known as Europe, and whose members eventually perfected the use of the marker "religion" to name a seemingly distinct domain of diverse (though not necessarily inherently related) items of human activity and production. The corollary to this should also be well known to members of this admittedly small group of researchers: people outside Europe were not spontaneously organizing themselves and their world in terms of what was and what was not religion or religious[7] – not, that is, until imperialism's advance guard (i.e., those who are colloquially known as explorers, traders, and yes, missionaries) arrived on distant shores and quite understandably tried to make sense of the strange by means of a classification system that divided up the so-called new world in a way that was entirely familiar to those arriving for the first time.

In a videotaped interview from 1999, filmed at Fairfield University and now available online, Jonathan Z. Smith phrased this point particularly well, drawing attention away from studying religion and

---

[7] I add the adjective here because some scholars make much of its difference from the noun, inasmuch as the adjective supposedly names a deeply human and thus universal quality of people rather than the noun, which is thought to name only reified, impersonal institutions (one would be correct, I think, to hear echoes of Wilfred Cantwell Smith's critique of "religion" in this widely used distinction). I would argue that this is purely a rhetorical distinction, as if saying that something is political (the adjective) amounts to something other than asserting that politics (the noun) exists. That the plurals of the noun – i.e., religions or Christianities – are often favored over the singular is an equally suspect move, for it effectively bypasses the question of definition and instead simply assumes a plurality. For example, speaking only of birds naturalizes the presumption (rather than defending it and elaborating on it) that the concept bird, in distinction from, say, fish or plant, is useful. Settling that question will take argumentation rather than a more detailed study of the variety of birds.

refocusing it on our habit – and it is just ours – with calling something religion:

> The biggest question would be why we in our sort of cultural complex have found it necessary, out of the complexity of human activities, to say we can find one in there that we want to call religion. It's a well-known conundrum; nobody else has a word remotely like that.... If you really want to falsify a translation, find the word religion in any other language. Now there's kind of a silly argument: if there's no word for it it's not there; that's not a very good argument. But it is the fact that we have been preoccupied for a long time with finding in this seamless web of human activities the capacity to break one out and say when they're doing that one they're doing religion.... In a way we're the only ones who think there's a big deal about defining religion, and why do we think that? And that's an honest question on my part because I haven't the foggiest idea why we decided to do that. But it certainly is distinctive that we think out of the web of things we do as humans, the web of relations and obligations, and so on, that we have as humans, we can actually underline one set of them and say,... "That's the political, you know, that's the legal sphere" – separation of powers, almost – I don't know anybody else who thinks they need to do things like that. And so that's a genuine puzzlement to me and I have never seen an answer that is remotely convincing on that question.[8]

As I said above, my hope is that it would be difficult to find a contemporary scholar in our field not familiar, at least to some extent, with the work done on this "puzzlement" – work done since the late 1990s when Smith gave this interview, and originally carried out by such scholars as Daniel Dubuisson, Tim Fitzgerald, Richard King, Tomoko Masuzawa, and myself. Although first aimed at critiquing the notion of irreducible and thus unexplainable religion, people have

[8] The interview is posted as a series of answers to discrete questions; the one I am quoting here, entitled "Dr. J Z Smith 00," is posted at: http://www.youtube.com/watch?v=iTVeX4Jp418 (accessed May 29, 2013). For a complete list of Smith interviews see also: http://digitalcommons.fairfield.edu/do/search/?q=Jonathan%20Z%20Smith&start=0&context=2385243 (accessed May 29, 2013).

since then turned their critical attention to the social work carried out by any attempt to use the category religion to find seemingly natural (as opposed to stipulative!) breaks in "the web of things we do as humans, the web of relations and obligations."[9]

But despite this critical turn away from seeing our object of study as somehow being a special case, we now find a thriving naturalistic industry developing a unique theory to discover the unique place in the brain or in the genome or in a collection of cognitive processes where the uniquely religious resides. The once and still popular "religious experience" has, however, now been replaced by Taves with a seemingly more inclusive, preferred term, "special experiences" – or, to be more accurate, experiences considered or, as she writes, *deemed*, special. But what is a special experience? To begin with, they are something other than ordinary experiences – they're "unusual sorts of experiences" (Taves 2009: xv) and "singular experiences" (ibid.: 10). Despite the reconsidered nomenclature, the so-called unusual experiences that Taves brings to the readers' attention are, of course, the usual suspects, for they still fall within a wide family resemblance domain familiar to anyone acquainted with the study of those experiences formerly known as religious, those that "people sometimes ascribe the special characteristics to things that we (as scholars) associate with terms such as 'religious,' 'magical,' 'mystical,' 'spiritual,' et cetera" (ibid.: 8). So, as with so many who focus on categorical critique but end up merely using new words to name old things – despite the change in name it is not clear that the data have been reconsidered all that much – we still end up finding people the world over who see "religion-like" things as like. The common (common to us, that is) limits of the folk taxon "religion," naming a distinct domain, are reproduced; once again, then, a local and therefore familiar folk

[9] Presumably it is because this was the focus of my first book, *Manufacturing Religion* (1997), that leads to it often being cited in many works by cognitivist scholars of religion, for such citations allow them to take as given that the notion of sui generis ought to be abandoned, thereby opening the door for their own explanatory work. That my subsequent work is rarely cited by these writers – work that has argued that *any* use of the category religion is a socio-political technique of management – is, perhaps, to be expected.

discourse has simply been adopted by scholars and uncritically elevated to the analytic level, and then used by them as if it described actual states of affairs in the world that need to be explained.

For some time I have been perplexed by how willing many otherwise serious scholars are to adopt an untheorized folk taxon, as if a classification used by a group we happen to study, or used within a group we happen to have been raised in ourselves, somehow corresponds to an actual aspect of reality that needs to be studied. After all, all groups of humans have complex taxonomic systems that they use to signify, classify, and thereby sort their world, yet scholars do not necessarily develop a scientific study of each of these taxons, thereby conceiving of them as universal properties of the human. To take one, rather silly example, there is no academic study of nerds despite the fact that my niece and her friends once called themselves "math nerds," in contradistinction to those who are not. Or, closer to our academic home, and recalling Pascal Boyer's *The Naturalness of Religious Ideas* (1994): I wonder what scholars here would make of a book originating from, say, a contemporary Polynesian author and arguing that mana was a natural part of the pan-human cognition and not simply a local term that is merely of ethnographic curiosity to those of us in Europe or North America – a book that explained the mana-like experiences that you and I have, despite our lacking the word in our local and thus understandably limited vocabulary? So why is it that scholars who happen to originate from a cultural context in which "religion" is used to name an aspect of the social world (and I do not just mean theologians or liberal humanists doing this work, as I might have earlier in my career, but also ardently reductionistic, naturalistic scholars)[10] continue to invest time in developing a theory of religion as if this word names a stable, cross-cultural reality?

For instance, consider the opening pages to his well received *Modes of Religiosity* (2004; see my review, McCutcheon 2006), in

[10] It must be said that the neurobiological toolbox has been equally useful to members of all three groups – for entirely different purposes, of course. Tracing the role of the Templeton Foundation in making this work possible, for members of all three seemingly distinct groups, would be a project well worth tackling.

which Harvey Whitehouse devotes a section to "What is Religion?" After acknowledging that "[t]he everyday meaning of the word 'religion' is not all that easy to pin down" he argues that, despite "a range of exemplary features" often being called upon to name something as religious, "[n]one of these features is necessary for the attribution of the label, but almost any combination is sufficient." He therefore concludes that this utterly vague and rather imprecise use of the folk term is sufficient warrant for the development of a scientific theory. But a scientific theory of what? Of other people's taxonomic imprecision or the very existence and effect of the taxon itself? If the former, then is the task of scholarship merely to systematize other people's folk taxons because those folks just got it wrong, despite their having had a pretty good intuition into a cross-cultural universal? I hardly think so – for me, the role of the scholar is not to systematize other people's folk knowledge. Of course, we might follow Smith and share his puzzlement and, instead, theorize why some humans (hardly all) use "religion" to name aspects of their social world, thereby studying the various ways in which the taxon (and its wider discourse) is used, and the practical effects of these uses (which amounts to developing a theory as to why "religion," and not religion, is so catchy). But I rarely see scholars going down this root – and even when they do they often historicize the word while somehow still knowing that an abiding, pre-discursive reality, let's call it faith or experience, lurks beneath it.

Opting instead to systematize folk notions, Whitehouse's work (like that of so many cognitivists) is premised on the old troublesome notion of religion equaling belief in superhuman agents and the actions grouped around these beliefs – this, of course, is no mere stipulation. The trouble is this: some of the people whom we study do indeed say that superhuman agents exist, and that a collection of beliefs, behaviors, and institutions relevant to these agents are somehow essentially connected one to another and thereby set apart from other aspects of culture, making this set of interrelated items "religious." But many of the people we study do not talk, write, act, or organize in this way at all – i.e., they do not claim that this or that origins tale is inherently linked to that rite of passage (e.g., baptism) but not this one (e.g., getting your driver's license). Taking just some of our research subjects' word for this set-apartness (a move that is likely linked to scholars feeling rather comfortable with a folk system in which they have themselves been reared), scholars then busily set about accounting for the actual existence of this distinct and cross-cultural domain – after all, they develop theories of religion and are not content to understand the thing that some of their research subjects call religion to be sufficiently explained by a higher order theory of something else entirely, of which those things grouped together as religion are but ethnographically and historically local instances (that Bloch [2008] is pushing in this direction is, however, encouraging). What if what attracted the scholarly imagination was not the taken-for-granted distinctness of that grouping of things some know as religion (thus requiring a specific theory to account for its existence as a unique domain of human practice) but (again, following Smith), instead, the fact of some people's compulsion to represent certain features of their social world *as* essentially interconnected and thus distinct, unique, set-apart, and, dare I say, special? Then, as already suggested, we would work on developing not a theory of religion but, instead, a theory of "religion" – a theory of the process of specialization (which, unlike religion, may very well turn out to be among the cognitive processes Geertz refers to as "the most fundamental aspects of human cognition" [2004: 385]). What's more, such an approach would simply be a component of a far wider theory of social classification/identity construction (in a word, a theory of signification, in the most general sense of the term). If *this* was our approach, then those who study the things called religion would quickly understand themselves to be part of a much larger study of how humans make and enforce meanings and identities in the world – the most supposedly mundane and ordinary of such would be no less central to the study than any other, since the process of centralization itself is the object of study. This would be a truly cross-disciplinary project, one affording none of its contributors the pretense of having data that holds a special place. Moreover, it strikes me that only such an approach would be truly scientific – if by "scientific" we mean an approach that studies all emic reports equally and according to etic procedures rather than one that elevates select emic terms to etic status (a selection process driven by a host of engines, from self-interest to academic sloppiness).

Since we can trace the history of "religion" and "religious experi-ence" as items of discourse – and by this I mean a genealogical study of the invention of religious experience as an agreed upon subset of the broader range of interior dispositions known as experiences – it is indeed odd to find naturalistic scholars so confident that they will find where this discursive construct resides in the brain of all human beings. This I find puzzling, for it could be persuasively argued that the only reason scholars find religion everywhere in the world, and thus religious experience in everyone's heads, is because those very scholars approach the world – better put, *make their* world – by using this term, defined broadly enough, so as always to find sufficient things that they can *deem* religion – suggesting to me that a theory of *deeming* (i.e., a theory of signification) is far more required than a theory of religion. For example, because so many scholars today understand "magic" or "cult" no longer to be analytically useful (inas-much as they are either linked to bygone concerns or to troublesome politics), a theory concerning why they were ever used (or continue to be used by some) makes far more sense than trying to develop a *new* theory of magic or a *better* theory of cults. It thus makes sense why titles such as *Phrenology Reconsidered* or *Rethinking the Phlogiston Theory of Combustion* are not appearing on our bookshelves anytime soon. Although I have some differences of opinion with parts of his thesis (e.g., see McCutcheon 2007a: 234–5; 2007b: 188, n. 12), this was what David Chidester so nicely did in his *Savage Systems* (1996): trace the history not of religion but, instead, of the deployment of consecutive (and, generally, ever-widening) definitions of religion, whereby an ever greater number of things people did and said on the colonial frontier got to count *as* religious.[11]

To come at the problem from another direction: just because we find people who self-identify as citizens all over the world does not mean that there is a necessary, evolutionary, cognitive basis to citizenship

---

[11] Elsewhere (e.g., McCutcheon 1999 and 2003) I draw distinction between my work and Chidester's – for instance, his assuming that colonial-ists somehow misportrayed the religion of the locals, rather than considering that the concept "religion," and thus the ability to think into existence the notion that the Other had religion of any sort, arrived with the colonialists.

(despite our apparent ease in projecting this modern concept backward in time *as if* it was eternal, e.g., "citizens of ancient Rome"). The very precise mode of social membership signaled by the concept of citizen as we know it is only as recent (and as successful) as the rise (and the unchecked coercive power) of the nation-state – one of the many ways in which human beings have organized social life. Or, to call on a more timely and, for some, emotionally potent example, because we know that there is no agreed upon definition of "terrorism" (i.e., the last time I checked the UN had no such definition; one group's freedom fighter is likely its opponent's terrorist) it would be far from sensible to look for a gene or a cognitive trigger that makes one a terrorist. Or because legislatures all over the world define and then, when it suits the majority or the powerful (not necessarily overlapping groups!), redefine what gets to count as a crime, looking for a neurobiological basis for criminality would be downright silly. Right? But – and *this* is the interesting thing! – given how high the stakes are in normalizing and thereby regulating competing forms of human behavior, just such fields *do indeed exist* – fields of study that naturalize, and in doing so substantialize, what others would simply "deem" as culturally produced (and perhaps even class-relevant) concepts and thus identities.[12] But in the face of the almost infinitely variable ways in which those things we call terror or criminality get defined – e.g., continually unexpected US drone strikes in some parts of the world might reasonably be defined by some as inciting terror, no? – nailing down a definition will, I conjecture, meet with as much success as the effort to ensure that we always mean just one thing by "sick."

If our object of study, such as terrorism and crime, is a product of competing, situationally-specific classification systems and choices driven by specific sets of social interests (i.e., making both discursive objects and *not* biological facts), then it makes sense that one would have great difficulty discovering "in the bones" some trait that identified one as either a terrorist or a criminal. In support of this, consider

---

[12] Murphy's (n.d.) attempt to provide a neurobiological approach to terrorism is questionable on many grounds but the growing field of biocriminology is being taken very seriously; for an overview, see Monaghan 2009.

one of the conclusions of the following 1999 report commissioned by the Federal Research Davison of the US Library of Congress:[13]

> In addition to having normal personalities and not being diagnosably mentally disturbed, a terrorist's other characteristics make him or her practically indistinguishable from normal people, at least in terms of outward appearance. (Hudson 1999: 61; see also Kershaw 2005)

Indeed; for what makes the so-called abnormal terrorist distinguishable from, say, the normal freedom fighter is (despite the above quote's insinuation of some invisible inner intention) the stipulative definition that is or is not applied to the act, *not* the inherent traits of the social actor so named. Identity, I would therefore argue, is a social attribution, a choice and an act, and not an interior disposition that is first felt and then given an "outward appearance."

Of course, if one were seeking to authorize one among many definitions and thereby legitimize the interests that it supported, then being able to lodge the features that you have decided ought to count as significant in the very fabric of the person's cognition and genes would be a pretty handy device for those doing the classifying. And, like controlling for all of the definitions of the signifier "sick," so as to normalize one and only one way of using the term, such scholars would likely have to develop ways to control the variability of social interests and language, so as to find a secure biological home for those otherwise immaterial discursive objects. Take, for example, this attempt to find a neurobiological basis to behavior understood as violent. But what counts as violence, you ask?

---

[13] From the report's opening: "The Federal Research Division is the [US] Library of Congress's primary fee-for-service research unit and has served United States Government agencies since 1948. At the request of Executive and Judicial branch agencies, and on a cost-recovery basis, the Division prepares customized studies and reports, chronologies, bibliographies, foreign-language abstracts, databases, and other directed-research products in hardcopy and electronic media. The research includes a broad spectrum of social sciences, physical sciences, and humanities topics using the collections of the Library of Congress and other information sources world-wide."

> For the purpose of this review, violent behavior is defined as overt and intentional physically aggressive behavior against another person. Examples include beating, kicking, choking, pushing, grabbing, throwing objects, using a weapon, threatening to use a weapon, and forcing sex. The definition does not include aggression against self. Violent crimes include murder, robbery, assault, and rape. In this review, I will not deal with organized state violence or ethnic warfare. (Volavka 1999; see also 2002: 2)

Although I would imagine violence could be defined as a far wider, and thus far more complex, thing than simply intentional, individual aggression coupled with low self-control (curiously, professional football linebackers escaped the scholar's net, and why not include war, suicide, genocide, or police violence?), such a narrow definition makes good analytical sense, for it produces a nicely manageable object of study that can be tackled and seemingly controlled with a small set of tools. What's more, the result of such work is an object that mirrors the taken-for-granted assumptions about the world that we had before embarking on the analysis (after all, we know what counts as violence, no?). Authors count on readers not recognizing this oddly self-serving nature of their work, of course – i.e., paying no attention to the stipulative "For the purpose of this review" that opened the previous indented quote. For instance, only because they all know what counts as terrorism will most readers see no problem with a *New York Times* reviewer making the following claim, in a review of recent works on "the terrorist mind": "Despite the lack of a single terrorist profile, researchers have largely agreed on the risk factors for involvement" (Kershaw 2010). Translation? We don't really know what a terrorist is, but we nonetheless know how you become one. In this one sentence, moving as it does from indecision to utter conviction, we see how easily a discursive object can be treated as a stable fact.

And this is the problem with the neurobiological approach – it takes a variable discursive object as a settled matter of biological fact, thereby interiorizing and thus normalizing what, at least some of us would argue, is a contestable and always ongoing social event. This is a point nicely made by Jeff Ferrell, a professor of sociology at Texas

Christian University and editor of the NYU Press series, *Alternative Criminology*. The discipline of Criminology's goal, as he understands it, has been to explain that what societies take to be criminal behavior is constructed out of historical and cultural forces. However, as he writes, the newly emerging subfield of Biocriminology, by looking inside human bodies rather than at the inherent ambiguity of crime's social context, "strikes me as misguided at a minimum, if not morally and politically questionable" (cited in Monaghan 2009).

And it is on this note that I return to the topic of a cognitive (or any other, for that matter) theory of religious experience: looking for the pan-human, pre-social constraints that make people religious is just as much of a misguided effort, for it amounts to taking but one local, recent, and folk classification system (i.e., "I'm religious, are you?") and universalizing it by finding (i.e., placing) it in all people's hearts and minds, as the old saying goes. That the category religion is a product of *our* folk system and that *we* are very comfortable living in the world its use helps to make possible, should not prevent us, as scholars, from recognizing its history, its utility, and its limits. Failing to do so, and instead, naturalizing this item of discourse – whether we say we study religion or special, religion-like things – will lead to that pesky old notion of sui generis religion re-entering our field, doing it this time through a new, biological back door.

References

Andresen, Jensine, ed. 2001. *Religion in Mind: Cognitive Perspectives on Religious Belief, Ritual, and Experience*. Cambridge: Cambridge University Press. http://dx.doi.org/10.1017/CBO9780511586330.

Bloch, Maurice. 2008. "Why Religion is Nothing Special but is Central." *Philosophical Transactions of the Royal Society* 363(1499): 2055–61. http://dx.doi.org/10.1098/rstb.2008.0007.

Boyer, Pascal. 1994. *The Naturalness of Religious Ideas: A Cognitive Theory of Religion*. Berkeley: University of California Press.

Chidester, David. 1996. *Savage Systems: Colonialism and Comparative Religion in Southern Africa*. Charlottesville: University Press of Virginia.

Geertz, Armin W. 2004. "Cognitive Approaches to the Study of Religion," in Peter Antes, Armin W. Geertz, and Randi R. Warne, eds., *New Approaches* to the Study of Religion, Vol 2. Textual, Comparative, Sociological, and Cognitive Approaches, 347–99. Berlin and New York: Walter de Gruyter.

Gregory, Justin P., and Justin L. Barrett. 2009. "Epistemology and Counterintuitiveness: Role and Relationship in Epidemiology of Cultural Representations." *Journal of Cognition and Culture* 9(3): 289–314. http://dx.doi.org/10.1163/156770909X12489459066381.

Hudson, Rex A. 1999. *The Sociology and Psychology of Terrorism: Who Becomes a Terrorist and Why? A Report Prepared Under an Interagency Agreement by the Federal Research Division.* Washington, DC: Library of Congress; http://www.loc.gov/rr/frd/pdf-files/Soc_Psych_of_Terrorism. pdf, accessed May 29, 2013.

Kershaw, Sarah. 2005. *The Sociology and Psychology of Terrorism: Who Becomes a Terrorist and Why?* Honolulu, Hawaii: University Press of the Pacific.

Kershaw, Sarah. 2010. "The Terrorist Mind: An Update." *The New York Times* (New York Edition), January 10: WK1. http://www.nytimes. com/2010/01/10/weekinreview/10kershaw.html, accessed May 29, 2013.

Martin, Craig, and Russell T. McCutcheon, eds. 2012. *Religious Experience: A Reader.* Durham, UK: Acumen.

McCutcheon, Russell T. 1997. *Manufacturing Religion: The Discourse on Sui Generis Religion and the Politics of Nostalgia.* New York: Oxford University Press.

McCutcheon, Russell T. 1999. "Book Review: *Savage Systems: Colonialism and Comparative Religion in Southern Africa*, David Chidester." *History of Religions* 39(1): 73–6. http://dx.doi.org/10.1086/463575.

McCutcheon, Russell T. 2003. "Filling in the Cracks with Resin: A Reply to John Burris''Text and Context in the Study of Religion'." *Method & Theory in the Study of Religion* 15(3): 284–303. http://dx.doi. org/10.1163/157006803322393404.

McCutcheon, Russell T. 2006. "Review of Harvey Whitehouse, *Modes of Religiosity: A Cognitive Theory of Religious Transmission*." *Journal of Contemporary Religion* 21(2): 261–2.

McCutcheon, Russell T. 2007a. "Africa on our Minds." In Theodore Trost, ed., *The African Diaspora and the Study of Religion*, 229–37. New York: Palgrave Macmillan.

McCutcheon, Russell T. 2007b. "They Licked the Platter Clean: On the Co-Dependency of the Religious and the Secular." *Method & Theory in the Study of Religion* 19: 173–99.

McNamara, Patrick. 2009. *The Neuroscience of Religious Experience.* Cambridge: Cambridge University Press. http://dx.doi.org/10.1017/ CBO9780511605529.

Monaghan, Peter. 2009. "Biocriminology." *The Chronicle of Higher Education* 55/32 (April 17): B4. http://chronicle.com/article/Biocriminology/17685, accessed May 29, 2013.

Murphy, Todd. (n.d.). *Neurobiology of Religious Terrorism.* http://www.shaktitechnology.com/terrorism.htm, accessed May 29, 2013.

Sperber, Dan. 1996. *Explaining Culture: A Naturalistic Approach.* Cambridge, MA: Blackwell Publishers.

Taves, Ann. 2009. *Religious Experience Reconsidered: A Building Block Approach to the Study of Religion and Other Special Things.* Princeton: Princeton University Press.

Volavka, Jan. 1999. "The Neurobiology of Violence." *Journal of Neuropsychiatry and Clinical Neurosciences* 11(3): 307–14. http://dx.doi.org/10.1176/jnp.11.3.307http://neuro.psychiatryonline.org/article.aspx?articleid=100304, accessed May 29, 2013.

Volavka, Jan. 2002. *The Neurobiology of Violence.* 2nd ed. Washington, DC: American Psychiatric Publishing.

Whitehouse, Harvey. 2004. *Modes of Religiosity: A Cognitive Theory of Religious Transmission.* Walnut Creek, CA: Alta Mira Press.

Russell T. McCutcheon is Professor and Chair of the Department of Religious Studies at the University of Alabama. His research focuses on the social and political implications of competing classification systems.

Topic II: Behind the "Ahistorical"

3. Everything is a Cemetery: On the History Behind the "Ahistorical"

Leslie Dorrough Smith

As I write this, the 150th anniversary of the Battle of Gettysburg has just passed. Gettysburg is remembered as one of the most pivotal moments in the United States' Civil War, in part for the decisive way that momentum shifted in favor of the Union forces, but also because a larger number of lives were lost there than in any other battle in the conflict. Today, the battle is often remembered in conjunction with Lincoln's famous Gettysburg Address, which occurred some four months after the clash that shares the same name. In that speech, Lincoln invoked the founding of the nation itself ("Four score and seven years ago…") as the start of an enterprise dedicated to the preservation of justice, equality, and freedom, one which the sacrifices of the Gettysburg dead continued to make possible, he noted, for they "gave their lives that a nation might live" (Lincoln 1863).

I was recently listening to a local radio talk show that was interviewing the author of a new book on the battle. The author described Gettysburg (now a national military park and major tourist draw) as "hallowed ground" because, he claimed, it is infused with a sacred aura due to the sheer number of people killed on the site. When the phone lines were opened up to the audience, many of the show's callers remarked on Gettysburg's "haunting" nature. One caller in particular (a self-described stoic) claimed that he found himself sobbing uncontrollably when he entered the park, a response he understood as an instinctual reaction to the sadness and the death that tangibly permeated that physical space. He was careful to note that he had never felt anything like that before in any other location, an evaluation with which many others on the show concurred.

These descriptions of Gettysburg show the critical role that an enormously popular narrative can play in normalizing the description of, and even sensations surrounding, a particular event or place. On the simplest analytical level, those who contributed to this conversation were asserting that the physical site of the battle holds distinction because so many died there – it reeks, some might say, with the emotions of death. To those who employ this sort of description, death (and particularly, mass death) is portrayed as a force that exposes things called "sacredness" and "hallowedness," states which, under this reading, comprise a wholly "other," ineffable experience.

It seems, however, that if Gettysburg had been left an unmarked, grassy field, uncontextualized as a vital part of a nation's (and by extension, its citizens') history, then it would likely conjure no emotions at all. Realistically speaking, those of us who live in a locale that has ever supported a population of any size are constantly walking, jogging, working, and simply *living* directly on the geographical sites where others – perhaps many, many others – have long ago died.

In this sense, everything is a cemetery. It is a common problem in certain regions of Greece, for instance, that when one wants to erect a new building, one will frequently unearth all sorts of artifacts and even human remains, the ruins of that country's many ancient population centers. The government then decides whether such artifacts are of any historical importance (i.e., whether they play a role in the nation's dominant cultural narrative), which then determines whether the building project may proceed.

This process of selective importance is instructive, for what this shows to the analytical scholar is that it is not particularly useful to describe "the sacred" as a substance that emanates universally from certain sources, but as, rather, a label that gets strategically deployed to distinguish certain phenomena from others. We can likely all agree that those who long ago died and may now lie buried underneath our backyards or the local shopping mall (to name a couple of mundane examples) were not any less alive than those who participated in Gettysburg. Rather, those more mundane places remain largely irrelevant precisely because those who died there are not a part of our social consciousness, and thus are not a part of our cultural or personal narratives. Moreover, their absence within these narratives means that they do not even register as a piece of data in our minds, the relative "sacredness" of which we might evaluate.

If "sacredness," then, is a term that does not so much describe an eternal, ahistorical essence as much as it labels the way that we presently appropriate importance to certain things, how and in what context we construct such labels (and the emotions that often accompany them) is worth considering. To be clear, taking up this question is not an implicit statement that those who visited Gettysburg were not feeling real emotions, nor does it suggest that they were not sincerely moved by whatever it was that they experienced there. Rather, it is to suggest, in the vein of Durkheim, that the emotional experiences that help create our perceptions of reality are not inward impulses that reveal deep-seated truths as much as they are learned responses that operate like teaching tools, reinforcing the values that cultures embrace – and thus pass on – to their members (1995: 217–20, 222)

Consider the multiple other labels that we are trained, in a sense, to feel. Our culture's obsession with thinness is not something that we're born with; one must be taught that body fat is disgusting before a close examination in the mirror conjures feelings of repulsion and worthlessness. So also some learn to be afraid of public speaking or harmless spiders, neither of which poses any sort of inherent physical threat. Similarly, one might think of the irony that so much of what is called "comfort food," if consumed in certain quantities over time, can kill. Although the sensations that we experience in these moments are "real" in the sense that they are measurable phenomena, this does not make them any less constructed.

It seems, then, that Gettysburg produces the emotions that it does because the story of the Civil War is a well-rehearsed, critical part of the American narrative that has been fundamental not only to politics past and present, but to everything from the nation's religious history and racial demographics to its real-estate patterns and culinary preferences. In this way, Americans have been trained to see Gettysburg as a place overwhelmed with emotion only because it is the backdrop in a story of a courageous president, freed slaves, liberties preserved, and the coming of age of a young and righteous nation.

There are other ways, of course, to think about Gettysburg and the Civil War. The white supremacist Confederate movements that still exist today likely contextualize events differently, as might those who trouble Lincoln's memorialization as the "Great Emancipator," instead highlighting the many examples of the President's overt racism. Had either one of these perspectives been mainstreamed as the central version of events we hear today, perhaps our recollections, attitudes, and even feelings about Gettysburg might be different. The fact that one version of the story has been widely popularized at the expense of other recollections of the same physical events, however, displays the very selective qualities of memory, history, and the emotional training that often follows from them.

Insomuch as one of our most basic acts as humans is the social dance of being taught and thereby adopting certain descriptions over others, then, particular accounts of reality operate as powerful pre-existing frames of reference that work not to simply describe a reality in neutral existence before us, but to craft the seemingly inevitable version of events (or the limited choices therein) that our culture's labels permit. With this in mind, perhaps a robust scholarly analysis depends on exercising a considerable amount of caution when encountering any descriptions of reality that presume self-evidence, universality, or any other claim of inexplicability that the aforementioned terms like "sacred" or "hallowed" invoke. Scholars may find this a rather obvious lesson when it comes to the categorization performed by cultures that strike us as illogical, inconsequential, or otherwise uncanny. It is much harder to keep this in mind, however, when the labels being employed are so widely popular and of such great cultural importance (to us, at least) that they are rendered virtually obvious.

This is the very sort of issue that the following essay considers regarding the highly influential work of Mircea Eliade. As McCutcheon argues, Eliade's popularization of the concept of "the sacred" has created what McCutcheon perceives to be a series of the discipline's most serious methodological contradictions. In addition to how one can analytically speak about a thing that is often described as beyond proof, Eliadian models also introduce concepts that push the critical scholar to consider how one should generally regard the logic used by insiders, the role and degree to which social and historical forces help create powerful and popular social concepts, and even how scholars' own socio-political locations contribute to their creation, interpretation, and analysis of categories like "the sacred."

This is an important lesson to keep in mind when thinking about historically prominent events such as Gettysburg, for sometimes the scholars responsible for the dominant narratives about those events with which we live become the very data worth studying. In Eliade's case, McCutcheon shows how the concept of an enduring, positive, universal force that remained above the political fray would have been a concept with great appeal to someone living in a time and place marred by political instability. Similarly, those who want to seriously consider why Gettysburg is described as a "sacred" site might look to the contexts of those scholars who deploy the term today rather than back to any special quality of Gettysburg itself. Only so long as Gettysburg remains a critical backdrop to the way that concepts like patriotism, liberties, sacrifice, and duty – to name just a popular few – are currently contextualized does its "sacred" label likely stand. In other words, the fact that a certain emotion stems from a certain concept that was inspired by certain social arrangements makes the resulting labels ("sacred," "hallowed," etc.) adjectives that are the product of the commingling of historical, temporal events, not descriptions of ahistorical, sui generis phenomena.

What this means, by extension, is that the way that we talk – and even the way we feel – about the past is always a matter of understanding the political negotiations of the present. We miss the ability to understand why such labels are both manufactured and applied to specific historical moments if we presume that they stand outside of history even as they describe it. To take the concept of "the sacred" as an indefinable, ineffable, ahistorical reality – a term thrown around and often used in the service of describing otherwise powerful emotions or things "beyond description" – ultimately arrests the scholarly conversation. For if the defining quality of the sacred is this fundamental ineffability, then scholars are disqualified from its study; as themselves products of culture, time, and place, scholars are left with no extra-cultural techniques of studying an extra-cultural thing. If, however, we can begin to think about "the sacred" as an identificatory strategy instead of an essence that defies analysis, then the conversation can begin, and with it the question of how a grassy field in Gettysburg, Pennsylvania has become, for some, a central character in a nation's self-representation.

References

Durkheim, Emile. 1995. *The Elementary Forms of Religious Life*. Trans. Karen Fields. New York: The Free Press.

Lincoln, Abraham. 1863. "Gettysburg Address (1863)," *Our Documents* Initiative Website, http://www.ourdocuments.gov/doc.php?flash=true&doc=36, accessed July 30, 2013.

Leslie Dorrough Smith is Assistant Professor of Religious Studies and Chair of the Women's and Gender Studies program at Avila University. Her current research examines the interplay between gender, sex, reproduction, and the politics of American evangelical groups.

4. The Melancholy Empire Builder: The Life and Works of Mircea Eliade[1]

Russell T. McCutcheon

> "I am telling you, that experience was so – so sacred that I never thought I could touch it again. So I put you out of time and space" [he said].... "Why do you speak of putting me beyond time and space? [she replied.] Have I become a ghost? In what dream world, in what obscure heaven do you live, Mircea?... Get rid of your escapist mentality." – Maitreyi Devi (1995 [1976]: 252–3)

Over the past 25 years, the career of the influential historian of religions, Mircea Eliade (1907–86), has become the fertile ground

[1] Although this essay was originally published in 1993, the version that is included here was first revised (and probably doubled in size) sometime in 2002, when I had considered including an updated version of it in the essay collection, *The Discipline of Religion* (2003). It is hardly a definitive overview of Eliade's life and the controversies surrounding it and his work (see McCutcheon 2001 for additional commentary on the controversies), but it has been cited in the literature around Eliade (inasmuch as it came out not long after the controversy on Eliade's life and work first developed); given the manner in which the depoliticized approach to his story often wins the day – as it often does with any tale purporting to tell an origins story or which addresses the exploits of someone considered to be a founder – this earlier essay also served as a useful springboard into a few wider issues, such as the manner in which those interested in such topics as religion and violence – a research area that has picked up speed considerably since the early 2000s – employ the same sort of rhetoric in their work on the causes of certain sorts of violent acts. For all of these reasons – plus the fact that it is not difficult to find people, 20 years after critiques like this were being first leveled, still aestheticizing our field's past – it seemed worth including here.

from which has sprung not only a minor industry in autobiographical and biographical writings, but a controversial body of secondary literature concerned with clarifying the extent of Eliade's apparent attraction to Romanian fascism between the first and second world wars. In particular, some scholars have investigated whether there is any relationship between Eliade's early politics and his subsequent empire building in the US discipline of the History of Religions. As was first argued by Ivan Strenski in what was then his ground-breaking *Four Theories of Myth in Twentieth-Century History: Cassirer, Eliade, Lévi-Strauss, and Malinowski* (1987), Eliade's political past in pre-World War II Romania could partly account for his unique theory of myths and his methods for conceptualizing and studying the religions of moderns as well as archaic people. This chapter rehearses some of that history, in an attempt to examine the wider context that helped to produce one of the most influential rhetoriticians of the newly emergent discipline. Eliade's story is one in which alienation and melancholy are very much at home, prompted by changing structural circumstances, all of which comprise the raw materials for new acts of social formation.

Labors of Love

As far as modern scholars of religion are concerned, Eliade's life is the only one to have received such elaborate attention. His unfinished two-volume autobiography (1988, 1990a), supplemented by his four published volumes of journals (1989a, 1989b, 1990b, 1990c; in one manner or another he kept notebooks and journals for most his life), and his translator, Mac Linscott Ricketts's extensively documented, 1,460-page biography of Eliade's early Romanian period (1988; Ricketts also translated the two-volume autobiography, along with a variety of other works by Elaide) provide the interested – perhaps devoted – reader with an account of one man's life, his influences, and his actions. The journals began publication with volume two in 1977 (originally under the title *No Souvenirs* and covering the years 1957–69) and contain only a small portion of Eliade's private notes, all of which are housed in the archives at the University of Chicago.[2]

Eliade's autobiography and journals are best read together since we are told that various passages scribbled in his notebooks and on various scraps of paper over the years were Eliade's only references when, many years later, he created a coherent narrative covering his early years in Romania. This serves to remind the wary reader of the concocted nature of narrative in general, and the autobiographical process in particular. Besides the expected mundane entries, the journals record details of his writing and working routines (he worked best throughout the night, a habit he picked up in his youth), his lectures and visitors, his increasing difficulties with poor health as he aged, and his recurring nostalgia for the Romania of his youth. In these pages, the reader can follow not only Eliade's books from their inception to their publication and eventual translation (see Smith 2000a and 2000b for his two essays using these resources to track Eliade's work on his still classic *Patterns in Comparative Religion* [1958]), but also his many travels across Europe, and to Japan and the United States. The degree to which the single word "melancholy" – "the feeling of the enormous vanity of all things," as he phrases it (1988: 21) – appears throughout the journals and autobiography, most notably in Eliade's last published journal (covering the years 1979–85), is enough to cause the reader to share the emotion. "How mediocre is the man who has never in his life known melancholy," he writes while on summer vacation in 1937 (1988: 44); "Melancholy," he concludes, is "a major instrument in cognition, the only one capable of disturbing and shaking the imperialistic security of theology...." In both volumes of his *Autobiography*, Eliade links his ability for adolescent, and in fact lifelong, fits of despair to his father's Moldavian roots – an example of his apparently lifelong preoccupation with obscured meanings, hidden roots, an insecurity concerning self-identity and

---

[2] Apart from a portion of the collection devoted to student grades, letters of reference written by Eliade, etc., the collection is now open for research. For more information, and a list of contents for the various parts of the collection, see: http://www.lib.uchicago.edu/e/scrc/findingaids/view.php?eadid=ICU.SPCL.ELIADEM (accessed May 24, 2013).

social importance, and the disaffection that comes of living on the margin as an exile, as a persona non grata (1988: 126).

If any reader must be vigilant for the undisclosed effects of the untheorized autobiographical process (i.e., the way in which writers construct a narrative of the past through a prism of present interests), this warning also goes for Eliade's biographical volumes. Ricketts, Eliade's biographer and the translator of two of his journals, who studied under the scholar at the University of Chicago from 1959 to 1964, has co-edited a collection of essays on Eliade (Girardot and Ricketts 1982) written from the 1960s through 1980s, on such topics as Eliade's place in the death of God debate of the 1960s and his relations to the theories of Jung (notably Eliade's talk of a transconscious and his specific use of the term *archetype*). Further, it was Ricketts who defended Eliade against the sharp attack on his methods and theories mounted by the anthropologist Edmund Leach (Leach 1966; Ricketts 1973). "Driven by some obscure demon," Ricketts informs his readers in the Introduction to his two thick biographical volumes (1988: 2), he acquired his reading knowledge of Romanian specifically for his study and translations of Eliade's work. What one will find in this work, begun in 1981, are verifications and clarifications (with some limited contestation) of Eliade's own recollections, accompanied by lengthy summaries of Eliade's many early stories, newspaper columns, novels, and novellas. But, alas, Ricketts's great adoration for Eliade (the biography has been described as "a labor of love" [Allen 1992: 174]) makes the critical utility of this work rather questionable.

Apart from the admittedly important contribution Ricketts has made by translating for the English reader material that formerly existed only in yellowing Romanian periodicals, his biographical volumes, and possibly Eliade's own for that matter, fail to pursue the sensitive questions. Both writers consistently portray Eliade as a politically naïve youth concerned with what, even in his old age, he still maintained were essentially spiritual and cultural matters – messianic or spiritual nationalism are favorite phrases of Eliade's defenders (akin to the slippery and self-beneficial distinction between dangerous nationalism and harmless patriotism, or perhaps the difference between supposedly mild wrongdoing and egregious wrongdoing)

– untainted by the messy workings of power and politics.[3] In spite of the rather obvious absence of any sort of critical scrutiny of his life, these volumes will have to do for now since there has yet to appear a critical biography on this influential yet controversial figure.

Scholar and Author of the Fantastic

Mircea Eliade is today known widely as one of the most influential modern Historians of Religions – as far back as 1978 he was the 43rd most cited author in all of the arts and humanities. Perhaps this is because his mature academic interests were diverse; they varied from what he termed the spiritual techniques of shamanism and yoga to alchemy and the interpretation of dreams, from the so-called religious dimensions of archaic civilizations to the role played by religious symbolism in modern cinema and fiction. What began in the form of his regular contributions to Romanian student periodicals on such topics as entomology and geology led to three years of study in India and the writing of his dissertation on yoga. His academic career culminated with his sweeping, yet unfinished, three-volume *A History of Religious Ideas* and his role as editor-in-chief of Macmillan's massive 16-volume *Encyclopedia of Religion*, published in 1987, the year after his death.

Sprinkled throughout his career of scholarly writing were his numerous fictional and fantastical works – in fact, by 30 he was a widely read Romanian author of some note. *Maitreyi* (1933; it was later published in English as *Bengal Nights* [1995]), his fictionalized account of his time in India, was named after his Indian host's 16-year-old daughter – Maitreyi Devi (d. 1990) – with whom the 23-year-old Eliade was apparently infatuated. Over 40 years later, upon learning for the first time of Eliade's fictionalized tale, Maitreyi published her own fictionalized version of events entitled, *It Does Not Die* (1995

---

[3] As Rennie writes in the *Encyclopedia of Religion*'s new edition, in a supplementary article on Eliade: "It is worthy of note that despite strident condemnations of Eliade's political past, this material [i.e., archival material recently unearthed concerning Eliade's past] has so far revealed no incontrovertible evidence of egregious wrongdoing" (2005: 2758).

[1976]) – from which I quoted this chapter's epigraph. Her book contests what she saw as Eliade's own self-serving and Romanticized version of the events; significantly, perhaps, whereas his book ends with the words, "I would like to be able to look Maitreyi in the eyes..." (1995: 176), her novel concludes with her fictional confrontation with the now old, and famous, Eliade who stands with his back to her in his University of Chicago office: "Turn around, Mircea, I want to see you," she writes (1995: 253).

The scandal of their brief and apparently innocent relationship, coupled with mandatory military service back in Romania, led to Eliade's early departure from India. At home the novel received an enthusiastic reception and helped to propel him to minor fame. It is of interest, however, that he never returned to India and that he and Maitreyi met again only in the "dream world" of their contesting narratives. His various novels and novellas, written mostly in Romanian, some of which have been translated into English (e.g., *The Forbidden Forest* and the collection *Youth Without Youth*) have only recently begun to receive the same academic scrutiny as his work in the history of religions.[4] Interestingly, he always felt that in North America and western Europe he was bound by convention either to become a scholar *or* a fiction author – but not both. Accordingly, Eliade's scholarly works (unlike his fiction) exist in numerous translations throughout the world and can be purchased not only in university book stores but, like his fellow mythologist and Jungian Eranos Conference participant Joseph Campbell, as mass-market paperbacks (on Eliade's involvement at Eranos, see Wasserstrom 1999).

Universal Aspirations

Eliade was born in Bucharest in 1907, a year after his brother Nicolaie and four years before his sister Cornelia. His father, Gheorghe, was a career officer in the Romanian infantry, eventually rising to the rank of captain. His mother, Ioana, was one of 14 children and born in

---

[4] For example, Francis Ford Coppola released his film adaptation of "Youth Without Youth," starring Tim Roth, in 2007.

Bucharest herself. It was from his father, Eliade often remarked, that he had inherited his spirit of Romanticism and from his mother that he acquired his energy and pragmatism. This apparent union of opposites is a theme that recurs throughout his writings, perhaps telling us why he frames his own narrative as he does, for he later came to believe that it comprised the very core of religious symbolism (what he termed the *coincidentia oppositorum*). As he represents himself, the young Eliade can only be described as a voracious reader. Hampered by the early diagnosis of myopia and his father's conclusion that his young eyes must not be strained by excessive reading for leisure, he was forced to stay up late into the night secretly reading in his attic bedroom. Gradually teaching himself a variety of ancient and modern languages, he made his way through many of what we would now consider the classics of late-19th-century learning, following what he believed to be an honorable tradition of the Romanian academics who aspired to have a cultural impact outside what they felt to be their sadly isolated, provincial country.

His passion for universal learning originally ran the route of the natural and life sciences, but, primarily as a result of reading the works of such early comparative religionists as F. Max Müller (1823–1900) and James G. Frazer (1854–1951), he quickly developed an interest in studying ancient myths, rituals, and languages. As well, Eliade demonstrated at an early age what were to become for him two lifelong preoccupations: the romance of the peasantry and the terrors of historical time. Even though he acknowledged elsewhere that he was brought up as part of the petit bourgeoisie, he remarks in his autobiography on how he Romanticized his own origins: "I liked knowing that I was descended from a family of Moldavian yeomen.... I was proud of the fact that I was only three generations removed from peasants – that, although born and bred in a city, I was still so close to the 'soul of the country'" (1990a: 16). Romanticizing the difficult life of early 20th-century Romanian peasants in a manner possible only for those who do not have to live such a life in reality, he goes on to write,

> Sometimes I regretted that I had not been reared in the country,
> that I did not know as a child the village life that seemed to me

to be the only true kind, and that now I was severed irrevocably
from that idyllic world. (1990a: 73)

These interests, with "things archaic" and the dehistoricized and thus
depoliticized peasant life, come together for Eliade to form his often
made claim that the peasant classes throughout Europe were a link
to a nobler, common past, housing within their contemporary myths
and stories basic human truths long forgotten by "Western" secular
society. There is an important irony here: despite seeming to be all too
provincial, within the rural peasantry survives essential, trans-human
meanings.

   After a somewhat meager existence during World War I – where
his youthful nationalist pride took the form of fantasies he recorded
involving camouflaged Romanian infantrymen to whom he says he
dreamed of passing messages on the movements of the German soldiers occupying his town and his home – Eliade began in earnest
his studies at the local *lyceé*. During these early student years Eliade
reports that he was preoccupied by a need to recapture time, yet
another theme of his later writings (or a later theme read backward in
time through the autobiographical process) and one possibly linked
to the repeated melancholy of his last years. Throughout his adoles-
cence, he records, in hindsight, how he devised a method whereby
he would defeat time by regaining several minutes from sleep each
night, thereby extending his nightly reading time. This "struggle
against sleep," as he phrased it years later, signified "a heroic attempt
to transcend the human condition" (1990a: 110) – a theme he reads
back onto these childhood disciplines after years of studying such
practices as yoga. Having achieved some limited victory in this early
struggle by lessening his sleep by an entire hour, he reports that he
would accustom himself to his new pattern for several weeks before
embarking on recapturing yet another precious hour. In this somewhat
driven manner, he states that he trained himself to sleep, at times only
three or four hours a night while working strenuously on his writing
(1990a: 63). And write he did – at first only brief articles in his early
student days, but eventually he had the tremendous energy to review
books, establish and edit journals, write novellas, and contribute to a
variety of newspapers, believing himself to be speaking on behalf of

his entire generation. Before he left for India in November of 1928, he had already become a minor writer of some note in the popular Romanian presses.

Eliade returned to Romania in 1931 after spending three years studying various aspects of Indian asceticism – topics of much interest to many other disillusioned Europeans of this period. Apart from his brief yet somewhat scandalous relationship with Maitreyi, this time of meditation and study seems to have been intellectually quite productive for him. His early interest in the seemingly simple life of the Romanian village was complemented nicely, and thus cultivated, by what he – and so many other equally alienated Europeans of this era – understood as the romance of the "East." In particular, Eliade focused upon what he understood to be the Hindu stress upon the need to return perpetually to archaic origins, in order to situate the present as meaningful. Through the study and practice of yoga, Eliade believed he had found a universally applicable spiritual technique which, much like the pre-Christian myths of the essentialized Romanian peasants, pre-dated the rise of Hinduism in the Indian subcontinent (1990a: 202–4). Yoga was, to him, but one technique for escaping from the bonds of the ever-repeating cycles of unmanageable historical existence. It was at this time that his belief in the basic yearning of all humans to escape history – the so-called heroic attempt to transcend the human condition – found its first systematic articulation. Looking back on the late-1930s, he wrote in his autobiography that

> [s]ome nationalistic intellectuals deplored my alienation, the fact that I had let myself be absorbed by exotic cultural phenomena instead of studying authentic Romanian creations. Now, to repeat myself, I believe that my efforts to understand the structures of archaic and Oriental thought contributed more genuinely to the decipherment of the values of the Romanian folk spirituality than, for instance, the exegesis of Kant or sociological interpretations based on the latest books from Germany, France, or the United States. (1988: 8, n. 2)

Insights from "the Orient" were thus the key for unlocking the supposed universality of the misleadingly provincial Romanian hinterlands. Later recollections of his onetime critics notwithstanding, Eliade's contributions to remaking the Romanian nation-state were, ironically perhaps, made possible only by his alienation and departure from it, which in turn allowed him to return home from the "mystic East" with insights he had reached about the relations between "our peasantry" and "the Human Condition."

The years leading up to World War II in Romania, as in much of Europe, were politically unstable, to say the least. Upon his return from India, Eliade's writing career was extremely productive, if not financially secure. He married his first wife, Nina, who was extremely supportive of his life as novelist, and his lecturing career began to blossom. However, during this time his long inbred nationalistic spirit seems to have grown considerably. By the close of the 1930s he was writing quite openly in support of the Legion of the Archangel Michael – the crypto-spiritual Romanian fascist movement founded in 1927 – and condemning the government as well as the king. However, a dark time soon arrived once the Legion temporarily lost power in 1938, and King Carol II set up his own dictatorship. Many Legion supporters were jailed and/or executed and, for a time, Eliade found himself in a political prison camp, but a possible illness landed him in a hospital from where he, somewhat anticlimactically but luckily for him, was released unharmed. Fortuitously, it seems that friends in high places soon ensured that he obtained a position as a Romanian diplomat in England, thereby allowing him to leave the country. As it turns out, Eliade lived in London for just a year, for there was some controversy as to his status as Romanian cultural attaché. After leaving London, he carried out diplomatic duties as a member of the Romanian delegation in neutral Lisbon, where he stayed for the duration of the war. Following the end of World War II, he chose to live what he would later call the life of an exile in Paris.

In 1945, not long after Nina's death from cancer, Georges Dumézil – the noted scholar of Indo-European myths – obtained for Eliade a teaching position at the École des hautes études, where he continued to write and publish the books that were to become synonymous with his particular approach to the study of religion: *Traité d'histoire des religions* (in 1947); *Le Mythe de l'éternel retour: archétypes et répétition* (in 1949, English translation 1974); *Le Chamanisme et les techniques archaiques de l'extase* (in 1951); and *Le Yoga: Immortalité et liberté* (in 1954) – in some quarters his early work on yoga and shamanism is still believed to set a standard rarely equaled in subsequent scholarship. Interestingly, the great fame Eliade attained in the United States was almost exclusively based upon these early works published prior to his arrival there.

In 1957, following the sudden death of the German sociologist of religion, Joachim Wach, Eliade was invited to remain at the University of Chicago and replace Wach as head of Chicago's History of Religions program – an institution with which Eliade's name is now intimately associated (e.g., the Mircea Eliade Distinguished Service Chair in the History of Religions, currently held by Wendy Doniger since its establishment in 1986). He had come to Chicago from Paris the previous year to deliver the divinity school's prestigious Haskell lectures (later published as *Birth and Rebirth* [1958]). After accepting Wach's former position and permanently moving to Chicago, Eliade, with the assistance of a variety of scholars (not least would be Wach's disciple, Joseph Kitagawa [1915–92], long credited by many with "working the phones" to ensure that Chicago graduates obtained positions around the country), ensured that the "Chicago school" quickly became the academic centre of gravity for the academic study of religion in North America. Many departments around the continent were gradually populated with Chicago graduates trained to realize Eliade's dream of universal scholars of religion schooled in studying any number of its historical manifestations. For as he notes in his autobiography (1988: 208), in the late 1950s there were

> only a few chairs of history of religions in American universities. Fifteen years later, their number had risen to twenty-five, almost all occupied by our former students who had obtained their doctorates at the University of Chicago.

Until his death in April of 1986, Eliade taught at Chicago, directed doctoral students, wrote and travelled extensively in the summer term, was highlighted in the national media, and lectured around the world.

"Happy Guilt"

Eliade's brief stay in London, begun after his departure from Bucharest in April 1940, is an issue that has initiated some debate. Based upon varied interpretations of British Foreign Office documents from this period, it is presently unclear whether or not Eliade was ever recognized by the British as having diplomatic status. Further, not only did the British apparently suspect Eliade of assisting the pro-Legionary Romanian government that came to power after the failure of King Carol II's dictatorship, but he may actually have been asked by the British government to leave for Lisbon. While it is true that such controversial revelations rely upon a rather uncritical acceptance of the Foreign Office's own propagandistic motivations in labeling the young Eliade as a fascist, this is a period in his life that still remains concealed to a large degree.

What *is* clear is that because of his pre-war associations – to whatever degree – with the fascist movement in Romania, Eliade was prevented from returning to his homeland under Communist rule following the end of the war. Although his subsequent fame in Romania appears to have varied with the country's political climate, Eliade declined to return to his homeland, and only after 1967 was he able occasionally to speak with his family by telephone. After a sleepless night in the Fall of 1984, Eliade wrote briefly in his journal of what he considered to be his "happy guilt": "I kept thinking of what I would have suffered had I remained in the homeland as professor and writer. If it hadn't been for that *felix culpa*: my adoration for Nae Ionescu and all the baleful consequences (in 1935–1940) of that relationship" (October 4, 1984; see 1988: 139).

Ironically, then, his relationship with Nae Ionescu (1890–1940), editor and professor of philosophy and logic who was Eliade's mentor (as well as considered by many to have been the chief ideologist of the Legionary movement), may have saved Eliade's life by preventing him from returning to Romania's tragic post-war Communist purges. From the vantage point of the second volume of his autobiography, Eliade reflected back on such topics as Romania's coups, counter-coups, and political assassinations of the late 1930s, Ionescu's arrest and dismissal from the university (entailing his own dismissal

as Ionescu's assistant), his own literary outpouring, and the imma-
nent, if only temporary, demise of the popular Legionary movement:

> That was why I had produced so much so fast; I knew that the
> leisure history had allowed us was limited. I had never imag-
> ined that we would find ourselves in such a situation due to a
> nationalistic student movement that in my university years I had
> viewed with indifference, and due to a young king whose com-
> ing to the throne I, like my whole generation, had considered
> providential. (1988: 13)

In this passage one can detect a variety of themes more than likely
important to an older man remembering himself as a younger man:
his belief that he embodied the aspirations of his entire generation;
his apparent political naïveté; his need to create culture through his
voluminous writing; his belief in destiny; and his terror of history.

Myths, Mysteries, and Terrors

Perhaps what Eliade is still most known for today is his work on myth
and ritual and the application of his theory of symbolism to a variety of other areas. As already mentioned, Eliade argued that humans
are preoccupied by what he often referred to as a "terror of history,"
an anxiety over the uncertainty of linear, temporal existence and the
dangers that accompany its unexpected – because unprecedented –
disruptions. To make sense of what generally appeared to be a chaotic
and uncertain historical existence, Eliade argued that archaic people
employed myths to narrate, and rituals to (re)enact, paradigmatic or
archetypal events in their past, i.e., in the age of ancestors or the time
when the gods walked the earth, which in turn functioned as models
and thus legitimators for their own behavior in the present. In the
hands of Eliade, the cosmogonic myth – accounts of the founding of
the universe present in a variety of cultures – became the exemplar of
all myths, providing the authoritative narration of how things came
to be and thus how things now *ought* to be. It thus provides people
with an existential orientation, a centre for action in the present and
the future based firmly upon traditional patterns (archetypes) of the

past. For this reason, Eliade placed great interpretive emphasis upon recurring images of the authoritative centre (e.g., center poles in tents or central pillars in temples) in what he considered to be virtually all religions and cultures.

Alongside his theory of myth, Eliade is also still well-known for his use of the sacred/profane pairing. However, unlike the sociologist, Émile Durkheim (1858–1917), who accounted for the sacred as a projection of the group itself (as a value created by policing otherwise mundane rule systems), Eliade can be read to have maintained that it was the ahistorical sacred – related to the "wholly other" of the German theologian Rudolph Otto (1869–1937) – which, through an intimate relationship with historical conditions, manifested itself within certain previously profane (and thus only seemingly mundane) items such as rocks, mountains, or human beings. Bringing his work on myth and the sacred together, Eliade held that it is primarily those exemplary creative moments – narrated in myths and acted out in rituals – that signal occasions when the sacred becomes incarnate within the profane world. He thus maintained that incursions of the sacred into history are always at the heart of the creation stories that provide human beings with an orientation for, and therefore meaning in, their present lives.[5]

To provide evidence for his theory, Eliade looked to the early ethnographic records of archaic or "primitive" civilizations, most notably the Australian aborigines, a group popular among late 19th- and early 20th-century European scholars intent on applying their theories of cultural deterioration or development.[6] Archaic humans, he believed, had yet to attempt to answer their terror of history through the strategy employed by the modern, technological, and largely Christian West – the development of the notion of a linear history that would someday end. Rather, so-called archaic people – and religious people in general, Eliade argues – cope with existential untidiness and the apparent meaninglessness of historical existence by interpreting the present in

[5] It is explicitly against Eliade's use of "sacred/profane" that Bill Arnal and I entitled our own book (2013).

[6] See Sam Gill's *Storytracking* (1998) for a fascinating study of the many conflicting versions through which these ethnographies went; on the development of Gill's own work, see Urban 2001.

terms of virtually endless past and future cycles, whereby meaning is created through reference to, and repetition of, timeless archetypes or patterns (i.e., appeals to and re-enactments of past events such as a golden age, as described at length by Plato in *The Republic*, or even the founding of the universe, much as a Brahmin priest's disciplined ritual recitations are said to re-create the universe). Such grand origins are then continually re-experienced by devotees through the stories and practices that narrate/enact the universe's (and hence their own group's) founding. Hence, the myth of the eternal return occupies a prominent place in Eliade's comparative studies.

Since he argued that an ahistorical sacred (a term that he, like some of his students, never adequately defined) was actually manifested in various profane conditions, Eliade employed a decontextualized comparative method to analyze the similarities in myths and rituals from many different historical periods, cultures, and contexts. Somewhat reminiscent of his late19th-century predecessors (e.g., James G. Frazer), images of the moon, rebirth, mountains, trees, snakes, etc., found in a variety of what other scholars would see to be disparate oral and textual sources, became the raw material in his search for the underlying, inner structures of the sacred – i.e., the logic of *hierophanies* or manifestations of the sacred. His reasoning: changeable history and culture influence the outward *form* of religious expression, but not its pre-contextual essence, and to understand the *essence*, the Historian of Religions needs to employ sensitive interpretive techniques that treat the religious phenomenon as something intrinsically *religious*, as opposed to *reducing* its supposedly deep meaning to what Eliade considered crude and simplistic social (structural) conditions, such as economics (Marx) or mere wish-fulfillment (Freud). An example of what he called the "banalization of history" (1989a: 55) can be seen in his view on the role context plays in determining the "creativity" of the artist or the state of "one's existence"; recalling his early poverty while attempting to write, he records:

> I refused to believe that poverty or wealth or the "environment" could sterilize a creative spirit.... I could not believe that an existence is modified according to scenery and characters.... For me, the style of one's existence was a continual inner creation that

had nothing to do either with material conditions or with the surroundings or setting in which circumstances had placed one. (1990a: 274)

In much the same manner, Eliade asserted that the academic discourse on religion was the exclusive province of Historians of Religions who were capable of re-creating the inner life of the sacred without being distracted by such non-essential matters of scenery, style, and context. It is understandable, therefore, (i) why anthropologists and psychologists (to name only two other groups who also study "things religious") have had great difficulty with Eliade's work and (ii) why his work has often been embraced by several generations of disaffected, liberal humanists and religious pluralists alike.

Regardless one's agreement with Eliade's approach, what he did accomplish is a long overdue revaluation of the category "primitive" while providing the slowly re-emerging North American discipline with a focal point, an already existent canon of his own texts, a hermeneutical method, and the much valued legitimacy of a European heritage. As recently phrased by John Burris:

> While Mircea Eliade's conceptions of the "archaic" or "primitive" have been dismissed as a degeneration into romanticism in many quarters, his work can also be viewed as a cognizance that there was something vital in the particular inquiry into the nature of the "primitive" that had not been adequately incorporated into the developing field of religion. (2001: 77)

As the product of a long and bloody colonial tradition that in many ways culminated in such 19th-century endeavors as Christian missions, anthropological reconnaissance work, and social Darwinist theories, the category of the contemporary primitive or archaic civilization was once often thought to be an unfortunate survival from our species' collective, childlike past. Of course, it must be said that it would not be difficult to argue that these so-called primitives, these Others, were the foils by which Europeans constructed the limits of their own self-definition. Unfortunately, as history can attest, cultural *decimation* often follows upon such cultural *discrimination*. By reversing the traditional priority through devaluing the technological and so-called secular era in favor of what he described as the exemplary mode of existence found both in archaic and religious persons, Eliade assisted in bringing about an interpretive revolution that may very well have some of its rumblings in the once popular New Age movement. But, as Burris suggests, because he simply inverted the modern/primitive binary, he can easily be critiqued for romanticizing and essentializing a certain type of human social organization.

Where Philosophy and Politics Meet

Unfortunately, such a devaluation of modern, technologized Western culture appears to have coalesced around a core of formative moments that took place in his native Romania. Eliade himself recalls how his "young generation," born between the two European wars of the 20th century, reaped the benefits of the post-World War I break-up of the Austro-Hungarian Empire, which resulted in Romanian expansion into Transylvania (interpreted by Eliade the young nationalist as the fated reunification of Romania). It was his generation that could dare to dream of transforming their traditionally isolated European nation into a global influence in culture and the arts.

> As I saw things, the differences between the "young generation" and those generations that had preceded it were due primarily to the fact that our forebears had realized their historic mission: the reintegration of the Romanian people who had been divided between the Austro-Hungarian and Czarist empires. But if the First World War had allowed Romania to consolidate itself nationally, it had also caused terrible contradictions for official Western ideology. The myth of infinite progress, the faith in the decisive role of science and industry to establish universal peace and social justice, the preeminence of rationalism and the prestige of agnosticism – all these had been swept away on the battlefront. The "irrationalism" that had made the war possible and had sustained it was now making itself felt in the spiritual and cultural life of the West.... The crisis upon which the Occidental world had entered proved to me that the ideology of the war generation was no longer valid. We, the "young generation," had to find our own goals.... In order not to slumber in

cultural provincialism or spiritual sterility, we had to know what was happening everywhere in the world, in our *own time.* (1990a: 131–2)

As has already been suggested, this dream of moving from so-called provincial to universal values – compelled, I would conjecture, by tremendous insecurity and alienation prompted by the social world of interwar Romania – is realized in his later writings. As observed by Strenski (1987), the shock that greeted such youthful optimism in the guise of the political upheavals in the late 1930s was enough to instill in Eliade his own personal terror for history – a terror he seems never to have exorcized. Unlike the French existentialists, fellow products of European upheaval, who found solace in accepting – even embracing – what they termed the absurdity of history, Eliade sought instead to authorize a very particular, local understanding of contemporary history and politics by legitimizing it through appeals to a supposed golden age, linked to rhetorics of universality, depth, and authenticity. Therefore, his preoccupation with the category of the "archaic" is not so much evidence of an interest in such things as aboriginal, small-scale societies as it is a codeword for his own political program.

It may therefore be understandable that the young Eliade was drawn towards the philosophical and political circle of Nae Ionescu and the Legion of the Archangel Michael – complete with its violent wing, the Iron Guard. Although he left Romania prior to the Iron Guard's physical terrorizing of Romanian Jews, Eliade's writings from this period and, in a subtle way, all his writings in general, seem to betray the all too familiar elements of nationalist ideologies (as argued in detail in McCutcheon 1997): the emphasis upon metaphors of the earth and soil; his belief in the genius of the peasants and the village as the "soul" of the nation; his references to the "historic mission" or "messianic destiny" of the nation; and the necessity for the nation's pure, authentic membership. Adriana Berger, Eliade's former research assistant in Chicago in the early 1980s, quotes Eliade's young nationalist sentiments:

> We stayed passively and watched how the Jewish element became stronger in Transylvanian cities ... how colonies of Jewish ploughmen were established in Maramures.... Instead

of cruelly eliminating the Bulgarian element from the entire
Dobrogea, we have colonized it with Bulgarian gardeners.
(Berger 1989: 458; see Rennie 1992 for his reply; see also
Berger 1994)

Here, Berger is quoting Eliade from his early article *"Pilotii ordii"*
("Blind Pilots" or "Blind Leaders"), published in the Romanian
periodical *Vremea* (September 13, 1937: 3).[7] Even in his autobiography, written with the luxury of hindsight, Eliade seems unaware
of the potential indictment contained in his language concerning
the historic mission of the Romanian people and his use of the
phrase, "the Jewish element." Despite such language, both Eliade
and Ricketts hold firmly (and perhaps understandably) to the interpretation that he was essentially naïve, spiritual, and apolitical
throughout his young career and was attracted to Ionescu and the
Legionary movement – "the only Romanian political movement"
Eliade maintained, "which took seriously Christianity and the
church" – through what he portrays as purely intellectual, cultural,
and spiritual interests. Eliade claimed that for Corneliu Codreanu,
the founder of the Legion who was eventually jailed and executed in
1938, "the Legionary movement did not constitute a political phenomenon but was, in its essence, ethical and religious" (1988: 65).
It was a movement that "had the structure and vocation of a mystical sect, not of a political movement" (ibid.: 69).

It is true (and quite understandable) that Codreanu's movement
relied on certain Romanian traditions and that it used much Orthodox
Christian symbolism and ritual – hence its very name – but as well, it
was responsible for much violence and terror. This, of course, is not
a contradiction if we see the rhetoric of religion as an ordinary means
for accomplishing social formation, regardless the group to whose
purposes it is put. Whether or not the social group is understood by

---

[7] Berger's work in organizing Eliade's library, his anger over how she
had supposedly "rearranged" and "ransacked" his files, and a mysterious fire
which began in his office desk on December 19, 1985, destroying old papers
and books, all of which are narrated in the final volume of his journals, is a
most intriguing case, well worth the read. See in particular the entries leading
up to April 6, 1984, as well as Doniger's epilogue (Eliade 1990c: 151).

itself or others as good or bad, so long as it successfully reproduces itself it employs the rhetoric all the same. But, it *is* a contradiction for those who see religion as essentially concerned with goodness, peacefulness, and tolerance (a view shared by many scholars of religion to this day). Hence Eliade – assuming religion to have something with enduring, timeless values fundamental to "the Human Condition" – must utilize a rhetoric of culture vs politics, spiritual vs political, or orthodox vs extremist to gloss over the apparent contradiction, along with employing the notion of so-called hooligans hijacking the movement to explain the eventual violence. Predictably, not very long after the tragic September 11, 2001 attacks on New York and Washington DC we saw this same rhetorical technique in use, when politicians, media commentators, and scholars of religion on both sides of the Atlantic quickly sought to distinguish "fanatical terrorists" from "peaceful and tolerant Muslims" – a useful technique for accounting for the apparently anomalous fact that seemingly "devout and pious" people had just flown jet airliners filled with passengers into crowded buildings, leading to the tragic deaths of approximately 3,000 people.[8] As made plain at the time by the British Prime Minister, Tony Blair, in his televised October 7, 2001 speech to the British people, calling those who carried out these attacks "Islamic terrorists" is an insult to true Islam.[9] In fact, it is more than an insult, for it is actually a contradiction in terms insomuch as "religion" is a classification that we only extend to "peaceful" and therefore "civil" social movements that do not conflict with our own. In fact, we now seem to have new classifications that reflect this: whereas a "Muslim" remains a peaceful, rational, politically neutral, and thus tolerant person, an "Islamisist" is an irrational person who puts into practice dangerous politics (e.g., Rushdie 2001). That the prime suspect in "masterminding" (i.e., we could instead just say organizing, to remove the sinister implications of "masterminding") these attacks, Osama bin Laden,

---

[8] This was the theme of my own 2005 book, *Religion and the Domestication of Dissent*.

[9] Find the text of the speech at: http://www.theguardian.com/world/2001/oct/07/afghanistan.terrorism11 (accessed May 23, 2013). The section I am referring to is 9 paragraphs from the end of the statement.

had been quoted extensively by European and US media as having very specific, rationally defensible – whether one agrees with them or not, of course – disagreements with US foreign policy (e.g., criticizing the continued US presence in Saudi Arabia; private Saudi ownership of oil reserves; United Nations economic sanctions against Iraq; US support of Israeli actions against Palestinians, etc.) is irrelevant to our understanding of this Manichean battle between the forces of Light and Darkness, Reason and Unreason.

What is particularly fascinating is not just that the same rhetorical techniques were used by each side in the days after the September 11, 2001 attacks (see Lincoln's brief but extremely important op-ed piece, from October 23, 2001, on this topic [reprinted as chapter two in Lincoln 2003, "Symmetrical Dualisms: Bush and bin Laden on October 7"]), but that they are also used to manage dissent closer to home. Take, for example, a 2002 scholarly article on the September 11 attacks in which the conservative US Christian news commentator and sometimes political candidate, Pat Robertson, is criticized for broadcasting that Islam is a dangerous religion. While Islam's defenders universalize one sense of this complex historical movement and thus fail to "take seriously" that there are indeed people who are self-designated Muslims (and Hindus and Christians and Jews, etc.) who resort to violence for reasons that they themselves understand as highly reasonable and commendable, such a criticism of Robertson also fails to take seriously that, *for him*, such groups are indeed dangerous. Instead of studying these socio-rhetorical mechanisms at work, such scholars dive into the interpretive fray, intent on rescuing, in this case, the real Islam from its right-wing detractors. To be honest, speaking as a scholar rather than an apologist, I have no idea what such a thing is. For instance, Pat Robertson seems to think he has the real Christianity, but my guess is so does the Pope; is it the scholar of religion's role to announce that one or the other is mistaken? Instead of trying to "help to change the voices of American Islam," as this one commentator suggests (Hussain 2002), could we not instead study these contesting voices and the techniques used to portray one as loudest and thus more authentic? While Robertson's demonization of all of Islam is far more ambitious and grandiose, it nonetheless plays precisely the same role in helping his group to reproduce itself as Tony Blair's comments helped members of his group to spiritualize, and thus argue away, specific forms of practical dissent and violent opposition – thus enabling them to embrace just those Others who least threaten liberal sentiments and standards of civility (not to mention our economic system as well). For certain sorts of opposition are so far removed from the commonsense realm of the acceptable that even labeling them "opposition" rather than "terrorism" might itself be seen as a form of traitorous collaboration.

My point in using the preceding example is neither to diminish and thus argue away the horrific nature of these attacks and counter-attacks, nor to take sides regarding the grievances that motivated such actions and reactions. It is simply to identify, in a still painfully recent and therefore fresh episode in the violent history of social for-mation, the intimate, intertwined, yet largely unrecognized relations between the discourses on religion, faith, freedom, belief, civility, economy, global interests, and the use of coercive violence. After all, as Bruce Lincoln has commented, "words are weapons in the pres-ent [post-September 11] struggle" (2003: 9). Despite the obviously shocking nature of these events, just who gets to count as a legitimate member of a group, what the precise meaning of "freedom" ought to be, and what is a "true Muslim" ought to be left up to the contest-ing group's various competing factions; scholars qua scholars ought not adjudicate the limits of group membership but, instead, study the manner in which members carry out their own self-policing activities.

The inability of some to study religion in this fashion is evidenced in the assumption that fuels the above rhetoric: those features of human society that we call religion are somehow said to be set apart from the natural world of historical (banal, in Eliade's words) happen-stance. Instead, they are above or beyond history and concerned with a person's inner goodness, emotion, aesthetic feeling, or morality, thus precluding violence and actions that aggressively challenge the status quo. (Is this not the assumption that drives the proliferation of "Religion and Non-violence" courses in our field?) This assumption is itself a political technique, however, for making certain types of modern groups and citizens. As Paul Christopher Johnson has argued, "Since the [September 11] terrorists were discredited as not 'real' Muslims – after all, some of them drank, smoked and had extramarital girlfriends – their action could only be considered 'political' or 'cultural,' making false use of 'religion' as a legitimating façade" (2002: 6). This distinction between inner piety and outer action drives much of the work in our field, even the work of those who try empathetically to "understand on its own terms" religious violence. I think here of the work of such writers as Mark Juergensmeyer whose book *Terror in the Mind of God* (2001), is premised on the apparent oxymoron "religious terrorism." "What puzzles me," Juergensmeyer writes in his opening chapter,

> is not why bad things are done by bad people, but rather why bad things are done by people who otherwise appear to be good – in cases of religious terrorism, by pious people dedicated to a moral vision of the world. (2001: 7)

If, instead, we took seriously the etymology of our own words – for example seeing "piety" in the above quotation as simply denoting (if we think back to a classical, Greco-Roman notion of piety) the ability to negotiate successfully issues of privilege and deference in complex, hierarchical social formations – then negotiating one's place within competing systems of social rank and material interest would, understandably at times, lead to violent conflict. To rephrase: if the thing we commonly call religion is seen as a rhetoric for legitimating social place and material interest – regardless whose place or what set of interests – then "religious violence" is not an oxymoron and the problematic that propelled many post-September 11 commentators, the problematic that prompted Eliade's hindsight efforts to sanitize the Legion by spiritualizing it, and that puzzles Juergensmeyer, is solved. For if the ability to name something *as* religion has nothing to do with *being* good but is, instead, a socio-rhetorical activity that is part of some people's repertoire of political strategies that efficiently and effectively police what (and thus who) *gets to count* as good, peaceful, tolerant, civil, and nonthreatening to the status quo, then coercion and violent conflict among competing interests, legitimized and propelled by certain sorts of rhetorics, are perhaps an inevitable part of all acts of social formation.

But such violence *is* a contradiction for those who re-create their group's identity by appeals to the essential spirituality of this thing we call religion and its normally separate status from those things we call politics. Appealing to Juergensmeyer once again, we quote from his influential book's concluding paragraph:

> This is one of history's ironies, that although religion has been used to justify violence, violence can also empower religion.... Religion gives spirit to public life and provides a beacon for moral order.... In a curious way, then, the cure for religious violence may ultimately lie in renewed appreciation for religion itself. (2001: 242–3).

Like all ironies and contradictions, this one is more slippery than it at first appears, for it is only an irony if religion is about being good and spiritual and *not* political. For example, after Eliade laments, in his autobiography, the persecution the essentially spiritual Legionary sympathizers received at the hands of the government of King Carol II between 1938 and '39, he has little choice but to acknowledge that very real, bloody violence was perpetrated by this group. Thus, a rather understated and unelaborated footnote appears in his text: "It should be recalled here that [from September to December of 1940] ... Legionary terrorists committed numerous horrible crimes" (1988: 66, n. 2). By that time they had assassinated four premiers, including the famous historian Nicolae Iorga – one of the young Eliade's academic idols. The Guardist attacks on Jewish inhabitants of Romania in late 1940 and '41 – culminating in June 1941, when "anti-Semitic atrocities in Romania peaked, with the massacre of perhaps 13,000 Jews in and around Iasi, near the disputed Russian border at the Prut River" (Rennie 2002: 172) – should alone disqualify readers from crediting Eliade's overly generous interpretation of the movement's essentially *mystical* goals and aspirations. But Eliade's rhetoric quickly recovers and enters a new phase; his hindsight rationalizations bring to mind Martin Heidegger's later explanation that he had been attracted to the *essence* of Nazism – an explanation Jurgen Habermas has termed "abstraction via essentialization" (1989: 449), whereby the particularities of historical and political events are glossed over in favor of some purported ahistorical core meaning ("the history of Being" in

Heidegger's case). For, although he does cite the Legion-sponsored murder of Iorga, going so far as to classify it as an "odious assassination," Eliade then immediately dehistoricizes this historic event by commenting: "But this tragedy too belongs to the *destiny* of the Romanian people, a people without luck" (1988: 69; emphasis added). As signaled rhetorically by his "But," what is given with one hand is quickly taken away with the other: a specific tragedy that eludes his initial rhetoric of "essential spiritualism" is ultimately and efficiently subsumed within a totalized, and thereby flattened, grand narrative of depersonalized, irresistible, nationalist "destiny" – that *longue longue durée* to which only some of us seem to have access. Whereas violent social fractures are more than apparent in political assassinations and victimization of Romanian Jews, the homogeneity and thus identity of a specific subgroup known as "the people" is, nonetheless, preserved. One part is thus efficiently elevated to the Whole. Within these few brief lines we see a master rhetorician at work. Only if we are persuaded by the rhetoric will we join Juergensmeyer in seeing the presence of religious jargon along with violence as "one of history's ironies." Instead, it might be one of history's engines.

To return more explicitly to the topics of this chapter, the academic controversy around Eliade's life really begins in earnest when scholars maintain that these early and obvious political commitments find their way into Eliade's mature scholarly productions. As already suggested, elements of a prototypical nationalist ideology seem to saturate Eliade's later texts (something argued in greater detail in McCutcheon 1997), as is evidenced by his preoccupation with *Volksreligion* and the paradigmatic importance of the myths of the peasants of eastern Europe; his Platonic, traditionalist epistemology, whereby meaning inheres in phenomena insomuch as they repeat paradigmatic events in the epic past (i.e., to know is to remember); his disdain for materialistic explanatory schemes that address historical and social factors (e.g., economics or politics); and his later preoccupation with establishing a "new, universal humanism," whereby Western technological society would be re-created in a form based upon the archaic exemplar of *Homo religiosus*. Whereas Eliade's contemporary defenders are preoccupied with issues of meaning, arguing over the correct *interpretation* of specific events in his life or disclosures in his texts, to date there have been few attempts to respond to the more general charges of political conservatism and philosophical idealism that inform his studies on religion; in fact, those who have attempted such a defense generally beg the very issues to which they are supposedly responding (e.g., see McCutcheon 2001).

The Security and Welfare of the United States

Given these possible links between Eliade's political past and his mature academic productions, what is most amazing about reading Eliade now is the apparently unblemished allure he yet holds for some modern students of religion. He is still held in high esteem by some of his fellow teachers and disciples from Chicago, who appear to minimalize what one former student of Eliade's once termed "the recent bout of Eliade bashing." (Somewhat akin to pundits sticking to their talking points on the TV news, his defenders often elect to use this metaphor when dismissing criticisms of Eliade's body of work.) One must surely ask what is at stake for contemporary scholars to continue to hold onto Eliade as the exemplar for their studies while ignoring, or in the least minimalizing, the politics of his sort of scholarship on religion.

It becomes more difficult to conceive of Eliade's work on understanding the Other, as well as his efforts to institute a new universal humanism, as anything but politically charged after learning how Eliade attained Permanent Resident status in the United States. His original two-year visitor's visa, which enabled him to deliver the Haskell lectures in Chicago in the late 1950s, was replaced on May 1, 1961, only after the University of Chicago was able to convince the US Defense Department that Professor Eliade's presence was "indispensable to the security and welfare of the United States." According to then Dean of the Chicago Divinity School, Jerald Brauer, the Department of Defense had noted that "Eliade's work had to do with the kind of humanistic matters that the United States desperately needed for its security" (Eliade 1988: 213, n. 15; see Brauer 1985: 25). As reported by Brauer, the representative of the Department of Defense commented that "[a]ll the others [granted this status] were people involved with weaponry and such." If the juxtaposition of the value of Eliade's scholarship with the value of weapons experts is not enough to prompt even the casual reader of this passage to reflect on the politics of scholarship, once placed within the appropriate Cold War "doublespeak" atmosphere of the late 1950s and early '60s, such language can challenge those who yet maintain that the study of religion, and other related humanistic and social scientific fields, are essentially neutral, apolitical enterprises. While it may be debatable precisely what or whom the US Defense Department is in the business of defending, it certainly is not in the business of spiritual exchange.

Eliade's link to mid-20th-century American foreign policy may be explained by his view on the importance of *understanding* the Other. On October 22, 1959, he wrote in his journal:

> The hermeneutic necessary for the revelation of the meanings and the messages hidden in myths, rites, symbols, will also help us to understand both depth psychology and the historical age into which we are entering and in which we will be not only surrounded but also dominated by the "foreigner," the non-Occidentals. It will be possible to decipher the "Unconscious," as well as the "Non-Western World," through the hermeneutic of the history of religions.

Or, as he recalled in his autobiography, in a talk given on November 3, 1959:

> I tried to show the importance of the history of religions in culture and even in contemporary American foreign policy. I insisted also on the fact that, today, when Asia has reentered history and when "primitive" societies are on the way to achieving independence, the study and correct understanding of the religious concepts that structure these exotic civilizations constitute a necessity in the political realm. Diplomats, economists, and technologists sent on missions in Asian countries, especially former European colonies, must be initiated beforehand, and not only by missionaries and anthropologists. (1988: 208)

Despite his professed sympathies for the symbols and myths of archaic people, Eliade correctly understood that matters of essential importance to the maintenance of nation-states had much to do with classifying and understanding the religions of those who were to be governed – those who, with a history of their own, were thus re-entering not simply history, in the generic sense portrayed in his above quotation, but re-entering *our* history and *our* way of organizing the world, thus necessitating that *our* classification systems and *our* foreign policy take account of *them*.

Potent Ideology or Tempest in a Teapot?

During a job interview in Canada in the early 1990s, a friend of mine reported that she had been asked, "What do you think of Eliade?" At one time such a question may have led to an academic discussion of methods and theories, criticizing him for his poor empirical techniques (as did the anthropologist Edmund Leach [1966] in an infamous critique of Eliade) or praising his bold synthetic skills and interpretive creativity. However, such a question – especially when it originates from within the rather imbalanced power relations of a job interview – takes on a highly-charged nature. That academics still talk about him and discuss his theories, that people's opinions of him play some role in getting them a job, is surely a testament to something. It is questionable, however, whether that testament is to the timeless value of his insights into the normally camouflaged presence of the sacred within the profane or to the ability of personal and political interests to become so evenly encoded within what some would have us believe to be essentially neutral scholarly activity – the life of the mind, as some call it. If nothing else, the modern preoccupation with applying the methods of the sociology of knowledge and ideology critique to intellectual biography has certainly invigorated Eliade studies, if for no other reason than to reread and reinterpret Eliade's work in his own defense – for example, see Bryan Rennie's effort to read Eliade "on his own terms," in *Reconstructing Eliade* (1996), or his edited collection, *Changing Religious Worlds: The Meaning and End of Mircea Eliade* (2001) as well as its companion

volume, devoted to international (i.e., non-American and from outside Western Europe) commentaries on Eliade's work (2007) – a volume that avoids discussing anything to do with the controversies that
today attend Eliade's work.[10] While some may consider the "Eliade
controversy" simply to be a tempest in a teapot, the surprising degree
to which much of the modern discourse on religion is represented by
his idealist approach to the study of religious *minds* (i.e., people's
beliefs) rather than social *practices and institutions*, seeing religion
as somehow set apart from history and culture and thereby interacting
with it in specific cases (such as the popularity now of talking about
"religion in the public sphere," as if the ability to define something
as religion or not was not always and already public and thus contestable) does warrant further investigation. The political critique of
Eliade surely opens up the possibility of a larger critique of the discourse on religion itself.

Perhaps Eliade's continued influence in a field whose members
still seem to feel marginalized within the academy, thereby prompting them to continue to justify themselves and their research interests
(especially now that the Humanities are felt to be under attack – the
division of the modern university in which the study of religion most
often falls), could be linked to his early exposure to, and use of, the
rhetoric of nationalism in the creation of shared identity. Such strategies as essentialization, universalization, and dehistoricization played
a primary role in his effort not only to concoct a coherent group for
the so-called "young generation" of heroically destined interwar
Romanians but also in his later scholarly work on religion where a
new group – a "total discipline" rather than the Fascist notion of a
"total man" – was successfully fashioned by means of his search for
the essence and his use of ahistoric, cross-cultural comparisons where
trans-human similarity trumped contextual difference at every turn.
Arriving in the United States in the late 1950s, when the academic
study of religion was, as we now know, on the verge of bridging the

---

[10] As Rennie succinctly writes in a freestanding paragraph in his
Introduction: "None of the present contributions specially address the ques-
tion of Eliade's political past," on which the reader can consult "Eliade,
Mircea: [Further Considerations]," in the second edition of the Macmillan
Encyclopedia (Rennie 2005: 1–2).

long-standing American separation between church and state (thereby allowing it to be taught in publicly funded, higher institutions – a change taking place throughout the 1960s), Eliade's nationalist strategies seem to have been very useful for his fellow scholars in this emergent discipline, intent upon differentiating themselves, not from the Transylvanians or the French, but from anthropologists and other social scientists.

Given the way in which the establishment of this academic discipline in the US failed just a few decades earlier (see McCutcheon 2003, chapter 2), his efforts to build on Wach's earlier momentum and re-establish the History of Religions as the exclusive disciplinary location of the discourse on religion was surprisingly successful. The important role played by his many "cultural creations" in this process – the various publishing projects in which he participated, such as methodological essay collections (e.g., Eliade and Kitagawa 1959), the Chicago journal *History of Religions* begun in 1961, his popularization through his personal journals and life-story, his numerous interviews in the popular press, not to mention the *Encyclopedia of Religion* – cannot be overlooked. Given the supposedly apolitical nature of this discipline, it is all the more ironic how print capitalism has been used quite effectively in setting the agenda and defining and disseminating the thinkable conditions in what has now become the dominant discourse in this area of study. It is therefore not misleading to speak of the Eliade industry – an industry ironically reproduced, to whatever degree, by this very chapter.

In his final years, suffering from rheumatoid arthritis in his hands and also from cataracts (and his lifelong battle with what he called his "galloping myopia"), Eliade seems to have found little time for anything but reading and writing – with great difficulty one might add – and lamenting the projects he would never finish, let alone those he knew he would never begin, such as the "short theoretical monograph...[to] explain the 'confusions and errors' for which I am reproached" by critics (September 15, 1985). If one can trust his written, and no doubt highly-edited, hindsight reflections, human beings populate increasingly small portions of his life. His second marriage, to Christinel in France in 1950, while only referred to in passing in his published journal, does inspire a chapter in the autobiography, although it concentrates mainly upon the writings that preoccupied him during this time.

Much like his biographer, then, Eliade seems also to have been driven until the end by some obscure demon. Writing in his journal in 1979, he notes how "at least once a week [a friend of mine] is preoccupied by the question: 'what will remain after my death?'" (July 2, 1979). Undoubtedly, Eliade demonstrates his resonance with such a question by the very act of recording it without comment. His terror thus lives on in his recorded fear of how he will be judged by those who follow him. But the question is not whether Eliade was or is culpable, and thus defenses of him based upon the invocation of subtle differences – like that of Rennie, which asserts (with no rationale or elaboration) that "*a distinction has to be made* between an involvement with the political right and anti-Semitism, and a brief period of political activity does not necessarily indicate a lifelong commitment" (2005: 2758; emphasis added) – entirely miss the point. Instead of lodging the issue with the guilty or innocent individual, the problem lies at the structural level, with how scholars of religion understand their object of study – whether it be a myth, a ritual, or the life of one of their own intellectual predecessors – and its relationship to the happenstance, contingent domains that we know as history and culture. For in defining "politics" so narrowly that one could be said only to have had a brief or benign relationship with it (i.e., party politics), thereby creating an apolitical zone supposedly free of interests and contests, strikes me as failing to take seriously that history is a stage where power is asserted and experienced. Of course such a zone is required if one wishes to argue for some sort of autonomy and thus privilege for one's object of study – be it a mythic founder or the sacred – but that strikes me as the invested work of identity formation rather than its study.[11]

---

[11] Portions from the original version of this essay were elaborated in greater detail in McCutcheon 1997.

References

Allen, Douglas. 1992. "Review of Mac Linscott Ricketts, *Mircea Eliade: The Romanian Roots.*" *Journal of the American Academy of Religion* 60:174–7. http://dx.doi.org/10.1093/jaarel/LX.1.174.

Arnal, William E., and Russell T. McCutcheon. 2013. *The Sacred is the Profane: The Political Nature of "Religion."* New York: Oxford University Press.

Berger, Adriana. 1989. "Fascism and Religion in Romania." *Annals of Scholarship* 6:455–65.

Berger, Adriana. 1994. "Mircea Eliade: Romanian Fascism and the History of Religions in the United States." In Nancy A. Harrowitz, ed., *Tainted Greatness: Antisemitism and Cultural Heroes*, 51–74. Philadelphia: Temple University Press.

Brauer, Jerald C. 1985. "Mircea Eliade and the Divinity School." *Criterion* 24(3): 25–6.

Burris, John P. 2001. *Exhibiting Religion: Colonialism and Spectacle at International Expositions, 1851–1893.* Charlottesville: University Press of Virginia.

Eliade, Mircea. 1958. *Patterns in Comparative Religion.* Trans. Rosemary Sheed. New York: Sheed & Ward.

Eliade, Mircea. 1974 (1949). *Myth of the Eternal Return.* Trans. Willard R. Trask. Princeton: Princeton University Press.

Eliade, Mircea, ed. 1987. *The Encyclopedia of Religion.* 16 vols. New York: Macmillan.

Eliade, Mircea. 1988. *Autobiography Vol. II, 1937–1960, Exile's Return.* Trans. Mac Linscott Ricketts. Chicago: University of Chicago Press.

Eliade, Mircea. 1989a. *Journal II: 1957–1969.* Trans. Fred H. Johnson. Chicago: University of Chicago Press.

Eliade, Mircea. 1989b. *Journal III: 1970–1978.* Trans. Teresa Lavender Fagan. Chicago: University of Chicago Press.

Eliade, Mircea. 1990a (1981). *Autobiography Vol. I, 1907–1937, Journey East, Journey West.* Trans. Mac Linscott Ricketts. Chicago: University of Chicago Press.

Eliade, Mircea. 1990b. *Journal I: 1945–1955.* Trans. Mac Linscott Ricketts. Chicago: University of Chicago Press.

Eliade, Mircea. 1990c. *Journal IV: 1979–1985.* Trans. Mac Linscott Ricketts. Chicago: University of Chicago Press.

Eliade, Mircea. 1995 (1933). *Bengal Nights.* Chicago: University of Chicago Press.

Eliade, Mircea, and Joseph M. Kitagawa, eds. 1959. *The History of Religions: Essays in Methodology.* Chicago: University of Chicago Press.

Gill, Sam. 1998. *Storytracking: Texts, Stories, and the Histories in Central Australia.* New York: Oxford University Press. http://dx.doi.org/10.1093/acprof:oso/9780195115871.001.0001.

Girardot, Norman, and Mac Linscott Ricketts, eds. 1982. *Imagination and Meaning: The Scholarly and Literary Worlds of Mircea Eliade.* New York: Seabury Press.

Habermas, Jürgen. 1989. "Work and *Weltanschauung*: The Heidegger Controversy from a German Perspective." Trans. John McCumber. *Critical Inquiry* 15(2): 431–56. http://dx.doi.org/10.1086/448492.

Hussain, Amir. 2002. "Death is a Master from...." *Religious Studies News* 17(2): 11.

Johnson, Paul C. 2002. "Death and Memory at Ground Zero: A Historian of Religion's Report." *Bulletin of the Council of Societies for the Study of Religion* 31(1): 3–7.

Juergensmeyer, Mark. 2001 (2000). *Terror in the Mind of God: The Global Rise of Religious Fundamentalism.* Berkeley: University of California Press.

Leach, Edmund (1966). "Sermons by a Man on a Ladder." *The New York Review of Books* 7/6 (October 20): 28–31.

Lincoln, Bruce. 2003. *Holy Terrors: Thinking about Religion after September 11.* Chicago: University of Chicago Press.

Maitreyi Devi. 1995 (1976). *It Does Not Die.* Chicago: University of Chicago Press.

McCutcheon, Russell T. 1997. *Manufacturing Religion: The Discourse on Sui Generis Religion and the Politics of Nostalgia.* New York: Oxford University Press.

McCutcheon, Russell T. 2001. "Methods, Theories, and the Terrors of History: Closing the Eliadean Era With Some Dignity." In Bryan S. Rennie, ed., *Reconsidering Eliade: The Meaning and End of Mircea Eliade,* 11–23. Albany, NY: State University of New York Press.

McCutcheon, Russell T. 2003. *The Discipline of Religion: Structure, Meaning, Rhetoric.* New York, London: Routledge. http://dx.doi.org/10.4324/9780203451793.

McCutcheon, Russell T. 2005. *Religion and the Domestication of Dissent, Or How to Live in a Less than Perfect Nation.* London: Equinox Publishers.

Rennie, Bryan S. 1992. "The Diplomatic Career of Mircea Eliade: A Response to Adriana Berger." *Religion* 22(4): 375–92. http://dx.doi.org/10.1016/0048-721X(92)90045-6.

Rennie, Bryan S. 1996. *Reconstructing Eliade: Making Sense of Religion.* Albany, NY: State University of New York Press.

Rennie, Bryan S., ed. 2001. *Changing Religious Worlds: The Meaning and End of Mircea Eliade.* Albany, NY: State University of New York Press.

Rennie, Bryan S. 2002. "Book Review: Mihail Sebastian, *Journal, 1935–1944: The Fascist Years.*" *Religion* 32(2): 172–5. http://dx.doi.org/10.1006/reli.2001.0403.

Rennie, Bryan S. 2005. "Eliade, Mircea: [Further Considerations]." In Lindsey Jones, ed., *Encyclopedia of Religion,* 2nd ed., Vol. 4, 2757–63. Detroit: Thomson Gale.

Rennie, Bryan S., ed. 2007. *The International Eliade.* Albany, NY: State University of New York Press.

Ricketts, Mac Linscott. 1973. "In Defense of Eliade: Bridging the Gap between Anthropology and the History of Religions." *Religion* 3(1): 13–34. http://dx.doi.org/10.1016/0048-721X(73)90041-9.

Ricketts, Mac Linscott. 1988. *Mircea Eliade: The Romanian Roots, 1907–1945.* 2 vols. Boulder, CO: East European Monographs.

Rushdie, Salman. 2001. "Yes, This is About Islam: How Radical Politics Co-opts a Faith." *The New York Times* (Friday, November 2): A25, cols. 1–4.

Smith, Jonathan Z. 2000a. "Acknowledgments: Morphology and History in Mircea Eliade's Patterns in Comparative Religion (1949–1999) Part 1: The Work and its Contexts." *History of Religions* 39(4): 315–21. http://dx.doi.org/10.1086/463598.

Smith, Jonathan Z. 2000b. "Acknowledgments: Morphology and History in Mircea Eliade's Patterns in Comparative Religion (1949–1999) Part 2: The Texture of the Work." *History of Religions* 39(4): 322–51.

Strenski, Ivan. 1987. *Four Theories of Myth in Twentieth-Century History: Cassirer, Eliade, Lévi-Strauss, and Malinowski.* Iowa City: University of Iowa Press.

Urban, Hugh. 2001. "Scholartracking: The Ethics and Politics of Studying 'Others' in the Work of Sam D. Gill." *Method & Theory in the Study of Religion* 13(1): 110–36. http://dx.doi.org/10.1163/157006801X00147.

Wasserstrom, Steven M. 1999. *Religion After Religion: Gershom Scholem, Mircea Eliade, and Henry Corbin at Eranos.* Princeton: Princeton University Press. http://dx.doi.org/10.1515/9781400823178.

Russell T. McCutcheon is Professor and Chair of the Department of Religious Studies at the University of Alabama. His research focuses on the social and political implications of competing classification systems.

Topic III: Theoretical and Methodological Cake

5. Who Is The Nigger?: *Strategies* of Using the "N" Word and Having It Both Ways

Monica R. Miller

"Sticks and stones may break my bones but words will never hurt me," goes the frequently rehearsed juvenile adage often quoted by children on playgrounds and in classrooms around the country. But the reality is, words, seemingly innocuous on surface level, do "hurt" given the "timeless" essence of meaning often placed upon them (and thus re-appropriated in the minds of social actors). What is considered injurious language relies upon the data mines of historical memory, cultural stasis, and revisionist accounts of historical trauma (after all, "historical" meanings of words are largely expected to guide their contemporary uses and applications). That is, words, according to this logic, *do* hurt because of what they're assumed to signify based on certain uses in cherry-picked historical moments by one group towards another. Here the "I" often becomes subsumed under the universalist "We" (thus, offering an illusion of protection when certain uses of words need to be fought and disputed). But, there's more to the story of (un)intended linguistic pain and injury and how such pain becomes perceived and projected onto the words that try to interpolate the identity of Others. Despite popular opinion, words can't and don't ever hurt on their *own*, as if they come pre-packaged with some sort of trans-historical self-evident and sui generis meaning and reality. Thus the violence commonly associated with particular uses of certain words towards certain individuals or people are managed by (and through) socially constructed codes – "rules" and "manuals" (material and ideological) which provide the guidelines and expectations of their use. Of course, it is quite often the case that "guidelines" (the social mores which govern what we can and cannot do in certain contexts) can't possibly govern (or account for) the unexpected difference (i.e., not all women agree the word "bitch" is harmful) among the perceived sameness (i.e., the word bitch is offensive to "women") of the uses (i.e., does it matter when a woman calls other women bitches verses when a man does so) in question.

Most recently, the "N" word, so vile and abhorrent that we have trouble spelling out the whole word *nigger*, yet again, makes its way into legal and public debate through the national cases of Paula Deen and Brandi Johnson which have sparked heated controversial dialogues over what this word *means*, *who* can say it, and *how* the law both protects and perpetuates harmful speech. While both cases above involve the "same" word, the varying responses to such cases by the public demonstrate the manner in which not all uses and words are created equal. That is, the debate around the public conversation of these cases, from media to in and out group politics, speaks not so much to *what* words mean, but rather, how *context* and competing *strategies of identification* become employed and thus manage the rules of such contests.

In a story first revealed in June 2013 by the *National Enquirer* based on court proceedings, Lisa Jackson, a Caucasian female and former restaurant employee of Uncle Bubba's Seafood and Oyster House owned by celebrity chef, cooking show host, and restaurateur Paula Deen and brother Earl "Bubba" Heirs, filed a lawsuit alleging racial discrimination and sexual harassment where she argued that racial epithets and discriminatory practices (such as the use of separate bathrooms for blacks and whites) were used against people of color in the restaurant owned by Deen and Heirs. Jackson argued that the maltreatment of blacks in the workplace caused her emotional damage, given that her nieces are biracial and have an African American father. In addition, she reported that Heirs often exposed women to pornography and they were frequently denigrated in the workplace. She also noted that Deen had asked black workers to dress up as slaves for a mock antebellum wedding in the restaurant. This case sparked a massive social media debate and public conversation, and consequently, Deen's contract with the Food Network was not renewed. In addition, in the same month, Smithfield Foods as well as Walmart, Target, QVC, and Kmart among others, dropped Deen as a spokesperson. A few months after the story broke a federal judge dismissed the allegations against Deen, ruling that the plaintiff couldn't sue for treatment that she *herself* didn't allegedly endure.

In another recent case (September 2013), a federal jury ruled that the "N" word cannot and should not be used in the workplace. This case involved 38-year-old African American Brandi Johnson who, with video evidence, claimed to be the target of her supervisor's (Rob Carmona – a black male of Puerto Rican descent) profanity-filled "four-minute nigger tirade," used to chastise her for inappropriate professional decorum. The court ruled that neither disparaging nor positive uses of the "N" word are appropriate in the workplace. Johnson sued both the employment centre (STRIVE, which Carmona founded in 1984) as well as Carmona personally who argued that the use of the word was part of a "tough love" culture. Unlike Deen, the charges against whom were dismissed, jurors awarded Johnson $250,000 in compensatory damages. This ruling sparked, once again, a public discourse and debate on the limits and boundaries that ought to govern what some see as hate speech on one end and a reclaimed, repurposed term of endearment on the other.

While Deen figured out her next move and how to handle the case now gone public, with collective wit and a taste for justice, "Black Twitter," in a matter of minutes, turned Deen into a viral social media meme with a **#paulasbestdishes** rant, which included racialized comedic delicacies such as "Lettuce from Birmingham Jail," "Coming Forth to Carry Me Home Fries," "Coon on a Cob," and "Field Negro Greens with a Light House Negro Vinaigrette" (it's okay to laugh), to name just a few. Of the social media takedown, one person tweeted in celebratory response, "I love my peeps, we find out that you are a raging racist, and we will use humor to let you know how we feel." The second case involving Carmona and Johnson didn't however receive such explosive and controversial attention by the black community beyond a public conversation about *if* and *when blacks* should ever use the word nigger.

In light of such highly charged allegations of racial discrimination involving the very public cases of Deen and the George Zimmerman trial for the murder of Trayvon Martin (an African American high school student), CNN hosted a special entitled *The "N" Word* which was hosted by Don Lemmon in July 2013. Lemmon has been rather public about his views on the usage of the word, arguing that journalists should always spell out the whole word. To this point, he stated, "I think someone should say, that person called someone 'nigger,' instead of saying 'the n-word,' because I think it sanitizes it." In addition, he also expressed his disgust for its misogynistic use in culture and music.

Collectively, these instances draw attention to a certain sort of public reflection on methods and contexts of use which highlight particular strategies used by insider and outsider groups to manage discourse on historical memory, agency, and constructed boundaries based on ontological distinctions grounded in over-determined categories of experience. In both cases, strategies of strategic essentialism *and* critical distance are used by both Deen and Carmona and reinforced in the public discussion that ensued (most notably seen in Deen's case), in an effort to have it, in my opinion, "both ways." In other words, this method of having it both ways in an effort to have it all is a technique that gives one the appearance of being both critic *and* apologist – to defend the self while giving the impression of standing *with* and speaking for/on behalf of the contested "Other." Such strategies are most notably seen in conversations and debates about misogyny in rap music where, on one hand, much like Deen, rappers are often called out and held accountable for violent lyrics towards women (e.g., Rick Ross and the Molly Date Rape Debate) at disproportionate rates compared to similar sorts of violence towards women espoused by female artists. In many instances, male rappers are expected to publically apologize, which usually evolves into an expectation of all men in hip hop to join the conversation and hold the said rapper likewise accountable while being warned that they cannot control the terms of such apology and conversation because they aren't women and can't fully "feel" what it's like to be the object of such violence. On the other hand, feminists often remind the public that the category "woman" cannot and should not be universalized and homogenized although *they* intend to speak for and on behalf of this category in critical moments.

This anecdote and the cases involving race above are made possible through strategies of strategic essentialism, claims to origins and uniqueness, access to intentionality, and celebrations of authenticity that give rise to particular wars of positions which seemingly say more about the interests of those involved than the very object they think they're discussing, defending, or denying (e.g., nigger). Take for instance Deen's claim that, "...*that's just not a word that we use as time has gone on.... Things have changed since the '60s in the South. And my children and my brother object to that word being used in any cruel or mean behavior. As well as I do.*" Here, Deen invokes history and geography in all-encompassing ways where the word nigger was once used in *a* particular moment in *a* particular way in *a* particular place and as such should stay put in the annals of history because times have changed and causes for its use are no more. She assumes that meanings of words don't change over time, that there is some trans-historical essence or "common meaning" of that word from long ago that would not hold up to who blacks are in society today. However, her historically contingent argument falls flat in the face of the instances exemplified in her current private usages (with her husband and in the workplace) and treatment of blacks (as slaves) in the workplace, as cited in court proceedings. Of course, the '60s didn't stop her usage of the term as suggested above, so she reaches for the strategy of re-appropriation to corroborate her post-'60s usage (on telling offensive jokes). On this point, Deen states, "*It's just what they are – they're jokes...most jokes are about Jewish people, rednecks, black folks.... Gays or straights, black, redneck, you know, I just don't know – I just don't know what to say. I can't, myself, determine what offends another person.*" Because Deen is unwilling to pay the price of charred status and reputation, here she presents a second viewpoint (seemingly different from her first) in her theory on the word nigger – one that is managed by the strategies of good intentions, social constructionism, and a reductionism of sameness while stepping back outside the system of difference through the category of experience to make clear that the *experience* of difference is one she can't possibly know. Deen is correct that it's impossible to determine what offends who because, despite her universalized logic that becomes strategically particular when needed, not all uses of the word nigger are created equal. Here, it is clear that Deen, when so needed, steps in and out of history, time, and social situativity when it benefits her at various moments of public interrogation. In her first comment above, she assumes that she can and does speak for and on behalf of blacks in the South – that her gift of empathy gives some agency back to blacks and will be well received. Perhaps enough empathy to at least discern when Deen is just kidding around and when she's not when telling jokes that draw on the same stereotypes and pejorative meanings of blacks. Regarding her request that middle-aged black male employees dress up as slaves for a mock antebellum-themed wedding she states, "...*it was really impressive. That restaurant represented a certain era in America...after the Civil War, during the Civil War, before the Civil War.... It was not only black men, it was black women...I would say they were slaves*," a strategy which helps keep alive a particular historical time in which she could see these black men *as* slaves – *as* niggers. Thus, Deen transforms the restaurant into a modern-day plantation where her treatment of black workers is justified according to her historical reimagining and revision of the workplace. In this, her antebellum mindset is front and centre.

In the end, Jackson was compensated for the claims of sexual harassment but not for the charge of racial discrimination. Once the race claims were dropped, both Deen and Jackson wished each other well. And, the black "Others" (who worked at Deen's restaurant), who bore much of the brunt of objectified representation throughout the Deen spectacle and were perceived to be given "voice" by Jackson in the uncovering of this scandal (by the public), in the end, never had a voice in this case from the beginning. Neither Deen (in her emotional and sappy apology) *nor* journalist Tracy Thompson (in her bearing witness and sticking up for family members and workers of color) in the end really spoke for or on behalf of the black workers, as presumed. They couldn't if they tried, despite their best *intentions*. Thus, the only *niggers* present here were the ones discursively created in and through the case itself – that is, the case by its very nature created the "Others" on which the case was built.

In the second case involving the "tough love" strategy of Carmona towards Johnson, an insider position is taken: *"You and (a previous employee) are just alike. Both of you are smart as s – , but dumb as s – . You know what it is...both of you are n – – , y'all act like n – – all the time."* Carmona continues by distinguishing the two-ness of acting like a nigger when he states, *"And I'm not saying the term n – – as derogatory; sometimes it's good to know when to act like a n – – , but y'all act like n – – all the time...both of you very bright, but both y'all act like n – – at inappropriate times."* In court he tearfully suggested that he's from a different historical time (much like Deen) and was only trying to help, adding that this case helped him to see that despite his age, he's got to be more careful in how he uses the term towards his own community in this day and time. Representative here in Carmona's testimony and transcript is a strategic use of essentialism, an attempt to have it both ways by situating himself as *both* insider (black person using tough love towards black people as a strategy of self-help) *and* a product of a particular historical moment which was, according to Carmona's testimony, much more open to such linguistic uses in service of aiding a community towards advancement and progress. In a way, Carmona saw his nigger tirade as a *gift* of sorts, one that, according to his claims, was an attempt to bear witness to and for the black community. Here, Carmona thought he could shift the playing field by switching hats – no longer just "boss" (outsider) to Johnson, he saw himself as having enough agency despite employment and workplace laws (discursive boundaries) and cultural capital to also play "friend" in his desire to help Johnson clean up her work image through a politics of respectability. Thus, in the end, the law (structures) reminds Johnson that despite his own good intentions, desires, and self-imposed "insider status," there's no room to step outside of the system (of the law) to bypass such legal boundaries. That is, the structures just simply can't, by their very nature, allow for such a movement. The ruling in the case exemplifies this limitation.

The methodological problem of wanting it all – or both ways – is an issue not exclusive to debates in the broader publics and counter-publics of society – it is also evident and a topic of concern in academic scholarship. The rise of identity-based politics in particular has placed the scholar in a precarious position, one that straddles realizing the great discursive gulf that separates scholars from their objects of study on one hand and the intentional efforts by some academics to challenge such a divide by playing both outsider/insider roles in their desire for transformation and agency of the Other. It is common academic parlance now in a variety of fields to ask questions such as: whom does the academic speak for and on behalf of, how can the academic offer agency to their research subjects, can the subaltern of scholarship speak, and can or should the scholar bear witness to the voice of the Other in their work? Can we, scholars, have it both ways? Are we cognizant of the fact that despite concern for the agency and subjectivity of our research subjects, scholarship will always create *its* others, discursively and invariably. Ultimately, the Other that has become the object of such concern in much of scholarly production today is quite often a category created by scholars themselves.

These issues are explored in the following essay where Russell T. McCutcheon raises critical questions related to the methodological problematic of scholars wanting it both ways in scholarship. That is, wanting to be *within* the system as rational scholar *and* a desire to be a Gnostic intellectual *outside* the system (in a trans-historical sort of way). In engaging these issues in Jeffrey Kripal's *The Serpent's Gift* (2007), we're confronted with methodological meditations on the limitations of the scholars' position. That is to say, McCutcheon sees Kripal as wanting to give agency to his research subjects and objects, (the "gift") which obscures, in many ways, the scholar's unwillingness to pay the price of the limitations of what scholarship can and cannot do. According to this desire, having it all means methodologically holding two simultaneous viewpoints within scholarship, where, in the end, bearing witness to our research subjects' agency becomes, in effect, an unobtainable scholarly weight.

As exemplified in the cases of Deen and Carmona above, despite their efforts and linguistic strategies, there was, in the end, no real way to "have it all" and "both ways." What we can glean from these cases in thinking about such (methodological) positions in the study of religion is that similar desires and strategies to have it all end up paying a price of not ever being able to satisfy the full concerns of our research subjects. The question that McCutcheon takes up here is whether or not such a position is possible – might such a gift (to the Other) ultimately produce, in the end, diminished returns? The strategies grounding the desire to have it both ways are highlighted in the cases of Deen and Carmona, the homogenizing strategies of (strategic) racial essentialism as adjudication always fell flat and short (despite goodwill). Notwithstanding the good intentions of Lisa Jackson (outsider) to speak for/on behalf of her black colleagues by claiming an injurious emotional pain of racism, Deen's (outsider) tearful apology and limits of historical situativity, much like Carmona's (insider) good intentions that led him to be reminded by his employee, Brandi Johnson (insider) that his vision of nigger was not valid for her despite her black identity, produced no gifts or mutual exchange. At best, these positionalities produced diminished returns.

On this point, McCutcheon adds: "...some of those interested today in the problem of agency recognize that a voice cannot be given, no matter how well intentioned the motivations behind the gift, for passively accepting other people's presents hardly leads to the sort of realigned power relations that many scholars on the humanistic left wish to establish." Thus, as seen in these instances, despite the strategies that ranged from over-determinism to social constructionism on behalf of the actors involved, there was in the end, despite a neoliberal (humanist) desire and project to have it both ways, a price to pay for trying to have it all. In the following essay, there's a way in which Kripal reduces difference and complexity for a bimodal sameness in human consciousness; yet, as exemplified in my examples, such a position was hardly achievable and Deen and Carmona's apologia for why they did what they did was based, in the end, on the irreducible nature of difference – the public reaction to both cases also corroborates this reality.

Great gulfs and chasms divide things such as racial politics – neither Deen nor Carmona could bridge these gaps that have long held the nation at too great a distance from itself to fully see itself in toto. Similar gaps exist in academia when meaning, identity, and agency are at stake – as demonstrated in Kripal's desire to bridge a gap between the rational reductionism of scholarly inquiry in the study of religion on one hand and the desire for the "much more" (which scholarly inquiry cannot speak to) on the other.

In this essay, McCutcheon asks (on behalf of the scholars' data), "who gets to say what I mean and who I am?" A look into a famous KQED interview with James Baldwin from the documentary *Take This Hammer* (1963) might offer some insight. On the topic of "Who is the Nigger?" Baldwin "gives back" to white America *their* problem when he eloquently states how he can't possibly be a nigger because that category of identity was created in the white imagination and mapped upon black subjectivity; thus, the issue of *who* the nigger is, is not *his*: "I give you your problem back. You're the nigger, baby, it isn't me." Here, Baldwin, unlike Deen, Carmona, and the public reacting to these cases, doesn't enter the contest on the *meaning* and *identity* of nigger as much as he reminds the classifiers (scholars and analysts alike) through a similar strategy, that he refuses to accept *their* classifications. Rather, he studies the contest itself. Thus, the analyst (journalist) in the Baldwin interview interested in the *meaning* of the word nigger gets reminded by the perceived nigger that that classification is an object of *their* own linguistic imagination. Thus, Baldwin turns the intellectual tables against the interviewer and becomes the analyst holding up the diagnostic mirror against the journalist himself. Theorist Jonathan Z. Smith famously reminded the field of religion that the category of religion (analogous here to nigger) is an object of the theorist's own imagining. Discourse has, according to McCutcheon, an interesting way of producing its *own* Others.

This perspective is given life in Baldwin's historic interview on whites' invention of the word nigger, when he cautions that talk of the Other is always talk of the self: "I'm not describing you when I talk about you, I'm describing me."

References

Baldwin, James. 1963. "Who is the Nigger?" From *Take This Hammer*, https://www.youtube.com/watch?v=L0L5fciA6AU, accessed July 25, 2013.

Cawthon, Erinn and Kristina Sguelia. 2013. "Black boss's n-word rant to black employee costs him, nonprofit $280,000" (September 4), https://www.cnn.com/2013/09/03/us/new-york-racial-slur-lawsuit/, accessed September 6, 2013.

Don, Lemon. 2013. "CNN Special: The N-Word" (July 01), https://politicslive.cnn.com/Event/CNN_Special_The_N-Word?Page=0, accessed July 25, 2013.

Gupta, Prachi. 2013. "Paula Deen's racism goes viral with #PaulasBestDishes" (June 19), https://www.salon.com/2013/06/19/paulas_best_dishes_are_racist_jokes_twitter/, accessed July 25, 2013.

Macatee, Rebecca. 2013. "Paula Deen's Accuser: 5 Things to Know About Lisa Jackson" (July 3), https://www.eonline.com/news/436227/paula-deen-s-accuser-5-things-to-know-about-lisa-jackson, accessed July 25, 2013.

Tepper, Rachel. 2013. "Paula Deen Racist Comments, Use Of N-Word Allegedly Caught On Video [UPDATED]" (June 21), https://www.huffingtonpost.com/2013/06/19/paula-deen-racist-comments-n-word-caught-on-video_n_3467287.html, accessed July 25, 2013.

Monica R. Miller is Assistant Professor of Religion and Africana Studies at Lehigh University and Director of Women, Gender and Sexuality Studies. Her research considers the intersections of religion in youth culture, popular culture, identity and difference, and theory and method in the study of black religions.

6. A Gift with Diminished Returns: On Jeff Kripal's *The Serpent's Gift*[1]

Russell T. McCutcheon

The invitation must be given, and must be accepted.
– Marcel Mauss (1990: 66)

The agency of their research subjects – the perennial Others – weighs heavily on the minds of some scholars of religion. This concern dates to around the time when unchecked speculations on the "savage mind" gave way to participant-observation, when grand theorizing was nudged aside in favor of thick descriptive studies, and when fieldwork and the acquisition of languages, rather than reading other people's travelogues, became the badge of the credentialed ethnographer. Anyone familiar with this story – what amounts to anthropology's early to mid-20th-century professionalization, and its impact on the nascent study of religion – will also know that "taking religion seriously," at the one end, and "reductionism," at the other, became the terminological shorthands, possibly slogans, for the limits of a debate that has now lasted for several academic generations. Although originally a dispute over the place and authority of religious participants' self-reports – a dispute in which naturalistic theorists were regularly accused of "throwing the baby [i.e., the religious meaning] out with

[1] I would like to thank *JAAR*'s book review editor (where this slightly revised essay was published in its original form), along with Will Arnal (University of Regina, Canada), Willi Braun (University of Alberta, Canada), J.E. Llewellyn (Missouri State, USA), as well as Jaci Gresham (then of the University of Alabama but now pursuing her MA at the University of Chicago) and Vaia Touna (then of Aristotle University, Greece, but now at the University of Alabama), for helpful comments on an earlier draft of this essay.

the bathwater [i.e., the contexts and manners of its expression]" – the issue became more complex with the rise of area studies. For now the so-called religious Other rapidly divided and subdivided into countless branches (evident in the proliferation of American Academy of Religion [AAR] program units over the past decade), with writers seeking to recover the silenced voices and meanings of yet other Others – everyone from the working class (in the case of social history) and women (in the case of Feminist theory) to minority groups (in the case of race and ethnicity studies) and gays and lesbians (in the case of Queer theory).

Although the disparate collection of critical approaches grouped together as postmodernism has been of use to those working along these lines – insofar as it has allowed them to historicize, and thereby undermine, approaches that were once presumed to have exclusive access to the archive of human doings – at about the same time yet other scholars, influenced by an even more radical, or at least a more thoroughgoing, brand of postmodernism, went in a rather different direction, arguing that scholarship actually creates its Other – with no authentic or pre-discursive remainder left over. The implication of this position was that, prior to the scholar arriving on the scene with assumptions, curiosities, and a travel grant, there might in fact be no coherent participant or insider of which to talk and write; for people fully immersed in living their lives are not the same as research subjects answering questions about what it *means* to live their lives. For such writers it is therefore no coincidence that Marxists' Others can end up being members of the working class or that Feminists' Others often end up being women. Because they hold that sets of interests specify what in the world will attract one's gaze (i.e., data is a product of discourse, thus ensuring that, without a map, there is no territory to navigate), this position maintains that the Other to whom one gives a voice is one's own creation; for the so-called recovered or empowered voice ends up sounding oddly familiar to anyone who listens carefully enough.

As a result of these back and forth critiques, some of those interested today in the problem of agency recognize that a voice cannot be given, no matter how well intentioned the motivations behind the gift, for passively accepting other people's presents hardly leads to the sort of realigned power relations that many scholars on the human-istic left wish to establish. Instead, as some now argue, a voice, and the identity that is thought to animate it, are one's natural posses-sions, needing merely to be expressed and registered. Drawing on this position, we now find people from around the world, many of whom have been schooled in what were once exclusively European, and then North American, academic methods, using these tools to register what seems to be a voice of their own – one that sometimes contests such things as how *their* faiths and *their* traditions are represented in *our* books and *our* classes – no matter how well-meaning *our* efforts to represent *them*. Academia's so-called Others, once far removed in both space and time from our armchair predecessors, now read and review our books, and write books of their own about, of all things, us and our efforts to represent them.

It is into this mix of meaning, identity, and agency – or what he elsewhere terms "the cross-cultural and theoretical complexities of what it would mean to study and write about someone else's secrets" (2001, xii) – that Jeffrey Kripal steps once again, this time with his book *The Serpent's Gift* (2007b).

Although he is the author or editor of eight books (the most recent of which, *Esalen: America and the Religion of No Religion*, was also published in 2007),[2] to some readers Kripal may be best known for the published version of his dissertation, *Kali's Child* (1995). Or, more correctly stated, he is perhaps best known by some for inhabiting the centre of a storm that followed upon his psychologically-informed study of the influential Bengali mystic, Sri Ramakrishna Paramahamsa (1836–86). Although his study of the relations between mysticism and eroticism was awarded the AAR's 1996 award for best first book in the History of Religions, his work was hardly received in the same generous spirit by some of those who hold a certain sort of memory of Ramakrishna quite dear. Although he has responded elsewhere, repeatedly and in admirably

---

[2] Kripal has an active publishing career; apart from edited and co-edited volumes, and a forthcoming introductory textbook on comparative religion, he has published two more books since *The Serpent's Gift* (see Kripal 2010 and 2011).

patient detail, to this controversy,[3] the meditations on methodology offered up in the essays collected in *The Serpent's Gift* read as the sort of book that might come from someone who has had little choice but to confront the sometimes dramatic gaps that lie between authorial best intentions and readers' responses.

Despite being directed at those "beyond the academy and its highly specialized debates" (182, n. 12), this is not a book for general, even if learned, readers; instead, it is firmly placed *within* the academy's specialized debates (the 30 pages of endnotes tell you as much). And of all the specialists in the field who might read it, it should attract the attention of methodologists and historians of the study of religion, for we have here one of the first open and self-conscious attempts to, as Kripal writes, have it both ways. Of course, for many years scholars studying religion have taken for granted that they could have it all, but rarely would they come right out and say it or, as Kripal does, defend their right to it. As was seen in an earlier generation, historians of religions apparently saw no contradiction in scolding their social scientific colleagues (i.e., reductionists), while their own work *reduced* the variety of, say, historically discrete water symbolisms to this or that essential, trans-historical *meaning* – a meaning that was, predictably perhaps, completely unknown to those who actually used water in their ceremonials. And here lies the crux of the issue in which Kripal's work, as well as his critics' responses, is immersed: a contest over the deep meaning of people's signifiers and the links between such symbols and their users' representations of self-identity. The critical question that ought to be in the back of our minds while reading this book is therefore a rephrasing of the one famously posed in the Christian Gospel of Matthew: who gets to say what I mean and who I am?

Traditionally, many scholars of religion have provided evidence of how they might answer such questions by freely interpreting *the* (and the definite article is important here) meaning of a symbol as if it pointed towards an otherwise obscured identity of the people under study, doing so as if they were merely describing a self-existing

---

[3] For example, see the website: http://www.ruf.rice.edu/~kalischi/ (accessed May 28, 2013).

fact floating free of their own scholarly curiosities and schemes. This is what "having it all" has implied; to paraphrase Jonathan Z. Smith's well known point, because they assumed that their observations and interpretations were not theory-driven (i.e., were not the result of interests, curiosities, assumptions, discourse, etc., exterior to some object of study), they saw little reason to pay any cost when doing their work (see Smith 2007: 77); they were thus able to make ambitious claims on unlimited depth, meaning, experience, and origins, having no need to, for example, recognize that a theory about X allows us to talk about some Y – a way of talking that precludes other possibly interesting things we could have said ("interesting" as judged from yet other starting points). Much like a perennial philosopher, many of our predecessors, not to mention a great deal of our contemporaries, often saw their work as cutting to the authentic heart of it all, tapping into a veritable god's-eye viewpoint, free of limiting perspective, agendas, and contexts. Having it all has therefore implied for many an unwillingness to pay any prices when going about their work, for in such scholarship what we end up saying about the world is not seen as a specific act of speech by a specific speaker in a specific place for specific reasons; instead, it almost amounts to bearing witness.

Of course there are benefits to not paying costs; for Kripal, the implication of having it all seems to be that we can finally bridge those gaps that he judges to have held the field back: between significance being the product of imported cognitive grids and intellectual structures, on the one hand, and it being something other or "much more" than we are able to make of it. Having it both ways, then, means keeping the gains in understanding that have resulted from applying rational, systematic tools to the study of religion (which, he makes plain on a number of occasions, he values quite highly, e.g., "I too want to reduce all religious language to human language" [87]) while also assuming that, as he also puts it, the full range or the full scope of being human is hardly exhausted by our various imported systems. Having it both ways therefore presupposes that two viewpoints can coexist in the same head: one from within a system (i.e., applying some local epistemological grid to make the world knowable) and the other from without (i.e., a universal perspective that lets us in on the secret knowledge that there is more than meets our perspective-bound eye), both of which are nicely captured in his double entendre of the term "Enlightenment" – scholars of religion, his readers are told, need to cultivate both a European rationalism *and* an Asian mysticism.

But just why is such a balance necessary for what he describes as an adequate theory of religion? As suggested in the above parenthetical quotation concerning reducing *religious* language to human language, Kripal answers by positing "the human" – variously referred to as human potential, human consciousness, human personality, human creativity, human experience, human flourishing, and "the metaphysical range of human being to which all religious phenomena are 'reduced'" (88). The human is comprised of two analytically separable moments: one socialized, empirical, and thus susceptible to systematic observation and study, whereas the other is a "complexly conscious field" which is rather more elusive, inspirational, libidinal, dynamic, and thus creative. If this thing that he refers to as "the human" is indeed founded upon two such forms of embodied consciousness, then failing to take both into account leads to an inadequate because skewed – he goes so far as to say prudish – scholarly study.

Somewhat like a latter-day Schleiermacher, Kripal therefore does not think that we ought to have to choose between the rational and the affective; in fact, the choice is illusory, he would likely say, which makes "choice" language part of the problem (yet for others, selection and exclusion provide the enabling conditions for all discourse). In his approach, one can be a critically-minded product of the European Enlightenment *and* religious, all at the same time:

> it is quite possible to be both an "insider" and an "outsider," to draw on the symbolic and ritual resources of a tradition without being slavishly bound to it, to love a religion and be deeply, publicly critical of its lies, to choose a form of consciousness that participates in both "faith" and "reason" but moves beyond both to a kind of modern "gnosis," even to imaginatively internalize and unite the depths of other religious traditions in one's own mystical body and its erotic energies. (119)

Or, to rephrase it a little more carefully, one can be both rational and religious *in a certain sort of way*, one that is unencumbered by what he describes as childish, literalist readings of myths, a way of being religious that is free of the apparent evils of certain forms of faith, ending up with what he and others describe as a mystical religion of no religion (somewhat akin to the old "I'm spiritual, not religious" distinction). I think that Kripal would therefore agree with the words of the Danish Prince, so long as we drop the bard's reference to what we now apparently know to be only a mythical paradise: "There are more things in ... earth, Horatio, than dreamt of in your philosophy."

As always, though, when it comes to generalizing about "human experience," the devil is in the particulars, for the problem with this universalist approach is in coming up with a way of justifying as anything but self-serving the criteria that one uses to distinguish the mature spiritual wheat from the infantile religious chaff. For the trouble, of course, is that others are making the same distinctions *for yet other purposes*, universalizing different criteria that entail other meanings and other consequences; because they are driven by different interests that prompt different choices, their picture of "the human" can end up looking rather different from our own – sometimes dramatically so.

Kripal's general conclusion concerning the bimodal consciousness of the human is supported by his book's four main chapters, each offering what he characterizes as creative rereadings of otherwise well known material: the two natures of Christ ("wholly man, wholly god"), Ludwig Feuerbach's thoughts on the two aspects of human beings (the individual as separable yet an instance of the collective human spirit – what Kripal terms a mystical humanism), the Indian mystical union of the self and the universe (i.e., the well-known Advaita Vedanta equation of *atman* with *Brahman*), and – departing from topics familiar to most scholars of religion – the comic-book superhero's true identity obscured beneath a mild-mannered disguise. In each of these examples Kripal finds evidence that, when taken together, seemingly separable ego and alter-ego comprise a "much more" than either on their own. Some of us have long known this, he writes, and they are called mystics. But others of us do not; although there is no one name for those who cannot "dispense with the common man's immature Feuerbachian projections and rest content with the innate beauty and pleasure of what he liked to call 'an oceanic feeling'" (as Kripal phrases it [166], describing the "religion of no religion" position of Freud's friend and correspondent, the French novelist, Romain Rolland [d. 1944]), some go by the name of philosophical idealists, literalists, or fundamentalists while yet others we know as philosophical materialists, naturalists, and reductionists. The trouble, he maintains, is that both sides only have part of the picture; having it all therefore means bridging what, at least to members of these two opposed sides, appears to be a gulf – the one that, when seen from Kripal's vantage point, prevents us from getting beyond some long-standing disputes over, say, essentialism versus social constructionism and between the theological and the naturalistic approaches to our data. Having it all therefore means appreciating the perspective-bound nature of the proverbial blind men while resting assured that, unbeknownst to those poor, groping souls, they were all experiencing the same "much more."

Those in the academy who understand that the deeply human, the erotic (meaning far more than, as his Introduction puts it, "sweet, delicious sex," of course, though a good dose of things that might make a prude blush are slipped in between the book's covers) constitutes just such a "much more," are, in Kripal's words, Gnostic intellectuals, well on track to realizing a "more fully actualized...human potential" (168). And the ability to work towards fulfilling this common potential is just what is meant by the book's title: knowledge of good and evil, knowledge of both our bodies and our minds as sites of the erotic – the much more than simple intellect vs affect – were, according to that old Hebrew tale, all priceless gifts given to our mythic ancestors by that mischievous but generous serpent.

When read "correctly," this old story therefore narrates our collective maturation as a species, a process that carries with it the price of freedom (i.e., we now know that we are all naked). Of course, this maturity is a controversial gift, for "not every culture is ready to leave its particular garden" (159), as Kripal writes near the close to the chapter on the X-Men comic books. For if people are not ready for it, then the humanist good news – that, for example,"Jesus, Feuerbach, and Ramakrishna were all basically correct, at least in a symbolic sense. The divine is (in) us. But as the rational study of religion has taught us equally well, so too is the demonic. As with the human body, there is a 'right' side to the sacred, and there is a 'left,' or sinister side. We would do well to keep both in mind." (161) – will likely be heard as not just unexpected but as rather transgressive (ideally in a transformative way, Kripal might add), somewhat akin to the effect of a ritualized hit or a koan in zazen (30). The difficulty, of course, is that a slap that is not invited is something other than a ritual. For it is one thing when it is delivered to the back of willing pupils by their Zen master; it is entirely another when it arrives uninvited, for then it can quite understandably be perceived as an insult and a challenge to one's honor, much as a slap with a glove might have once resulted in a duel.

As should be evident, Kripal's transformative position – one in which we each "take off the mask, look in the mirror, and see both this villain and this hero" (161) – is very much concerned with the realization of what it is to be human and defining the conditions for creating more Gnostic intellectuals who are capable of this type of self-realization. It is for this reason that I see his book as part of the now dominant liberal humanist tradition in the field. For it is a tradition that sees *some* historically particular instances of meaning-making as examples of wider, trans-historical values (i.e., one cannot forget that not all religious viewpoints are created equal, for some are judged to be improperly literalist). Although transcendence is a prominent theme in his volume, Kripal's position is not rightly termed theological (if by theology we strictly mean a rational discourse on God or the Gods) because all we have to presume is an essentially shared human nature or species consciousness (whatever that may in fact be) and the ability, through sexual reproduction (i.e., consciousness and body are thus inextricably linked!), to carry this common essence from the past to the future. With no need to posit an external agent of any sort (whether a fatherly, loving God or the philosopher's more abstract unmoved mover), we see why the old divide between theology and religious studies no longer strikes those who subscribe to this position as worth worrying over (case in point: the related position of self-described secular theologians who are currently trying to kick-start the once edgy death of God theology). But for those in the academy wary of too quickly moving from the particular to the general for genealogical, rather than analogical, purposes, for those concerned not to move from identifying similarities and differences among various ways of being human to drawing conclusions concerning the definitive way of being human (after all, how many dogs with spots do we need to see before we make confident conclusions about the nature of all dogs?), there is still much utility to distinguishing between those whose studies focus on the historical and the contingent and those, whether theological or not, who are more interested in the ahistorical, the necessary, and the essential.

In describing Kripal's stance, it would be unfair to liken it too much to the work of such intellectual forerunners as, say, Joseph Campbell, though readers familiar with the latter's still popular application of Jungian psychology to the study of myths may find the news that we are all both hero and villain somewhat familiar. But with our academic predecessors in mind I should note that, while reading *The Serpent's Gift*, I could not help but think of, on the one hand, Mircea Eliade's hope for a new humanism that helps scholars to realize "total man" and, on the other, Wendy Doniger's therapeutic approach to the study of myth (1986). As for the former, recall how Eliade's self-described creative hermeneutics could – or so he asserted (a word I purposefully choose for I am unsure how one would persuasively argue for such a totalizing stand) – re-create within the scholar the existential situation that must have led to some archaic artifact's original production, making the history of religions a mining exercise working with a rich deposit of deeply meaningful human intentions and existential situations that are prone to disappear without the careful conservator's interpretative efforts. As for the latter, recall Doniger's famous line, from her 1985 AAR Presidential address: "The Uses and Misuses of Other People's Myths":

> Their myths become our myths whether we like it or not, particularly when, as often happens, we discover that their myths have always been our myths, though we may not have known it; we recognize ourselves in those myths more vividly than we have ever recognized ourselves in the myths of our own culture.
> (Doniger O'Flaherty 1986: 224)

Somewhat akin to Eliade's "philosophical anthropology" (as described, for example, in his essay, "A New Humanism" [1984: 1–11]), Kripal's mystical anthropology (adding a phenomenology of consciousness to our theoretical toolbox results in the addition of these particular adjectives to the noun "anthropology") implicitly draws on the work of his two Chicago predecessors; all three would, I think, agree that the task of not simply studying but also nurturing and realizing human potential is particularly well suited to scholars of religion inasmuch as we have access to a body of data that, when its constitutive parts are each read allegorically or symbolically, through the proper lens (for Kripal that would be one that bends the light in what he might characterize as a post-postmodern psychoanalytic way), exemplify for us – all of us, I gather – what it is to be human. For, as Kripal tells his readers, any story about the so-called *full range* of being human must include "the altered states of trauma, trance, psychical phenomena, psychedelic states, certain types of erotic rapture, numinous dream, vision, and near death events"; the modern study of religion, with its rich collection of such evidence, is – rather like it was for Eliade – especially well positioned to "help us to recognize the wise snake, the lovely loving couple, and the angry jealous god among us. The garden of delight, it turns out, much like Jesus's kingdom of heaven, is still with(in) us, if only we can learn to open our eyes and have the courage to act accordingly" (165, 4).

At a time when, as phrased on the book's back cover, "domestic and geopolitical events have become increasingly dominated by intolerant forms of religious thought and action" such tolerant eye-opening is, apparently, more necessary than ever (suggesting a curious link between the insights of the Gnostic intellectual and certain forms of geopolitics). And once our eyes are open what we will see is not "a thousand premodern gardens of imagined ethnic, religious, and political purity" (10), but, instead, we will come to understand

> that those levels of human experience that first seem separate are in fact intimately related, even united, on some deeper level or hyperdimension. The male and the female, the heteroerotic and homoerotic, Adam and Eve, the sexual and the spiritual, faith and reason, East and West, sameness and difference, the reader and the author, the premodern and the postmodern, "high" and

"low" culture – all of these binarisms collapse in the (post)mod-
ern gnosis of the serpent's gift offered here. (27)

However, despite Kripal's postmodern sympathies, it seems that
modernism eventually wins out in his project, for the serpent's gift
apparently helps us to overcome what are seen to be unfortunate
compartmentalization and fragmentation, what Kripal describes as
the oppressive dualisms that come with this modern world of ours.
For we are then able to realize a universal and thus shared humanity
that transcends time (i.e., history) and place (i.e., culture, nation, race,
generation, etc.). For we now can apparently know that there is in fact
an enduring presence beneath all re-presentations, and it is none other
than our own. So, like the narrator's privileged knowledge that the
blind men are all feeling the same pachyderm, this secret knowledge
of "the human" lies outside all other perspectives, somehow being
more than just an additional perspective.

But surely all claims to knowledge are themselves parts of discourses that have a history, an author, and an audience, no? So, unless
readers are willing to grant to Kripal that his words are authorized
merely in their being spoken – and some readers may be very willing
to grant him this – perhaps we ought to inquire as to just who this
"our" refers and who constitutes his "the human."

In his Introduction, Kripal offers a few autobiographical disclosures that help us to begin to answer such questions (see also 119–20),
such as observing how, after the publication of *Kali's Child*, he "was
viciously attacked for eight years in the Indian media, in the Indian
Parliament, and on the Internet as an archrationalist, as a despised
Freudian, and as an embodiment of all that is 'neocolonialist' and
'hegemonic' about 'Western' reason and the Enlightenment tradition"
(17). Such a response from readers would be terribly unsettling to any
scholar – and I have no wish to appear to diminish the seriousness of
this and other such recent episodes of scholars coming under attack.
But such criticisms must be especially troubling for those working in
the liberal humanist tradition, inasmuch as their work explicitly aims
to recover the authentically human dimension of both themselves *and*
their research subjects, thereby surpassing what is now seen as the
condescending and dismissive nature of much previous scholarship

on the Other; for instead of explaining away their tales, as others might have, we now come to see that *their* myths have always been *our* myths, "whether we like it or not," as Doniger wrote. Scholarship in this vein eliciting such a vicious response from some who identify with the object under study must therefore strike scholars as utterly puzzling.

But if we are interested in trying to understand the clash between scholars and readers that, according to Kripal, lies in the background of *The Serpent's Gift*, perhaps we ought not to overlook what lies unstated in Doniger's seemingly benign claim of inclusivity: *our* identification with and ownership of *their* tales results not just whether *we* like it or not but, more significantly perhaps, *whether they like it or not.* In fact, recognizing this might provide the opening for making some sense of the highly critical reception that some scholars' works have recently received; for in their efforts to find the deep or hidden meaning of a symbol, action, or text such scholars are heard by some as saying that those whose identity, self-worth, and social interests have been closely linked with their own reading and use of these symbols cannot properly interpret them for themselves (something, our research subjects might reply, they have been doing for quite some time before we showed up with our notebooks). Such scholarship can therefore come across as, well, just a little presumptuous, much like that person in a meeting who, when someone finishes her comment, pipes up and says, "What I think she meant to say is…." Regardless such speakers' good intentions, their uninvited paraphrases and translations usually do not sit well with those who thought that they were representing their meanings fine on their own.

With the interpreter's good will in mind, it is therefore understandable that some might find it odd for Kripal's critics – a heterogeneous group with diverse political agendas of their own, of course – to see his work as representative of the archrationalist tradition. I too find such a characterization odd, for, in my reading, his hermeneutical approach directed towards a form of politically liberal and socially permissive interreligious/intercultural dialogue, doing so by recovering "the deepest and most transformative meanings of texts, meanings that often go directly against the assumed 'obvious,' commonsense, or literal readings that have more or less captured the conservative

ideologies" (29), places his work far from those so-called reductionists whom humanists and theologians alike still criticize for their
insensitive studies of human beings as mere grist for their theoretical
mills (i.e., the human as data). But if we recognize that all scholarship
translates one meaning system into another, and that *scholarship on
people's lives* (whether explanatory or interpretive) is rather different
from *simply living one's life*, then his critics' portrait of his work as
archrationalist makes a little more sense; for, despite the distinctions
that some might draw between his interpretive method and the more
harshly rationalist, explanatory methods found elsewhere in the field,
it is sensible that the differences between these approaches melt away
for those who focus mainly on the fact that both conclude that the
people under study (whether they know it or not) are saying something quite other than what they themselves think they are saying. But
what does not make sense is that scholarship that has traditionally
been criticized here at home as reductionistic, as not taking religion
seriously, has not received such criticisms from those, for example,
who are intent on reclaiming Hinduism from the humanists. It may
therefore seem ironic that those reductionists who openly attempt
to *explain* human behaviors by appeals to mechanisms possibly
unknown to participants (think here of cognitive scientists theorizing ritual) seem not to attract impassioned criticisms from the people whom they study; unless I am mistaken, only liberal humanists,
intent on articulating the deepest *meaning* of the trans-cultural human
experience that is said to unite us all, find themselves mired in such
controversies. Why?

   Answering this question will require us to examine what happens
when the people about whom we write fail to recognize their meanings in the diagnostic mirror that we hold up to them. To do so, we
might begin by asking why these people are being diagnosed in the
first place; for, as I once heard Jonathan Smith observe, in a conversation about the psychoanalytic method, Freud's patients *came to him*
because they felt something to be askew in their lives; he didn't take
his couch, uninvited, to them (though, admittedly, Freud certainly
was fond of generalizing his findings to large groups of people and
the species as a whole; perhaps this is the speculative shortcoming
of his work). Recent uses of Freud's theories by some scholars of

religion therefore seem to lack one of the crucial parties necessary for proper psychoanalytic treatment: the willing patient, whose own insights and interpretations, as Smith also noted, brings part of the "talking cure" to the couch (i.e., it takes two to have a conversation). So where, we might ask, is the prudish patient's agency in such studies? Moreover, do *they* think that they're being prudes?

After asking this sort of question, we might then inquire as to just which (or, better put, *whose*) criteria were used to determine the limits of our common human potential (i.e., who constitutes the limits of the "our" and what counts as a conversation?). That is, who gets to say who's the prude? Taking for granted that our so-called sexual freedom ought to be the progressive standard is not quite so easy after the work of Michel Foucault, for he persuaded some that the one who talks *most freely* and frequently about sex may turn out to be the *most repressed* of all (i.e., talk about sex is itself a form of bio-management). Of course there are certain accidental features of the society into which we happen to have been born and socialized that we no doubt come to appreciate and probably take for granted (such as, say, gender and generational relations, views on sexuality, definitions of the human, forms of economic relations, etc.), but using them as the bar against which to measure all human potential might understandably be seen as just a little self-serving by those who happen to measure themselves by other (surely no less contingent) standards. For I assume that the sentiments and social worlds of other people are taken by them to be just as grounded in reality as we take our own to be – whether the "they" of that sentence are politically conservative evangelicals in the United States intent on recovering the Christian values upon which the nation was supposedly founded, or well educated, politically liberal, and upwardly mobile members of India's worldwide diaspora community (or what others might rephrase as its "brain drain") intent on taking back their nation and their religious heritage from both European and North American scholars, on the one hand, and so-called extremist Hindu nationalists back in India, on the other. Much as politically and theologically liberal scholars don't appreciate such groups' attempts to export and impose their systems on us (I think here of the work of Americans United for the Separation of Church and State, to name but one prominent local example), quite understandably these groups do not respond well to being told that *we* know what ails *them* and that, despite their readings and use of their own symbols, we know what they actually mean and what they ought to entail – their response being particularly evident when it comes to such things as our commentary on their prudish views on such matters as gender relations and sexuality.

Inquiring into just these sorts of topics – an inquiry that goes to the heart of scholarly method – might then shed some light on why we find such a difference between some readers' reception of various forms of European and North American scholarship. Anything more than a good guess as to what we'll find when we do this sort of work will have to await another day (or the next chapter in this collection), but for the time being let me say that my suspicion is that theory-based, explanatory work – work that seeks not to nurture the Other's agency, define what it is to be human, or determine the deep or trans-human meaning of this or that symbol really is, but which, instead, seeks to satisfy systematically organized curiosities that may only be our own, doing so by drawing on some instance of human belief, behavior, or institution as an exemplum whose essence or value is not part of the analysis – is *not* seen as a threat because it has nothing at stake in the duel that inevitably results when one set of deep-seated meanings and values diagnoses another, all in the service of establishing our sense of a common humanity. To borrow a distinction from Bruce Lincoln (2003: 123, n. 5), cross-cultural work helps us to see that both our and their *values* (represented by members of all groups as static and eternal) are nothing more or less than *preferences* (i.e., circumstantial and a matter of choice), indicative of practical interests and social contexts/contests. Trouble therefore results when one side in this equation is demoted from self-evident value to contestable preference while the other is simultaneously elevated, not simply from a preference to a value, but from one among many values to the measure for all human experience (a category that, I admit, I was surprised to find in Kripal's book; one would think that today it would be rather more difficult to boil the species down to some essentially common interior disposition); such work may therefore end up, quite reasonably perhaps, being seen by some as rather more transgressive than intended by the well-meaning therapists trying to persuade their research subjects that they are in fact patients in need of our diagnostic skills. No wonder our generous gifts sometimes fail to prompt any display of gratitude.

And it is with the notion of an unreciprocated gift in mind that I think it is worth revisiting what a century of exchange theory *should have* taught us; a gift is only one of three elements: both the giver as well as the recipient must be taken into account in studying any exchange (somewhat like the need to have Freud's analyst *and* patient willingly present in the same room). Whereas *The Serpent's Gift* tells readers much about the assumptions and goals of the agent doing the giving (Kripal's psychoanalytically-inclined and liberated Gnostic intellectual), as well as the nature of the gift being given (a certain sort of politically liberal and humanistic view on the intertwined nature of critical thought, open sexuality, and human potential), we learn far less about the recipient. I therefore could not help but wonder about whether this gift was invited by them and, if not, what one does when an unanticipated analysis falls into the lap of those who fail to recognize themselves as patients. Should they share the interests of the Gnostic intellectual (as in the case of a growing trans-national consensus among an educated, mobile, middle class with economic and social aspirations and some degree of access to capital), then they may not mind the critique of the childish literalism that they feel to plague some of their "narrow minded" compatriots; but should their preferences deviate from those which the intellectual takes for granted, should they see Gnostic intellectuals' views on the human to be in direct competition with their own, then they'll likely be rather perturbed by a gift that they see to be less than generously given.

My point? While having no sympathies for the rhetorics of authenticity and origins now being used by peoples throughout the world, and from all across the political spectrum, to authorize various sorts of politically useful notions of, for example, "India" and its supposed past, and thus while having no interest whatsoever to be seen as supporting their causes, I cannot help but see that the necessary reciprocity of giver and recipient is wholly absent from much liberal humanist work that aims to encounter and pay due respect to the Other; the reciprocal nature of all good gifts is therefore missing, confirming that sometimes a gift is an imposition that, predictably enough, solicits no grateful "thank you" in reply – somewhat like newlyweds pondering what to do with their three toasters. Although drawing attention to this serious shortcoming in some of my peers' works risks me being seen as either naïve or having no regard for the political (as claimed by Pennington [2005: 182]), I think it quite the opposite; for the critique that I am offering invites scholars who claim to be interested in issue of empowerment and disenfranchisement to assess their own role in power politics – even if they think that their role is simply to uncover timeless meanings and deep experiences. For in looking over some such works, I find an ironic absence of the very agency in the Other that such humanists claim to be trying to recover. And while it may go unnoticed by them, it is a lack that is more than apparent to those in parts of the world who, until recently, have had no choice but to accept unsolicited colonial presents (e.g., languages, legal and economic systems, trading relationships, etc.) – so-called gifts for which they may have had little or no use.

But, as evidenced in the critical (in some cases, passionately critical and even sadly violent) responses elicited by some to recent liberal humanists' works, one of the effects of our globalized world is that such people now have choices; the Other is therefore electing to talk back, doing so in a language that scholars understand and in a variety of voices and styles that reflect an even wider variety of practical interests, exercising an agency we had not planned on. As already noted, while some are found in rallies and marches taking place far from North American centers of learning, yet others are on the web signing petitions, attending our classes, and working in the profession itself, using the familiar rules of argumentation and rhetoric of the European and North American institutions in which many of their authors were trained (i.e., the Other is now not simply in our midst but is in fact us!). I have in mind such works as the multi-author collection, *Invading the Sacred: An Analysis of Hinduism Studies in America* (Ramaswamy et al. 2007). As S.N. Balagangadhara writes in its Foreword (viii): "Many of them [i.e., Indian intellectuals] realize that Western explanations of their religions and culture trivialize their lived experiences; by distorting, such explanations transform these, and this denies Indians access to their own experiences."

Rather than taking sides in this debate over meaning, agency, experience, and identity (and thereby entering the contest over the limits of what counts as legitimately or authentically human), perhaps scholars ought to shift the ground and study the contest itself and refrain from seeing the results of their work as a gift to humankind; if we make such a shift, then we might notice that the same tools are being used by those on either side of this debate: we hear the familiar pairing of West vs East – as if this analytic helps us to understand something about the world rather than about our need to demarcate it into zones of local and exotic – we find the distinction between distorted vs pristine as well as experience vs expression. And of course we find the Latin-based word/concept religion, coupled with the presumption of apolitical interiority, now being used all across the world – from Balagangadhara's Foreword to, for example, Buddhist monks protesting for their "religious freedom" in Myanmar back in the Fall of 2007. Taking stock of how these once exclusively European tools are now being used worldwide will enable us to become curious about those who contest humanists' claims concerning, say, "Indian religion" (such as the contributors to *Invading the Sacred*) *not* by asserting that "religion" is an alien import of no relevance to how they think and act themselves into groups but, instead, by informing scholars as to what their religion and experience *really are*; what may strike us as curious is that such writers seem not to realize that the very game they are playing (i.e., religion/not religion) is itself a colonial import that they have adopted and modified to suit their own local purposes.

It is with great irony, then, that I close by recalling something written by Eliade:

> We may expect that sometime in the near future the intelligentsia of the former colonial peoples will regard many social scientists as camouflaged apologists for Western culture. Because these scientists insist so persistently on the sociopolitical origin and character of the "primitive" messianic movements, they may be suspected of a Western superiority complex…. (1984: 7)

What he had not foreseen in his familiar criticism of social scientists was that formerly colonized peoples would one day adopt the tools of the humanist and use them to study not only themselves but also us, just as we had long studied them; and, in the process, that they would bite the hand that had provided them with a their technical discourse. For in worrying so much over giving the gift of agency by pursuing the study of deeply felt, trans-historical meaning, scholars have empowered the Other by alienating them from the selves that they had long thought they were; the Other is now bold enough to use the same tools that we employ in this contest over meaning and identity and, in using them, they not only pursue ends that we had never dreamed of but ends which we do not approve of. Yet this is precisely the risk that having one's own agency entails, no?

But in opposing some scholarly choices and thereby speaking for themselves, will these Others ever recognize that, in responding to what they see to be outsiders' misrepresentations of their lives by means of such no less alien imports as "religion," "experience," "nation," and "citizenship," they provide strong evidence that, in a globalized world in which a colonial language, English, has become the lingua franca and in which a colonial economic system, capitalism, has won the day, they are no longer capable of thinking themselves into action except by means of imported concepts – tools they may think of as being expressions of internal states and obviously existing realities but which have a manufacturing history that long pre-dates their retooled appearance on distant shores? If not, then their failure to see how they have adopted and transformed what was once an uninvited imposition, making it into what is now portrayed as their own natural resource, will mark the true victory of colonialism; for if our critics continue to fail to see their own reactions to liberal humanist scholars as being part of the same discourse, then a specific group, with specific interests, encoded in their classifications of the world, will continue to set the terms by means of which postcolonial peoples think their agency into practice. For the very form of their protests empowers *us* to continue to say who *they* are.

References

Doniger O'Flaherty, Wendy. 1986. "The Uses and Misuses of Other People's Myths." *Journal of the American Academy of Religion* 54(2): 219–39. http://dx.doi.org/10.1093/jaarel/LIV.2.219.

Eliade, Mircea. 1984. *The Quest: History and Meaning in Religion.* Chicago: University of Chicago Press.

Kripal, Jeffrey J. 1995. *Kali's Child: The Mystical and the Erotic in the Life and Teachings of Ramakrishna.* Chicago: University of Chicago Press.

Kripal, Jeffrey J. 2001. *Roads of Excess, Palaces of Wisdom: Eroticism & Reflexivity in the Study of Mysticism.* Chicago: University of Chicago Press.

Kripal, Jeffrey J. 2007a. *Esalen: America and the Religion of No Religion.* Chicago: University of Chicago Press.

Kripal, Jeffrey J. 2007b. *The Serpent's Gift: Gnostic Reflections on the Study of Religion.* Chicago: University of Chicago Press.

Kripal, Jeffrey J. 2010. *Authors of the Impossible: The Paranormal and the Sacred.* Chicago: University of Chicago Press. http://dx.doi.org/10.7208/chicago/9780226453897.001.0001.

Kripal, Jeffrey J. 2011. *Mutants and Mystics: Science Fiction, Superhero Comics, and the Paranormal.* Chicago: University of Chicago Press. http://dx.doi.org/10.7208/chicago/9780226453859.001.0001.

Lincoln, Bruce. 2003. *Holy Terrors: Thinking about Religion after September 11.* Chicago: University of Chicago Press.

Mauss, Marcel. 1990 (1950). *The Gift: The Form and Reason for Exchange in Archaic Societies.* Trans. W.D. Hall. New York: W.W. Norton.

Pennington, Brian K. 2005. *Was Hinduism Invented: Britons, Indians, and the Colonial Construction of Religion.* New York: Oxford University Press. http://dx.doi.org/10.1093/0195166558.001.0001.

Ramaswamy, Krishnan, et al., eds. 2007. *Invading the Sacred: An Analysis of Hinduism Studies in America.* New Delhi: Rupa & Co.

Smith, Jonathan Z. 2007. "The Necessary Lie: Duplicity in the Disciplines." In Russell T.McCutcheon, *Studying Religion: An Introduction*, 73–80. London: Equinox Publishers.

Russell T. McCutcheon is Professor and Chair of the Department of Religious Studies at the University of Alabama. His research focuses on the social and political implications of competing classification systems.

Topic IV: Costs of Conceptual Colonialism

7. Conceptual Colonialism: How Descriptions Carry Explanations

Craig Martin

By what criteria do we determine a person's sexual orientation? Should we take individuals at their word? Can we impose identities onto people that they publicly reject? Consider the American documentary *Outrage* (Magnolia Pictures, 2009), which suggests that there are many closeted homosexual men in the Republican party who, in order to protect their closeted status, consistently vote against legislation supporting gay rights. The film begins with the story of Senator Larry Craig – a Republican from the state of Idaho – who was arrested in 2007 for soliciting sex from another man in an airport restroom. Despite Craig's longtime marriage to his wife, Suzanne, and his insistence at a press conference that "I'm not gay; I never have been gay," the documentary insists that he is a hypocrite, a liar, and a traitor to his own – i.e., homosexual – people. The documentary excoriates Craig and similar closeted Republican men for treason against their own kind.

According to the documentary, there are apparently only two sexual orientations – gay and straight – and any man who has a sexual relation with another man is, by definition, gay. This is, it seems, a clear and obvious truth, no matter the protestations of those on whom the descriptor "gay" is applied.

In a sense, this is conceptual colonialism at work. Colonialism is the practice of expanding an empire through the acquisition of foreign land or resources and exploiting those in the interests of the empire. I propose the phrase "conceptual colonialism" for the practice of applying concepts onto foreign social contexts where those concepts are not used, in order to serve the interests of those applying the concepts. Here we have a case of gay rights activists projecting the concept "homosexual" onto persons who reject the application of the term, and explicitly in support of the interests of those *applying* the term rather than the interests of those *on whom* the term is applied (the activists in this case express the hope that gay Republicans will come "out of the closet" and end their "homophobic" voting record). There is nothing intrinsically wrong with such conceptual colonialism; while ancient Greeks didn't have the concept of H_2O, I have little doubt that they drank it. However, we must be attentive to the politics of conceptual colonialism.

Scholars are often explicitly careful in the application of foreign terminology, even when they see it as appropriate. In *Christianity, Social Tolerance, and Homosexuality*, historian John Boswell (1980) cautions readers to beware of allowing modern homophobia to determine how we read the past; we should not unreflectively project our ideas or social fears onto ancient contexts, and should beware of conceptual anachronism. According to Boswell, the terms "gay" and "homosexual" are both of modern vintage – and the term "homosexual" was originally tied to medical literature that pathologized homosexuality. However, despite his warnings about anachronism, Boswell goes on to talk about "homosexuals" and "gays" in ancient Greece, ancient Rome, late antiquity, and the European Middle Ages; indeed, his book stops short of the modern period to which the terms themselves date. Boswell discourages his readers from projecting anachronisms onto the past, but nevertheless finds gays and homosexuals throughout antiquity.

How can we find "homosexuals" and "gays" in the past, prior to the existence of the concepts themselves? In his chapter on "Definitions," Boswell notes that the sizeable gap between our understanding of the world and that of the ancients prompts us to wonder "whether the dichotomy suggested by the terms 'homosexual' and 'heterosexual' corresponds to any reality at all" (1980: 58). How can the ancients not have noted this distinction, which seems so obvious to us? Quite simply, Boswell's answer is that there is a distinction between *appearance* and *reality*: that is, the reality of homosexuality has always existed; there has never been a time without a "ground" or perhaps "foundation" to the reality this concept picks up; however, only some social groups have a need to draw attention to that ground. Homosexuals have always existed as a percentage of the human population (like "left-handed people" [ibid.: 59]), but perhaps only moderns – given their particular heteronormative anxieties and social fears – perceive them fully. Much like the documentarians who "out" secretly gay politicians, Boswell knows the true sexual orientation of premodern homosexuals for whom the concept "homosexual" was not available. In addition, he similarly seems to hope that "outing" premodern gays will encourage tolerance by presenting as natural what others view as unnatural and by denaturalizing modern homophobia.

By contrast, in *Sexing the Body: Gender Politics and the Construction of Sexuality*, Anne Fausto-Sterling (2000) argues – coming from the perspective of Michel Foucault and Judith Butler – that sex identities and sexuality are products of discursive regimes and do not pre-exist them. On this view, a person who might have been a "gender invert" or a "sapphist" in the past might nevertheless be a "heterosexual" today. For Fausto-Sterling, the conceptual scheme in which individuals are interpellated has a constitutive role in the shape of their sexuality, sexual attraction, and sexual practices. For Boswell, however, sexuality is apparently pre-discursive, real, and innate, and is only "interpreted" or identified differently in different discourses. Fausto-Sterling writes, "Suppose for a minute that we had a few time-traveling clones – genetically identical humans living in ancient Greece, in seventeenth-century Europe, and in the contemporary United States. Boswell would say that if a particular clone was homosexual in ancient Greece, he would also be homosexual in the seventeenth century or today" (Fausto-Sterling 2000: 15–16). For Boswell, transfer a person to a new social context and their real sexuality remains the same; by contrast, for Fausto-Sterling, transfer a person to a new social context and a new sexuality may be brought into existence. Presumably for Boswell, Larry Craig is, deep down, essentially gay, no matter what he or his community of friends and family call him. For Fausto-Sterling, he might just be a self-identified straight man who enjoys having sex with other men on occasion – the identification he uses to describe himself and its relation to his sexual practices might bring into existence a new form of sexuality that's neither heterosexual nor homosexual.

To turn back to the question of conceptual colonialism: whether we side with Boswell's or Fausto-Sterling's account, our descriptions of what's going on with Craig involve the application of foreign concepts and assumptions. Boswell's description of homosexuals in ancient Greece assumes a particular type of causal explanation of their existence – homosexuality is caused by nature or biology, not produced by culture or discursive regimes, which is why we can use an anachronistic, modern concept to talk about them. Fausto-Sterling's description, following Foucault and Butler, also assumes a causal explanation – in her view, subjectivity and sexuality are not merely biological but also products of power, social relations, and discourses used to interpellate subjects. Two descriptions, then, both of which smuggle in foreign concepts and assumptions. Neither approach is likely to be approved by Craig himself.

In the essay following, Russell T. McCutcheon uncovers just such a case of conceptual contraband. McCutcheon looks closely at Robert Orsi's critique of Dennis Covington's account of snake-handling churches. In *Salvation on Sand Mountain: Snake Handling and Redemption in Southern Appalachia*, Covington (1995) proposes what McCutcheon calls a "loosely Marxist explanation" of the snake handling phenomenon, according to which the practice provides those who participate with some variety of an opiate of the masses. It is unlikely that the leader of the snake-handling church, Punkin' Brown, would appreciate his religion being reduced to an opiate of the masses any more than Craig appreciated being called a homosexual. By contrast, in *Between Heaven and Earth: The Religious Worlds People Make and the Scholars Who Study Them*, Orsi (2005) encourages us to listen not to a reductive Marxist interpretation but rather to the words of Punkin' Brown, himself. Orsi writes,

> Brown believed that it was God present before him that caused
> him to pick up snakes at meetings; he embodied, in other words,
> the enduring power of sacred presence in the modern world and

in modern persons' imaginations and memories, from which presence is disallowed. (2005: 182)

On the one hand we have a foreign explanation that posits the cause of this practice as the disenfranchisement of impoverished Alabamans; on the other hand we have what seems to be a mere description of Punkin' Brown's view, according to which God's presence "caused him to pick up snakes."

For McCutcheon, as readers will see below, perhaps Orsi's account is not a mere description. McCutcheon notes that Orsi's "description" smuggles in the language of 20th-century phenomenology of religion; the phrase "enduring power of sacred presence" sounds more like Rudolph Otto or Mircea Eliade than Alabaman fundamentalists, and carries with it a causal account that utilizes phenomenology's essence-and-manifestation framework. Perhaps translation is necessarily treason, and perhaps it is impossible *not* to use our own explanatory framework when recounting the words – and deeds – of others. McCutcheon writes, "I bet that we all do precisely what Orsi does in the above quotation: we put *our* words into *their* mouths and, for whatever reason, fail to recognize the sound of our own voices." Perhaps conceptual colonialism is unavoidable. Despite the phenomenologist's intention to bracket explanation, foreign explanations magically appear within our descriptions themselves, the contraband somehow miraculously transported from beyond the brackets holding them at bay. Rather than attempt to bracket explanation, perhaps we, as scholars, should attempt to be as reflexively self-aware as we can be, to note rather than obscure the explanations our descriptions perform.

Was Larry Craig gay? Was Brown in touch with "the Sacred"? Perhaps our goal – as scholars – should not be to attempt definitive answers to such questions but rather to be as attentive as possible to whose interests are served by the colonial endeavors under analysis.

References

Boswell, John. 1980. *Christianity, Social Tolerance, and Homosexuality: Gay People in Western Europe from the Beginning of the Christian Era to the Fourteenth Century*. Chicago: University of Chicago Press.

Covington, Dennis. 1995. *Salvation on Sand Mountain: Snake Handling and Redemption in Southern Appalachia*. New York: Penguin; 2009 reprint, Philadelphia: Da Capo Press.

Fausto-Sterling, Anne. 2000. *Sexing the Body: Gender Politics and the Construction of Sexuality*. New York: Basic Books.

Magnolia Pictures. 2009. *Outrage*.

Orsi, Robert A. 2005. *Between Heaven and Earth: The Religious Worlds People Make and the Scholars Who Study Them*. Princeton: Princeton University Press.

Craig Martin is Associate Professor of Religious Studies at St Thomas Aquinas College. His research focuses on theory and method in the study of religion.

8. "It's a Lie. There's No Truth in It! It's a Sin!": The Costs of Saving Others from Themselves[1]

Russell T. McCutcheon

> How many things have to happen to you before something occurs to you? – Robert Frost[2]

If, as Jonathan Z. Smith has so often told us, gains in knowledge come about by means of provocative juxtapositions – quoting a teacher of his own, Smith has referred to this method as "an exaggeration in the direction of truth"[3] – then I'd like to place alongside each other two recent scholarly texts concerned with methodology – texts that,

[1] Earlier versions of this essay were presented as lectures in the Fall of 2005 and Spring of 2006 at the University of Copenhagen, The University of Southern Denmark (my thanks to Tim Jensen for arranging this visit to Denmark), the University of Virginia (my thanks to Kurtis Schaeffer for arranging this visit), the Institute for the Advanced Study of Religion at Trinity College, Toronto (my thanks to Donald Wiebe for the invitation to speak), Universität Berne (thanks to Jens Schlieter for making the arrangements), and Universität Zürich (my thanks to Dorothea Lüddeckens for arranging the lecture). My thanks also go to those in attendance who offered comments on the paper and, most importantly, to Jeppe Sinding Jensen, of Aarhus University, Denmark, for his formal reply at the Toronto session. Finally, I wish to acknowledge *JAAR*'s editor and two anonymous reviewers, all of whom offered helpful comments on an earlier draft.
[2] Quoted by the US poet Edward Hirsch, as recounted to him by the American poet, William Meridith; Hirsch's full National Public Radio interview is available at: http://www.npr.org/templates/story/story.php?storyId=5331955 (accessed May 29, 2013).
[3] This is quoted from an online essay of Smith's entitled "The Necessary Lie: Duplicity in the Disciplines," posted at a University of Chicago site

when first reading them, prompted me to consider some of the costs to be paid when scholars of religion attempt to negotiate and thereby resolve issues of difference.

First, there was an essay written by Robert Orsi, devoted to reviewing my own 2003 book, *The Discipline of Religion*. Commenting on the manner in which the beliefs, behaviors, and institutions of human subjects are described in my book by means of that four-lettered word, "data,"[4] Orsi evaluated the book's method as "chilling," noting how dehumanizing it is to study people in ways they themselves have not authorized. When it comes to the scholar who thinks it necessary to subject human behaviors to such theoretical analysis, he asks:

> From what authoritative and normative vantage point (or political or intellectual imperatives) is this need identified? ... [N]owhere – absolutely nowhere – in this volume is any reference made to the moral requirement of obtaining the consent of those upon whom this theoretical action is to be performed.... Rather, the assumption appears to be that the scholar of religion by virtue of his or her normative epistemology, theoretical acuity, and political knowingness, has the authority and the right to make the lives of others the objects of his or her scrutiny. He or she theorizes them. (Orsi 2004: 88)

To drive home his critique, Orsi draws on a few hypothetical examples:

> a devout working class man who kneels to pray at his wife's grave, suddenly uncertain and afraid at the end of his own life of what lies ahead, has attained the status of data; he has become

---

intended for incoming graduate teaching assistants: http://teaching.uchicago. edu/?/ctl-archive/course-design-tutorials/assessing-and-improving/smith (accessed May 29, 2013; see also Smith 2007). Elsewhere Smith has spoken of "the cognitive power of distortion" (1996: 19). On Smith's body of work see McCutcheon 2006a.

[4] See Smith 1997 for another example of a scholar of religion content with naming human behavior, in this case that of theologians, as data. Or consider Lincoln's routine use of the term (most recently, 2012: 95 or 122). Curiously, Orsi has not gone after these rather higher-profile scholars for their supposed ethical lapses.

a fit candidate for theorization. A suburban Pentecostal woman speaking in tongues, an Orthodox family preparing for high holy days, a Mexican migrant imploring Guadalupe for a healing, a pilgrim to the shrine of the imprint of Krishna's foot: these are our specimens, their words [according to McCutcheon] *"heuristically useful, everyday rhetorical fictions."* Do the theorized have any voice to speak back to the italicizing theorizer? Can they challenge the assertion that they are in need of theorization or this construal of their lives? Can they protest being made into a theoretician's "fair game"? If they do, McCutcheon never says so, which is a serious omission: the data remain silent, as one might expect of data. A book that sets out to call attention to the dynamics of power/knowledge in the study of religion winds up proposing the most egregious exercise of power as the disciplines' fundamental work. And once again, religious studies can't look its subject in the eyes.

It strikes me that Orsi is here presenting an updated version of the late Wilfred Cantwell Smith's well known methodological rule of thumb which presumed that, insomuch as they share a common human nature and thus dignity, both scholar and religious participant are involved in a consensual conversation. As famously stated in Cantwell Smith's now classic essay, "The Comparative Study of Religion: Whither – and Why?" it goes: "no statement about a religion is valid unless it can be acknowledged by that religion's believers" (1959: 42).[5] For Orsi, much as with Cantwell Smith, scholars risk presenting a false, and thereby potentially harmful image of their research subjects if those subjects have not first signed-off on scholarly representations (what I take him to mean by "the moral requirement of obtaining the consent" of those whom we study). As already suggested, implicit here is the assumption that scholarship is a type of

[5] Or, as my late colleague, Tim Murphy, once noted, this position is also nicely represented by the Dutch phenomenologist, W. Brede Kristensen who, half a century ago, phrased it as follows (in the words of Eric Sharpe's English translation of Kristensen's 1954 work, *Religionshistoriskstudium*): "if our opinion about another religion differs from the opinion and evaluation of the believers, then we are no longer talking about their religion" (Sharpe 1986: 228).

Habermasian conversation, comprised of a series of goodwill negotiations between partners, in which the goal is to arrive at some sort
of mutual understanding that at least addresses, if not resolves, the
differences between potentially competing systems of representation.
Anything short of this and scholars can legitimately be classified as
immoral or – judging from their inability, at least in Orsi's estimation,
to look their subject straight in the eye – perhaps embarrassed or even
cowardly. For Orsi, then, it appears that scholars play the role of disciples and prophets, speaking only insomuch as they are authorized
by an Other.

Of course there are those occasions when Others do indeed speak
up (and sometimes even act up), as exemplified in the second text
that I would like to consider alongside Orsi's review essay: a brief
article by Paul Courtright which, though first published in Emory's
in-house periodical, *Academic Exchange*, was later re-published in the
American Academy of Religion's *Religious Studies News* (Courtright
2004). Entitled "Studying Religion in an Age of Terror," this article
makes obvious use of the now well known rhetoric of terror by means
of which Courtright reflects on the wider issues involved in the furor
created by some people within the US-based South Asian community
when his award-winning 1985 book, *Ganeśa: Lord of Obstacles, Lord
of Beginnings*, was reprinted in India in 2001. With a cover depicting
a small statue of a nude infant Ganesha, the elephant-headed Hindu
god, and a small portion of the text offering a Freudian analysis of
Shiva and Ganesha's complex and, at times, violent father/son relationship (e.g., Courtright 2001: 114 ff.), the controversy prompted
by this reprint[6] calls to mind the similarly angry reactions to, among
others, Jeffrey Kripal's 1995 book, *Kali's Child: The Mystical and
the Erotic in the Life and Teachings of Ramakrishna*, James Laine's
little 2003 book, *Shivaji: Hindu King in Islamic India*, along with
such incidents as the egg reportedly flung at Wendy Doniger during

---

[6] The controversy ranged from an online petition posted by the Hindu
Students' Council of the University of Louisiana that attracted several thousand signatures, to anger expressed to Emory University's President by some
well placed members of Atlanta's local South Asian population, as well as
actual threats against Courtright himself.

her November 2003 public lecture at the London School of Oriental and African Studies.[7]

Although one could draw on a number of incidents and articles (many of which are available on the web) that exemplify what greeted Courtright's reprinted book, consider just this one review that can easily be found at amazon.com. In an August 17, 2004 posting, we read:

> A reading of this book revealed to me how Courtright, a professor of religion, who teaches Hinduism in a Christian university in the South, is so absurdly prejudiced – anti-Hindu. He has written utter profanities of a gross sexual nature, totally a fabrication originating from his filthy mind, like a pornographic novel, with no basis in any Hindu literature or source document. This is the most stupid book I have read on the subject. It is astounding how such bigotted [sic] professors are allowed to teach the religion they despise. He should be let go of the university so he can follow his true calling as an evangelical missionary in some remote corner of the world where he can fool some illeterate [sic] people to convert them to christianity [sic]

[7] As an aside, I should say that one of this paper's original anonymous reviewers placed importance on such things as the fact that, in some of the cases here cited, people other than those about whom the scholarly work was written took offense, implying that this essay's analysis is insufficient since the cited cases are all rather different from one another. To me, highlighting this point in an attempt to ungroup the cases here placed alongside each other (i.e., in an attempt to correct this paper's "simplistic" approach) is most dubious, for it implies that scholars are in the position to decide who can legitimately be offended by their work. This, in turn, presupposes that one can rather easily settle issues of authenticity among the groups we study. However, this issue of authenticity (explored in greater detail in McCutcheon 2003: 167–88; and 2005b) can itself be understood as but one strategy to minimize and thereby manage a broad range of dissent, for it enables one to ignore those voices determined (by whom and using what criteria?) as coming from some illegitimate fringe. Case in point: noting that Courtright's detractors were not from the group he studied normalizes one set of standards for who gets to be counted as members of the offended group – a set of standards that certainly favors one way of portraying the issue by de-authorizing those US-based South Asians who seem to have felt so offended.

– rather than practicing his craft in a university that I am sure receives government funding in some way – that is: my taxes are going to support this hate mongering university professor. What a travesty of noble concepts like democracy, separation of church and state and academic freedom. This guy has trashed all these noble concepts in pursuit of his perverse agenda.

Reflecting on the affair of which this one scathing review is but a brief illustration, Courtright's own article describes how

> well-financed and organized groups on the political and religious right want to control the memory of India's past in ways that suit their own ideological agendas. Consequently, scholars within or outside India who challenge those constructions become targets of attack.

Because, as he puts it, "[t]o write is to resist the sloth of familiar forms of knowing and being in the world," Courtright understands scholarship long to have been "suspect by orthodoxies of one sort or another in many cultures." His brush with angry readers – though one never knows who, among his critics, has actually read his book – therefore provides evidence that, as he phrases it, "service to the pursuit of knowledge and understanding" can be dangerous business. Indeed.

Echoing Courtright's assessment of this controversy over what we often call "the insider/outsider problem,"[8] Wendy Doniger (who wrote forewords to both Courtright's and Kripal's books) has observed that, in the case of Hindu nationalists at least, it is asserted that "no one who is not a Hindu has the right to speak about Hinduism at all" (Vedantam 2004: A01; see also Braverman 2004). For William Dalrymple, writing in *The New York Review of Books* (2005), this amounts to nothing less than a war over India's history, a war that has profound contemporary political implications, none more central than

---

[8] The very fact that differing viewpoints are considered a "problem" is itself the issue that requires attention; on this, see McCutcheon 2005b: 16–32. See also the forthcoming new edition of my own *The Insider/Outsider Problem in the Study of Religion: A Reader*, co-edited with Suzanne Owen (Equinox Publishers).

the topic of concern here: the scholar's role when it comes to differing systems of representation.

Elaborating on what he sees this role to be, Courtright's brief article (2004) continues:

> as a scholar and interpreter, my intent is not to demean, dismantle, or offend. Rather, it is to explore, probe, and imagine, using whatever approaches the content of the religious tradition and the tradition of critical inquiry call upon – even drawing on forms of interpretation that may not be indigenous to that tradition itself but may be illuminating and novel.

Unlike Orsi's use of the language of *morality* to sanction one set of representations – those said to be in accord with, or at least sanctioned by the consent of, the subject's own self-representations[9] – Courtright speaks the language of *integrity* to legitimize yet another set – those of the scholar, potentially writing contrary to participant self-representations – concluding that: "The integrity of what we do must be protected" from the "self-appointed guardians of sentiment." And what scholars *do*, Courtright notes, is engage in "the pursuit of knowledge," otherwise described as "critical inquiry" – the sort of work that results in what one commentator has described as the "accessible, well-written, and balanced histories of India" (Dalrymple 2005: 65) that are, in this one reviewer's estimation, so badly needed in contemporary Indian schools.[10] To abandon the effort to produce

[9] As an aside, let me say that I recognize that Orsi does not say that participants must agree with our representations, but I have difficulty imagining many of our research subjects consenting to be – at least in their opinion – misrepresented, misquoted, and used for ends with which they disagree (e.g., submitting to naturalistic studies of their religion). The issue of *consent*, therefore, implicitly raises the issue of *assent*.

[10] Not to give away the punchline to my essay, but (as intimated in an earlier note) who gets to determine this *need*, how do we decide what counts as *well written*, and, most importantly perhaps, what constitutes *balance* (interestingly, this is the same argument creationists use to try to include their views in biology curricula) – these are *the* questions that are unaddressed when we presume an authentic Other to exist in contradistinction to illegitimate Others. Such questions are unaddressed because scrutinizing

scholarship when our conclusions offend against the so-called self-appointed, local guardians of sentiment is – Courtright concludes, drawing once again on a vocabulary well known to anyone who has watched the evening news in the post-September 11 world – "to give victory to the vigilantes. To remain silent is to abandon our students and surrender ourselves to those who seek, through terror, *to erase us*" (italics added).

These two texts – Orsi's and Courtright's – are both meditations on a basic and well known methodological problem; though basic, the issues involved are surely complex and no single essay can hope to juxtapose them in any adequate manner. Nonetheless, I wish to have readers consider why their two positions differ so much despite both having originated from within the same liberal humanistic tradition in the study of religion. By this I mean one that understands religion's significance – as well as the significance of the study of religion practiced as a form of conversation – to have something to do with its being both deeply human *and* humane. Although I would not be so flippant as to say that what we have here are simply modern-day instances of Mircea Eliade's well known notion of a new humanism – in which the scholar is thought vicariously to re-experience the supposedly deep existential situations contained in the remnants and artifacts of other people's lives (e.g., see Eliade 1984) – I *would* argue that both Orsi's work and at least Courtright's early work are premised on the classic liberal humanist assumption, found all throughout the field, that scholars share a foundational commonality with their research subjects – call it "the human condition," if you will

---

the apparently self-evident criteria commentators, such as Dalrymple, use to determine the elements that constitute this balance would betray that *all* sides in these controversies are comprised of political actors (including scholars) working to normalize sets of local interests that are not necessarily shared universally. Simply put, there are very real interests at stake *on all sides* concerning, at least in the case at hand, what India's current socio-political and economic structure, and its citizens' sense of their past, ought to look like – an "ought" likely based on contemporary geopolitic interests rather than on the passive recognition of stable, factual self-evidencies. Sadly, it goes well beyond this already excessively long essay to explore the geopolitical aspect of the issue here being investigated.

– making them all participants in a common dialogue that addresses and, ideally, overcomes the particularities that might otherwise divide them. This is a view aptly summed up by Arvind Sharma, when, in an article on these controversies, he is quoted as saying something akin to the old religious pluralist's parable of the blind men and the elephant: "[b]oth the insider and the outsider see the truth...but genuine understanding may be said to arise at the point of their intersection" (quoted in Braverman 2004). Although not accessible to any single one of us, there apparently is a big picture and collaborative representations are our best hope for getting at a "balanced" picture of it.[11]

I place Orsi's work into this tradition of seeking a balanced, genuine understanding not only because of his strong commitment to the moral requirement to obtain the consent of our research subjects[12] but also because of his interest, as expressed in the closing chapter to his 2005 collection of essays, in entering a mutual conversation with the Other "in order to discover something about human life and culture, about religion, and about ourselves" (Orsi 2005: 178). This theme of using the study of religion to bridge the gap between Self and Other is found all throughout the humanistic study of religion; for example, recall Wendy Doniger's conclusion that what drives the study of other people's stories is the realization that "their myths have always been our myths, though we may not have known it. We recognize ourselves

[11] At the level of logic, it is unclear how those who hold this viewpoint arrive at it in the first place for, if we grant their premise (that local perspectives prevent one from seeing the whole), then how can any local actor even know that there is a whole worth seeing? Simply put, the sort of "god's-eye" perspective that this view says we do not have must be assumed from the outset for this position even to make sense to those who hold it. For additional comments on the parable of the blind men and the elephant, see McCutcheon 1997: 109–11.

[12] Let me say at this point that I am not sure how this moral requirement can be applied to the artifacts we study which have been left either by recently or long-departed human actors. Presumably, one would have to invoke a hermeneutical principle – such as authorial intention? – capable of portraying one reading of an artifact as the authentic understanding, which could then be used to judge the accuracy, and thus adequacy, of scholarly readings. The problems involved in this interpretive move should be more than apparent to readers.

in those myths more vividly than we have ever recognized ourselves in the myths of our own culture" (Doniger O'Flaherty 1986: 224). Or think no further than José Cabezón's commissioned *JAAR* essay which redefines "theory" in order to pave the way towards a specific sort of pluralism, one that would allow elite religious participants to contribute what he terms their "indigenous theory" to our collective, scholarly conversation – an inclusion whose intended effect is the "weakening of the structures that under gird a facile Self/Other dichotomy" (2006: 25).[13]

With this scholarly goal of overcoming the gap between Self and Other in mind, I turn to the unenviable position in which Paul Courtright found himself, in which an Other vehemently disagreed with his representations and threatened to do something about it. What strikes me as curious in all this is that, his most recent views on intellectual autonomy notwithstanding, in his earlier work we find the same liberal humanist viewpoint motivating his work as apparently does Orsi's. For instance, consider the preface to the Indian reprint of his book on the elephant-headed god. To pick but one simple yet telling example, in thinking back on his earlier fieldwork in India, somewhat like Sharma and Cabezón, Courtright acknowledges a plurality of "ways of knowing" by saying that "my categories of knowing and seeing do not exhaust all possible ways

---

[13] Unlike the technical understanding of "theory" as a systematically related set of propositions with predictive capability (which necessitates that they are empirically testable), Cabezón defines theory merely as critical, self-reflexive awareness (unfortunately, his essay does not offer a basis for distinguishing what constitutes critique). Such a redefinition of the category of theory has also been the preferred strategy of those aiming to have creationism included in the high school biology curriculum (an approach that was *not* persuasive in the recent case of Kitzmiller et al. v. Dover Area School District et al.; Judge John E. Jones's December 20, 2005 decision against teaching creation science in science classrooms – a decision premised on its utter inability to be empirically testable and, thus, its not being a theory – is available at: http://news.findlaw.com/hdocs/docs/educate/ktzmllrdvr122005opn.pdf). On the effort to change the long-standing technical understanding of "theory" so as to break down traditional distinctions between scholar and data, insider and outsider, see McCutcheon 2001: 103–21.

of knowing and seeing." This recognition prompts him to wish that, as a scholar, he could "find ways for people to represent themselves and be subject to less interpretation from me" (2001: xii, x). Because Courtright's book came to my attention only after first reading his later article on methodology, I was perplexed to learn that the goal which he had once shared with many of his scholarly peers (of working towards ways of allowing the Other to represent him- or herself, unimpeded by scholarly intermediaries) had been dropped from his post-controversy article, in which Courtright warns readers not about the dangers of silencing the Other but, rather, of the very different danger of our own possible erasure!

So, to sum up: unlike Orsi's – and perhaps we should also add Courtright's pre-controversy – idea of the scholar, one whose legitimacy is linked to the degree to which she enters into a mutually beneficial dialogue with a consenting Other, Courtright's post-controversy idea of the scholar is legitimized by her autonomy, insomuch as she does *not* measure the adequacy of her own work in terms of any one set of participant self-interests – for, given the variety of people we as scholars study, it is easy to imagine such interests threatening our academic institutions and the people who work within them. Instead, she is free, as Courtright phrases it, to employ "forms of interpretation that may not be indigenous to that tradition." His post-controversy idea of the scholar therefore treats the self-representations of living or past subjects (such things as texts, verbal reports, behaviors, architecture, etc.) as primary source materials that comprise the basis for subsequent scholarly acts of historicization and theorization (what I take him to mean by his term "interpretation")[14] all of which follows the established conventions of the academy – conventions that can exist in sharp contradistinction to those of the groups under study. Yet these are

---

[14] A further issue that could be raised involves teasing out the possible significance of assuming that the scholar is free to interpret *meanings* in human artifacts that subjects themselves have not understood, on the one hand, and, on the other, a scholar's freedom to offer causal explanations for participant self-perceptions and actions. That is to say, although it is significant that he argues for scholarly autonomy, the apparent assumption that our task is essentially interpretive may signal Courtright's continued position within the liberal humanist tradition.

the very conventions (the authoritative and normative vantage point, as Orsi names it) that scholars such as Orsi and Cabezón – and, ironically perhaps, those nationalists so angered by Courtright's, Kripal's, and Laine's books[15] – understand as imperialist strategies that dehumanize the participants by ignoring their agency and own right to self-interpretation.[16]

So it was with Orsi's and Courtright's scholarly texts in front of me that I was struck by just how much they differed from one another, despite both being written from within the same scholarly tradition and both being deeply concerned with the practical ramifications of scholarship on the Other. For while Orsi occupies the *moral* high ground and chastises scholars who silence the Other, the post-controversy Courtright claims the *intellectual* high ground and laments when Others – or, to be more accurate, when a specific subgroup that Martin Marty, in an article on this very topic, identifies as "militants" (2004) – look us squarely in the eye and speak for themselves. For Orsi, the people we study are our conversation partners while for the post-controversy Courtright – though I do not believe he uses this particular four-lettered word – our research subjects comprise our *data* and there is no moral requirement whatsoever for us to converse with them so as to reach any mutually beneficial understanding. Rather, or so Courtright argues, as scholars we have

[15] To read an article that argues that, "whereas elite colleges in the West teach great respect for Greek and other Western Classics as being the bedrock of their civilization, it has become fashionable for elitist (i.e., Westernized) Indians to denigrate their own Indian Classics," which amounts to a postcolonialist attempt to "reclaim" representations of India from scholars, see the New Jersey-based businessman, Rajiv Malhotra's long web article, "Wendy's Child Syndrome," posted at: http://creative.sulekha.com/risa-lila-1-wendy-s-child-syndrome_103338_blog (accessed May 29, 2013). The site at which this is posted, named "Sulekha," was established in 1998 and is an online community for what could be called members of the worldwide, professional Indian diaspora.

[16] To avoid these outcomes we need, according to Cabezón (2006), to encourage a dialogue intended to arrive at what he terms "theory parity" (31); if not, he asserts that such negative consequences as denigration and manipulation will result (29, 30), both of which amount to scholarship that dismisses the Other (30, n. 25).

an intellectual and institutional imperative to, at times, study people *precisely* in ways unwelcome by them. For we do not study other people's myths because they embody our own hopes and dreams or because studying the "theories" that are implicit in them helps us "to challenge our theoretical parochialism" (Cabezón 2006: 30); instead, scholars study the artifacts of other people's worlds – regardless who created them or who claims to own their meanings – because they are the curious site at which they can use analytic methods of their own devising, to answer questions that are theirs, and not necessarily anyone else's.[17]

So I think it fair to ask: What *is* the scholar's role when it comes to difference and disagreement – either between their research subjects (e.g., the question much asked since September 11, 2001, "Whose version of Islam counts as authentic Islam?") or between their research subject and themselves? When are we in a conversation with the Other and when do we suspend the Other's right to his or her first-person interpretive authority (see Godlove 1994)? As suggested earlier, to answer such questions we must first determine which Others we're talking about and this involves determining which differences are *too* different – and what criteria do we use to make *this* judgment? For, judging from the lack of controversy that Courtright's 2004 *Religious Studies News* article's strong advocacy of scholarly autonomy generated among North American scholars who might otherwise argue that our role is to enter a collaborative and collegial dialogue with our research subjects, it appears that there are indeed times when scholars

[17] There is a fascinating triumphalism to those who see scholarship's goal to be overcoming parochialism; instead, as will become apparent below, I am suggesting quite the opposite: all human systems of knowing and acting are best understood as parochial, through and through, and scholars would be wise to consider their own interests as hardly coterminous with the interests of those whom they study. To presume otherwise – to presume that one's interests set the parameters of the so-called level playing field, thereby providing the terms in which all representations can be assessed – strikes me as the height of imperialism. That scholars compare across cultures is beyond dispute; the question is: are such comparisons and generalizations a product of their own curiosities and the theories that they develop to pursue them or are their comparisons getting at deeply essential traits? I advise opting for the former.

are allowed, perhaps even encouraged, to suspend Orsi's rules of order, without facing the risk that our methods, and those of us who use them, might be classified by our peers as inhuman or cowardly.[18]

To begin to investigate the issue of consent and the limits of difference, we need to look a little more closely at the specific Others studied by our two representative scholars. Although Courtright's subjects – or better put, the interests of these research subjects and those who identify with them – are quite obviously removed from many North American scholars, in the case of Orsi, much of his work remains rather close to home – specifically, close to his own often disclosed social identity as a contemporary US Roman Catholic. On a variety of occasions his work contains semi-autobiographical elements and is explicitly concerned with the relationships between himself and people who, "always and already" (as Louis Althusser might have phrased it), understand themselves to share deep social affinities. They are those to whom, in the Acknowledgments to his earlier, *The Madonna of 115th Street: Faith and Community in Italian Harlem*, he says he owes "a very special debt of gratitude" for their "gracious cooperation," for it was they who, as he puts it, "sat me down at kitchen tables, in empty churches,...in living rooms and offices, candy stores and restaurants, and told me the stories of their lives" (1985: x).[19] As anyone (from an anthropologist doing fieldwork to a stand-up comedian) can likely report, obtaining the consent of those whom one

---

[18] In fact, instead of seeing as immoral his efforts to study Others in ways that are highly unacceptable to the research subjects themselves, Courtright reports in his 2004 *RSN* article that "[c]olleagues in my own association, the American Academy of Religion, have been extraordinarily supportive in both the administrative leadership of the organization and also in the scholarly conventions specific to my area of inquiry." A request made to the AAR for copies of "any and all letters written by the Executive of the AAR in support of colleagues – such as Paul Courtright, Jeffrey Kripal, and James Laine – whose work has come under fire by members of the public" did not produce any results since, as I was told by the AAR's head office, such correspondence, whether or not it exists, is not public.

[19] I am indebted to one anonymous reviewer for pointing out that, in the Introduction to his earlier book's second edition (2002), Orsi points out that he too has had subjects contest his work. Specifically, he reports that "a

holds dear prior to making their disclosures public is undoubtedly a requirement, for to use their stories – or to tell your own stories about them – in any public venue risks betraying what might otherwise be seen as a shared confidence, possibly damaging a social relationship beyond the point of repair.[20] With just such social affinities in mind it is undoubtedly significant that, in his more recent book, Orsi felt the need to report that his Uncle Sal, who is the subject for the first chapter (2005: 19–47), read the article shortly before his death "and liked it" (2005: 3).

Although I do not wish to appear to minimize the no doubt important sentiment behind this disclosure (after all, who among us has not thought about dedicating a book to a family member?), I still feel compelled to ask, what are readers to do with it? What does this

---

woman named Antoinette" seeks him out each year that he attends the fiesta of the Madonna (that he now regularly attends). Orsi reports that, given the fact that the event now thrives, she asks when he will take out of his book the conjecture that the festival was waning when he studied it in the early to mid-1980s. "She is very passionate about this," he concludes, before informing his reader that her "accusation has long troubled me" (2002: xxix). Pointing out this minor though no doubt interesting disagreement, as did my anonymous reviewer, strikes me as begging the issues raised in this paper, for despite her so-called passion, this disagreement has none of the passion of those in the other cases cited in this essay. Moreover, the fact that Orsi takes the following few paragraphs in his Introduction to explain and qualify his earlier and, as it turns out, mistaken conjecture demonstrates his own affinity for these research subjects. (Aside: here, he informs his readers that more Haitian immigrants now attend the fiesta than do Catholics of Italian descent, which suggests that Orsi was indeed correct in his earlier conjecture, for the event he studied two decades ago has indeed waned and been reconstituted as a new event, complete with formerly unheard of Vodou elements. The point being that the supposed homogeneity of the various instantiations of the event is obviously apparent to a participant such as Antoinette; however, one would hope that the specificity and historicity of each is more than apparent to the scholar.)

[20] This is precisely the premise of comedian Mike Birbiglia's 2012 movie, *Sleep Walk with Me*, in which the career of a small-time stand-up comedian takes off when, without his girlfriend's knowledge, he begins discussing on stage the struggles of their relationship.

seal of approval signal? What does having one's research subjects approve of one's work have to do with assessing whether its analysis is persuasive or produces new knowledge?

Although Courtright's thoughts on methodology came in the context of a no less social situation than Orsi's, its context was characterized not by affinity but by severe estrangement – for they had also read what he wrote but they didn't like it one bit. So, instead of being invited to swap tales while seated around a homey kitchen table,[21] Courtright became the object of verbal assaults and was threatened with physical violence. In such a circumstance it is difficult to imagine any scholar still wishing that he could, as Courtright had previously stated, "find ways for people to represent themselves and be subject to less interpretation from me." Instead, Courtright seems to have been understandably unable to overlook the differences between himself and the people about whom he was writing for they have had no trouble representing themselves – it just happens that their representations resisted efforts to collapse Self/Other; and this resistance is perceived by us as threatening the institutions in which our efforts are carried out. Quite understandably, then, all of this leaves the no doubt well-meaning scholar with little choice but to attempt to interpret or explain the motives of his or her *detractors* (note: they are no longer *interlocutors*) in ways that they themselves would likely not sanction.[22] But does it all come down simply to shared interests and sentiments of affinity and estrangement (categories I borrow from Bruce

---

[21] See McCutcheon 2005b: 16–17 for an illustration of how storytelling can make evident social limits that, formerly, might not have been apparent to members of a group.

[22] I am reminded here of a session at the March 10–12, 2006 regional AAR meeting in Atlanta, during which we were told that studying Others in the world religions class requires empathy and a serious commitment to dialogue. Such qualities, though, apparently ended when, as part of a paper on teaching the world religions class, the presenter described his school's local setting, which prompted several members of the audience, along with the presenter, to laugh at his portrait of the traditional patriarchal and rural/hunting values of his regional university's surrounding community. Apparently these people were (due to their unenlightened ways, perhaps?) undeserving of being taken as seriously as those studied in our classes. Laughter at

Lincoln [1989]; see also McCutcheon 2005a)? Do our methods differ, all depending on who it is we're studying? Are we only able to say nice things about those who have already said something nice about us? Or, as our parents might have taught us, if we can't say something nice about someone, should we just keep our scholarly mouths shut?

To start answering some of these questions, consider the selection that resulted in Orsi's list of examples, quoted at the outset of this essay: the distraught widower, the suburban Pentecostal woman, the Orthodox family, the Mexican migrant, and the pious Hindu pilgrim; they all present what appears to be a rather uncontroversial face of the Other, thereby easily allowing us to collapse any perceived difference between each of them (the means whereby such a collection is created in the first place), let alone between "them" as an apparently uniform group (i.e., each are an instance of what we might term "the faithful") and ourselves as their observers – differences that are overcome by means of our appeal to a presumably deeply shared sentiment that unites us all (either faith or human nature). Accordingly, each member of this list exemplifies what I shall term the "no cost Other" – those whose toleration requires little or no investment on our part. Case in point: who would not first seek these people's consent before sharing with others the stories they may have told to us over a cup of coffee in their homes? They are not so-called agitators, revolutionaries, militants, or vigilantes; instead, they are crying, in pain, and engaged in the ritual (as opposed to political?) behaviors that strike many of us as being of such obviously universal significance that the inevitable distance between some posited "us" and "them" is inconsequential.[23] Much like the case of a politician being in favor of an ill-defined "freedom," there is no cost in identifying with the

---

scholarly panels such as this sometimes functions as an important, though unintentional, indicator of taken-for-granted norms and transgressions. Because the presumed norm can just as easily be seen as odd, in the words of Jean-François Bayart, "we should not smirk too readily" (2005: 199).

[23] I say "inevitable" because, to cite but one quick example, documenting the lives of Mexican migrants seeking healing presupposes scholars who have access to material resources unavailable to the migrant him/herself (e.g., the affluent ability to travel, often on someone else's dime).

grieving widower. But what if the hypothetical widower was kneeling at a grave somewhere in, let's just say for the sake of the argument, modern-day Iraq? What if we, as empathetic scholars, did not find his grief so easily universalizable? To press my counter-example further, what if this other grieving widower's uncertainty and fear were, instead, utter certainty and anger – directed at the people whose tax dollars and political leaders made possible a series of events that, from his viewpoint, had taken his wife away from him, forever? What then would the empathetic scholar make of the grieving widower? Would this man even tolerate such a scholar's efforts to engage him in conversation? And if he did not, what would prevent us from labeling him a radical for his unwillingness to converse?

As should by now be apparent, the no-cost Other with whom some in our field so easily presume themselves to share such deep affinities hardly exhausts the people whom we, as scholars, routinely study. For there are other voices out there that cannot so easily be catalogued in the "easy listening" section, for their voices strike our ears as strident and harsh; they are *too* Other for their own good, for their differences from us are rather difficult to overlook. Although there is little cost incurred when paying attention to the stories of the Orthodox family members preparing for their ritual celebrations, being attentive to these *other* Others potentially carries considerable cost – ask Courtright, Kripal, and Laine. So, switching to those with whom Courtright ended up interacting – not the people whom, early on, he wished he could *let* represent themselves (and notice that it is *always* the scholar who is doing the "letting" – not an insignificant point)[24] but, instead, those whom his representations seem to

---

[24] My larger theoretical point, as will become apparent below, is that human beings do not usually engage in self-representation; instead, more than likely they are simply immersed in, and thereby performing, their complex socio-semantic worlds. Only as a result of the non-participant arriving on the scene, making novel claims and asking unanticipated questions, does the so-called authentic Other engage in acts of self-conscious self-representation. As many before me have argued, the creation of Self/Other is therefore a complexly intertwined process, but this fact does not necessarily mean that the two parties are involved in a collegial conversation.

have so deeply offended – we should ask why *they* are so ripe for the kind of theorization from which we must refrain when studying the politically harmless. Or, to rephrase it, how would the work of such scholars as Courtright, Kripal, Laine, and Doniger fare in the hands of scholars who put Orsi's rules of order to use? Would such scholars condemn as "chilling" Courtright's assessment of his vocal critics? For, if we grant to modern-day Hindu nationalists the same sort of descriptive generosity that we are called upon to grant to the grieving widower – i.e., one that suspends speculating on sincerity, ulterior motives, or subconscious desires and, instead, takes them *seriously*, as anti-reductionists once told us we ought to do – then I seriously doubt whether they see themselves as a well-financed, right-wing, international cabal intent on controlling India's image to suit their own idiosyncratic, ideological (i.e., unbalanced) purposes. Although I'm willing to entertain that I'm being terribly naïve here, being descriptively generous I would say that they likely see themselves as not being ideological but simply correct, righteous, and expressing a self-evidency about India, Hinduism, world affairs, or even reality as such. If I am indeed correct, then, apart from our estrangement from what a university administrator might call such people's "goals and strategies," what warrant do we, as scholars, have for instituting a different set of rules for their study? Why do we so easily suspend this particular group's right to describe themselves, thereby failing to entertain that their views are but one more "indigenous theory" that sheds light on our own sad parochialism?

For instance, what would a scholar in Orsi's camp think of Bruce Lincoln (2003: 93–8) for making data of the texts that were left behind by, and which purport to communicate the self-understand-ings of, the September 11 hijackers? Although his work indicates that these disclosures can be read as – regardless how the hijack-ers themselves may have understood them or how their remaining allies might understand them – highly useful rhetorics that accom-plished practical, emotive/socio-political ends, I cannot imagine colleagues calling Lincoln's method "chilling" for the way it avoids ever addressing the need to obtain such Others' consent for his use

of their texts.[25] I find it equally difficult to imagine colleagues criticizing a scholar such as, say, Mark Juergensmeyer, who, despite
working very hard to take seriously the self-reports of actors who
engage in what he terms religious violence, concludes that

> [religious violence] has much to do with the nature of the reli-
> gious imagination, which always has had a propensity to abso-
> lutize and to project images of cosmic war. It also has much to
> do with social tensions of this moment of history that cry out for
> absolute solutions, and the sense of political humiliation experi-
> enced by men who long to restore an integrity they perceive as
> lost in the wake of virtually global social and political conflicts.
> (2001: 242)

Despite how enlightening these words may have been to many of his
readers, it seems clear to me that the people studied by Juergensmeyer
were not themselves talking about "the nature of the religious imagination," nor were they talking about cosmic war being merely an
"image," and they certainly were not self-diagnosing their actions as
attempts to compensate for feelings of humiliation. As with Lincoln,
so too in the case of Jurgensmeyer: these are both instances of higher-order theorization that takes as its starting point – as its data, if you
will – the disclosures and behaviors of a specific group of human subjects. However, our ability to do this sort of higher-order theoretical
work is threatened by Orsi's sense of morality, for the research subject's right to challenge what Orsi characterized as scholars' "assertions" means that we will have to entertain quite seriously that, in the
case of those who engage in acts of religious violence (or what some
of them might simply call righteous violence or divine retribution
– and here you see the kernel of my point: classification matters!),
they might report that they do it simply because this or that powerful, nonempirical being told them to. Period. Full stop. End of story.
This is what it means to entertain the allowing of research subjects to
represent themselves in competition with scholarly representations. It

[25] Instead, some US readers (such as Kurson 2003) might have been
angered by the fact that Lincoln found similarities in the rhetorical conventions used in speeches by Osama bin Laden and George W. Bush (e.g.,
Lincoln 2003: 19–32).

means the end of the human sciences as we know them, for it implies using different methods for different people, all depending on how closely they agree with – well, let's just be honest for a change – some posited "us."

Although I admit that I fear belaboring the point (something I realize I have already done, but, given Orsi's prominent position in our field [i.e., an award-winning author and former president of the AAR], I believe that his charge must be taken very seriously), it is worth considering the issue from yet another angle. As my former colleague Kurtis Schaeffer, who himself studies the politics of medieval Tibetan Buddhism, phrased the issue to me one day last year, because the collection of behaviors we have come to know since the 19th century as "Tantrism" is widely known by scholars to be regarded by its practitioners as based on secret teachings, is someone such as André Padoux (1987a; 1987b) to be criticized for letting some indigenous cat out of the bag by writing not one but two encyclopedia articles on it? I have a feeling that those who adopt Orsi's position would likely not bat an eyelid when it came to assessing the legitimacy of scholarship on Tantra for they likely do not feel bound to keep this particular secret (but why not?).[26] And they probably would have no difficulty when,

[26] The question is, must "their" secret be "ours" as well? If so, what do we make of the tremendous body of scholarly, not to mention popular, literature (i.e., everything from self-help manuals to titillation) that today exists on this thing we all seem to know as Tantrism – Mircea Eliade's classic work *Yoga: Immortality and Freedom* (1990) alone has 84 index entries on the topic, one of which is a 73-page chapter entitled "Yoga and Tantrism" which informs readers that "Tantric texts are often composed in an "intentional language" (*sandhā-bhāsā*), a secret, dark, ambiguous language...[that] seeks to conceal the doctrine form the noninitiate" (249–50). That examples such as this, drawn from the works of some of the most influential scholars in our field, could be reproduced virtually without end should be obvious; examples pertaining to recent literature on Tantra alone are numerous, for we could cite Kripal's *Kali's Child*, in which it is argued that the text English readers know as *The Gospel of Sri Ramakrishna* is structured as it is "in order to conceal, however intentionally, a secret" (1998: 3), David White's examination of the "widely advertised secret practices prescribed and described in sacred and secular literature" in his *Kiss of the Yogini* (2003: 126), as well as Hugh Urban's recent contributions to Tantric studies (2001a, 2001b,

for instance, they read Jeffrey Kripal concluding, in the preface to the second edition of his book on Ramakrishna, that the vocal critics of his book's first edition are deeply conflicted, *"whether they know it or not"* (1998: xiii; emphasis added). Used in this case, the normative epistemology – at least as a scholar such as Orsi might phrase it – that some would say is signaled by such "whether they know it or not"-statements would, at least to some of our peers, more than likely be unproblematic, and thus hardly imperialist.[27] Such a statement is likely unproblematic because it reflects a confidence, more than probably shared among many current members of the academy, that sexuality ought not to be considered to be a taboo, shameful, or embarrassing topic and, therefore, that it rightly ought to be but one more lens through which we, as scholars, are entitled to view the lives of other people – whether these other people like it or not.[28] So, despite the fact such Others no doubt take their own self-understandings

---

2003). Are these scholars also to be chided for failing to get the consent form signed before they spilled the beans? See Urban 2001a: 15–19 for a useful discussion of the ethics of research on Tantra: "Either...we must leave these traditions alone...or we must risk doing violence to ancient esoteric traditions to which we have no right" (19). Drawing on the work of Pierre Bourdieu and Michel Foucault, the solution Urban offers to what he describes as an insoluble problem is to study not the secrets themselves (i.e., content) but the strategies that create the phenomenon known as secrecy (i.e., form). With all this in mind, it is curious to ponder the implication Orsi's proposed methodological rule might have for how we view Eliade's entire corpus, given his oft-repeated attempt to disclose and then compare instances of what he termed the concealed and camouflaged sacred.

[27] Readers must be clear: I am not making this charge but trying to imagine how those scholars who wish to (re)authorize the participant would react to statements that presuppose the scholar's so-called privileged insight into other people's subconscious motives.

[28] That is to say, some scholars likely see their role not simply to be that of using a category such as sexuality as a legitimate scholarly lens through which to study other people's worlds (i.e., it is part of a scholarly toolbox) but, also, to be that of persuading the so-called inhibited or repressed occupants of these very worlds that they are wrong in seeing it to be out of bounds. *My suspicion is that our research subjects detect this distinction and are justifiably angered by those who adopt the latter position.*

as seriously as might Orsi's hypothetical widower, the people who angrily contested Courtright's psychological reading of Shiva and Ganesha's relationship, those who contested Kripal's discussion of homoerotic themes in the life and writings of Ramakrishna, or those who stormed the library in India where Laine worked on the history of "Islamic India," are easily judged by us to have mis-read and mis-performed their own traditions, leaving them wide open for experts to try to account for their puzzling distance from the so-called orthodoxy (as is done whenever we hear such categories as "Fundamentalism" and "political religion" being invoked in contemporary geopolitical analysis). Much like the flawed human beings in Isaac Asimov's first collection of short science fiction stories, *I, Robot*, all of these people therefore need to be saved from themselves. For Asimov, robots were up to the challenge and they set about systematically eliminating us; in the cases I am discussing here, it is the liberal humanist scholar who is prepared to make the tough calls and distinguish between the toothless pious and the radical fanatics, authorizing the former while paving the way towards dispensing with the latter by defining them out of "the faithful" – which is nothing other than excommunication by other means.

It therefore appears to me that those who speak back *indecently* (i.e., those who are unwilling to put up with our presumed ability to speak and act as we wish) are no longer counted among the sincere and are therefore fair game for theorization – and just what are the limits of decency, how are they judged, established, and authorized, these are the questions that ought to attract our attention as social theorists! My hunch, therefore, is that those who adopt Orsi's methodological rule would likely not critique the above-mentioned colleagues for their strong advocacy of a brand of theory-based re-descriptive scholarship that unapologetically deviates from a participant's own self-representations and self-interests – so long as these research subjects failed to play by *our* rules, for in such a case we already know that their self-representations are insincere, inauthentic, duplicitous, fanatical, militant, and maybe even criminal.

To bring home my point, consider what a scholar in Orsi's tradition would make of the privilege that Orsi himself exercises when, in the opening pages to his 2005 book, he has the following to say about his own colleagues:

Whether contemporary Americans working to understand particular religious phenomena *know it or not*, they bring to their
inquiries local histories.... Built into the very tools of analysis
are *hidden* normativities, *implicit* distinctions between "good"
and "bad" religions, and these *need* to be unpacked. (2005: 6;
emphasis added)

Have his research subjects consented to this much-needed unpack-
ing? If so, as a scholar of religion working in the USA – the research
subjects about whom Orsi seems to be making the above claim – I
admit that I do not recall signing the form (aside: exactly how does
one seek the consent of national groupings we might study?). Or,
instead, is this need based on Orsi's own intellectual and political
interests, regardless what his subjects think is in their own best interest? Like a house guest coming to stay for the weekend, do we, as
scholars, unpack our subjects' baggage only with their consent, or, as
seems to be the case here, is some baggage so obviously messy that,
as good hosts, we have every right to tidy it up, whether invited or
not? Come to think of it, because we are told in the above quotation
that this baggage is hidden to the people about whom he writes (echoing that earlier "whether they know it or not" statement), it makes
little sense even to think of asking them about it – much less seeking
their permission to neaten it up – for, by definition, they don't even
know it's there, much less that it isn't neatly ordered.[29] If, as Orsi
goes on to write, "religious practitioners usually do not like to hear"
what he characterizes as his own "critical, analytic questions" (2005:
12), then given the moral requirement to seek subjects' consent, what
warrant does he have for subjecting the material of their lives to what
he acknowledges to be unwanted scrutiny? Moreover, what reason
could he have to invoke the supreme privilege, as he does, of presuming that his research subjects have an active subconscious where the

---

[29] We see here some indication of why the use of Freudian theory by some
of those scholars in question may have sparked such controversy, for it necessarily presupposes that the scholar's object of study is unknown to participants themselves. When this assumption can, and cannot, be invoked is the
interesting question that requires attention (as already begun by Godlove).

latent source of the issue lies, undetected by the very people whom he studies? How is this any less chilling than any other methodology that treats human disclosures as data in need of theorization?

To see how all this plays out in his own scholarship, consider the last chapter of Orsi's *Between Heaven and Earth* (2005), which critiques an Alabama journalist, Dennis Covington (1995), for silencing the people about whom he wrote in his widely read book on snake-handling Pentecostal churches in the Appalachian region of the USA. In this chapter, Orsi describes Covington's explanation for why the people he met, who live in rural northeast Alabama's Sand Mountain region, take the last verses of the Gospel of Mark, concerning the various signs of a true believer, so seriously:

> [Covington] came to see snake handling as a way for poor, displaced people in a ravaged land to contend with and to surmount, at least once in a while, with the snakes in their hands, the violence and danger that bore down on them in their everyday lives. (Orsi 2005: 180)

Then, a few pages later, relying on Covington's ethnographic narrative as his own primary source, Orsi describes how one of the leaders of a local church who befriended Covington – a man named Punkin' Brown – himself sees it:

> Brown believed that it was God present before him that caused him to pick up snakes at meetings; he embodied, in other words, the enduring power of sacred presence in the modern world and in modern persons' imaginations and memories, from which presence is disallowed. (2005: 182)

Indeed, there is considerable distance between the journalist's loosely Marxist explanation, on the one hand, and, on the other, Orsi's re-description of Covington's description of this one participant's reported self-understanding concerning a powerful being who controls the universe ensuring that the following words be written in the Gospel of Mark – and taken by followers with deadly seriousness:

> And these signs will accompany those who believe: in my name they will cast out demons; they will speak in new tongues; they

will pick up serpents, and if they drink any deadly thing, it will
not hurt them; they will lay their hands on the sick, and they will
recover. (Mark 16: 17–18)

But are these two accounts in competition (i.e., what, exactly, is the
problem with the so-called insider/outsider problem)? If so, then there
must exist some vantage point, some fulcrum, from which these differences can be weighed, a point from which one could work towards
having Dennis Covington and Punkin' Brown arrive at a balanced
understanding and thereby mutual respect. Like many an ethnographer before him, this is the assumption that Covington employs in
first making contact with his research subjects (i.e., he engages in
participant-observation); he befriends his hosts and, eventually, handles snakes in a service and preaches a spontaneous sermon or two of
his own. This strategy is of considerable utility to the journalist (providing him with the sort of access that made it possible to obtain his
book's many engaging stories) – until, that is, its limit becomes painfully apparent to him. For, taking a little too seriously the impression
of unity that was created by his participation in the group, Covington
reports, towards the end of his book, how he blundered by making
a series of impromptu, public statements during a worship service
concerning his strong views on gender equality, statements that he no
doubt took as inspired and self-evident but which, once spoken as part
of his sermon, provided the occasion for the local male leadership to
cast him out of the group; for they ceased their echoes of his preach-
ing with shouts of "You're in the Word" and "Amen" and, instead,
replaced them with cold silence. "You're out of the Word," Covington
was finally told, just before Punkin' Brown took the microphone from
him and preached an impassioned sermon of his own on the false
doctrine of women having authority over men (Covington 1995: 226
ff.). As Covington records it, Punkin' Brown's sermon ended with
the preacher catching his eye, saying: "It's a lie, Dennis.... There's no
truth in it! It's a sin!" (ibid.: 235).

As is all too evident from this brief episode, there is a tremendous price to be paid when we try to overcome the significant gaps
and see the study of the Other as an opportunity for nurturing solidarity. When the gap is too great to overlook – and what constitutes

"significant" and "too great," now that's the $64,000 question that social theorists need to study – then what do we do? Do we champion the right of participants to interpret and represent their own words and worlds, recognizing that our shared humanity requires us just to sit politely and – recalling that lesson our parents taught us so long ago – keep quiet? Being a scholar myself, I suspect that just listening respectfully is not actually an option. Instead, I bet that we all do precisely what Orsi does in the above quotation: we put *our* words into *their* mouths and, for whatever reason, fail to recognize the sound of our own voices. So let me repeat Orsi's report of Punkin' Brown's understanding of snake handling, and, this time, pay careful attention to the important shift signaled by the phrase, "in other words":

> Brown believed that it was God present before him that caused
> him to pick up snakes at meetings; he embodied, *in other words*,
> the enduring power of sacred presence in the modern world and
> in modern persons' imaginations and memories, from which
> presence is disallowed. (emphasis added)

This is a fascinating rhetorical move, especially given the manner in which Covington, just earlier in Orsi's chapter, is criticized rather harshly for offering what Orsi describes as a "humiliating" representation of "Punkin' Brown" – a name that Orsi here places in quotation marks, presumably to distinguish Covington's mere representation from Punkin' Brown himself, thereby signaling to Orsi's reader the way the preacher was "constructed" and "rendered," as Orsi phrases it, into Covington's *version* of "Punkin' Brown" (Orsi 2005: 182) – a stereotyped, exotic character that, as Orsi puts it, "makes the world safe again for Covington and his readers" (181).

But paying a little more attention to Orsi's text demonstrates that he has made a classic error common to a number of liberal humanist scholars, what Wayne Proudfoot has famously called the confusion of descriptive reductionism, which scholars all agree must be avoided, with the explanatory reduction that inevitably characterizes every scholar's work (1985: 96 ff.). For immediately following his attempt to describe (i.e., to present) what a research subject might say about his own motives for handling snakes (i.e., he handles them because God told him to), Orsi signals a transition by means of "in other words" (i.e., to re-present), and then goes on to do just that: *he offers words other than those the research subject might himself offer, all in the guise of describing things from the indigenous subject's point of view.* Moreover, the *other words* Orsi offers are those of a Eliadean cross-cultural comparativist who understands local practices as a disguised instance of an otherwise uniform sacred presence, one that is manifested in the actions and artifacts of a diverse collection of others, *whether or not* these people themselves understand their behaviors to be but one relative node in a cross-cultural system of signification – at least I seriously doubt whether someone such as Punkin' Brown, what little I've read of the man, sees it this way. In fact, upon hearing Orsi's thoughts on how both snake handler and the Hindu pilgrim at the shrine of the imprint of Krishna's foot, "embodied...the enduring power of sacred presence in the modern world," I can only imagine that Punkin' Brown would catch Orsi's eye and sternly reply: "It's a lie, Bob, There's no truth in it! It's a sin."

For, at least according to my ears, snake handlers say something remarkably different from a scholarly observer such as Orsi. For instance, consider the following quotation, transcribed from an explanation offered by Jimmy Williams – the main informant in *They Shall Take Up Serpents*, a well known 1973 documentary on snake handling in east Tennessee. Speaking directly to the camera, beside the bed of a man who was "serpent bit" at that evening's service, he says:

> The reason that we take these serpents up is the Bible recommends to do it and all the apostles did it – everyone that believes. Jesus said these signs shall follow them that believe. He said, "In my name shall they cast out devils, they shall speak with new tongues, they shall take up serpents, and if they drink any deadly thing it shall not hurt them. They shall lay hands on the sick and they shall recover." Now, we believe that this interpretation of the scripture is for them that believe. In other words, them that believe, they shall take up serpents.[30]

[30] *They Shall Take Up Serpents*, John E. Schrader and Thomas G. Burton, Producers. Johnson City, TN: Eastern Tennessee State University, 1973. This documentary was filmed in early 1973 in Newport, Tennessee. Anyone familiar with this film knows that, at its end, viewers are informed

What's his "indigenous theory," as Cabezón might name it? The
Bible says to do it, which means that Jesus said to do it. And all of the
apostles did it. Therefore we do it. Simple as that.[31]

At least as I see it, then, Orsi's "other words" concerning the
enduring power of sacred presence are therefore just that, different words placed into a subject's mouth, *as if* they expressed sentiments lodged deep within a subject's subconscious and therefore
known only to the careful (i.e., privileged) interpreter. To my way of
thinking, they are Othering words, *as is the case with all language
and all representation* – and this is the point that many in the liberal
humanist tradition, in their efforts to speak on behalf of humanity
ansich, utterly fail to comprehend! – and not an innocent paraphrase
of a universal subject's own self-perceptions. Instead, like all acts
of signification, Orsi's "other words" are a translation of one set of
claims into a language that is itself no closer than any other to some
presumably authentic source of the Nile. To put it simply, all "Punkin'
Brown"s ought to be written in quotation marks, not just Covington's
but Orsi's and my own as well – for how could either mine or Orsi's
representation be any closer to the authentic man, for both of our
readings are based on Covington's text. Come to think of it, even
Punkin' Brown's own sense(s) of himself deserve the same quotation
marks – a point nicely made by Jorge Louis Borges in a little piece
entitled "Borges and I" in which, alienated from his own persona as

<hr>

that Jimmy Williams died on April 8, 1973, while attending a service and
ingesting strychnine. My thanks to Jennifer Goodman (then a student in our
Department) for transcribing this segment of the film.

[31] That the ethnographer who has obviously posed some such question
to him as, "Why do you handle snakes in your worship service," is not
seen in the film exemplifies the problems examined in this paper. Students
viewing the film will quite reasonably come away thinking that participants
spontaneously and authentically engage in acts of self-representation; our
task is therefore merely to listen carefully and faithfully record their words.
However, taking into account the presence of the filmmakers/fieldworker (as
a previous generation of anthropologists, e.g., James Clifford et al., told us
so convincingly) makes it evident that the so-called participant is in fact a
creation of the observer.

famous author, he remarks: "I live, I allow myself to live, so that Borges can spin out his literature" (1999: 324).

With this in mind, we can say that mistaking a representation for the real – and if Jean Baudrillard is to be trusted, then all we have are representations, each competing for the chance to stand in for a Real that never was present to begin with – was also a problem with Orsi's description of the "devout working class man who kneels to pray at his wife's grave, suddenly uncertain and afraid at the end of his own life of what lies ahead." Like most readers, I too have experienced the deaths of loved ones, but how does one generalize from this to read this one man's mind? I suspect that there are any number of things going through this hypothetical widower's head, including the uncertainly and fear that Orsi qua privileged narrator somehow intuits, along with panic, desperation, loneliness, anger, even guilt – who knows what else. In fact, we may be in error in approaching our speculative thought experiment in the manner of Orsi, for I'm not even sure that, at the moment he catches the scholar's attention – and becomes an item of discourse – anything much is actually going through this man's head. Not that he's oblivious to his surroundings or "overcome by emotion," as we sometimes say, but that, much of the time, human beings are completely immersed in their social worlds in rather unreflective ways, with nothing in particular in their heads, as it were, with no stories to tell, let alone criteria to use in distinguishing a generic happening from an occurrence (recalling the words attributed to Robert Frost that appear as this essay's epigraph). Case in point, I presume that, although many readers are by now wondering when I will signal that my essay is drawing to a close – which will be soon, but not quite yet – few are now contemplating the significance of, say, their use of English grammar to make the symbols that appear on this page into units of meaning – though, now that the nonparticipant to their so-called reading experience has made this apparent commonplace of their world curious to them, no doubt readers are mulling it over and could go on at some length about it. But scholars of signification will likely not measure the adequacy of their work in light of the participant's hindsight reflections on their reading experience (i.e., despite both being engaged in signification, at least to the scholar they are not necessarily working towards the same goal and are therefore *not* in competition with each other); instead, such scholars will set about describing and then analyzing a series of observable behaviors of which the participant may be completely unaware, seeing the participant's self-reflections on the process, if there are any, as but one more piece of data in need of analysis.

What I have in mind here is precisely what the mid-20th-century British novelist, Bryan Stanley Johnson, wrote about in his 1973 memoir:

> Life does not tell stories. Life is chaotic, fluid, random; it leaves myriads of ends untied, untidily. Writers can extract a story from life only by strict, close selection, and this must mean falsification. Telling stories really is telling lies. (Johnson 1973: 14)

If, as I'm suggesting, readers are not necessarily spontaneously doing the choosing, highlighting, and ignoring that produces a narrative about the occurrence of their current subject-position as "readers" – but, instead, are immersed in a series of happenings and thereby acting out a subjectivity not of their making – then scholarship is not a matter of an observer qua stenographer respectfully recording the widower's dictated reflections on his grief. Instead, it is more a matter of an observer, much like an ethnographic filmmaker, interrupting this man's world by posing unanticipated questions that prompt him to articulate something that wasn't necessarily in his head to begin with, prompting him to fabricate a story that, prior to being given its starting point – such as, "Why are you crying?" – wasn't a story at all, at least not to him. If this is the case, if the complexity of this thing we call reality is only experienceable (i.e., as a series of occurrences rather than disjointed happenings) once a non-indigenous framework is brought to bear (i.e., made into an item of discourse), then Orsi's methodological rule, which on the surface appears to protect the meek, is nothing other than a cleverly disguised paternal strategy that enables scholars to portray themselves as being in solidarity with the Other while retaining the right not only to distinguish Others from other Others, but also to inform both groups where their stories ought to start and end. For this methodological rule, like that of Cantwell Smith, is a triumphalistic move ensuring the scholar's absolute monopoly over the means of representation, for such scholars both speak and record their own other words, all the while attributing them to their research subjects. It is somewhat akin to the manner in which government officials sometimes leak information to the press then turn around and publicly quote the reported leak in support of the position they are advocating; it strategically exercises a passive aggressive form of authority in which the supposedly authentic human subjects – to borrow some of Orsi's own words – remain silent despite the humanist's claims of listening carefully and empathetically. Much as in his critique of my own work, apparently Orsi's "other words" require no rationale or defense, for, to paraphrase him once again, the liberal humanist, by virtue of his or her normative epistemology, theoretical acuity, and political knowingness, apparently has the authority and the right to be a ventriloquist, for he or she speaks for those others who do not have the good sense or ability to recognize their misplaced emphasis on difference and particularity.[32]

But if, as Bryan Stanley Johnson claims, all representation is inevitably a form of falsification – regardless who is doing the storytelling – then we, as scholars, should be a little more careful of the tales we choose to tell and in whose voice they are being told. Recognizing that much comes down to the act of choice[33] prompts us to adopt a rather more humble scholarly approach than we often find in the work of liberal humanist mind-readers in our field; for, despite the proclaimed empathy for their subjects of study, like everyone else they have no choice but to deploy concepts and interests alien to their object of study; it's just that they seem to assume that their language and their interests are coterminous with reality, allowing them

---

[32] It is worth noting that, when responding orally to an earlier version of this essay, Jeppe Sinding Jensen thought the image of a cannibal more apt than a ventriloquist.

[33] Although his thoughts on religion being "solely the creation of the scholar's study" have certainly influenced my own work in profound ways, I now think that the far more important insight contained in the opening pages to J.Z. Smith's *Imagining Religion* appear a little lower on the page, concerning this topic of choice: "The student of religion must be able to articulate clearly why 'this' rather than 'that' was chosen as an exemplum. His primary skill is concentrated in this choice" (1982: xi).

unimpeded access to the grieving widower's heart.[34] And it's just this self-serving assumption, obviously detected by those research subjects who fail to recognize themselves in the supposed mirror held up to them by liberal humanists, that likely angers some people so much; the limits of the liberal humanist bait and switch are more than apparent to them.

To return to the many rhetorical questions posed earlier, I fear that I have gone on far too long with hints, and, instead, owe readers a straightforward answer: so here it is. When it comes to the liberal humanists whom I have studied, they diligently work to sanction those Others towards whom they either already feel affinity or towards whom they feel very little estrangement – those Others whose differences from some posited "us" and our interests and norms can either be explained away or, because they strike us as utterly inconsequential, simply overlooked altogether. It is easy, of course, to tolerate those whom one feels to be inconsequential. However, when the differences of historical existence cannot be ignored, when the estrangements are painfully apparent because they strike at what the classic Marxist might once have termed the Base, then we understand these other Others to have relinquished their right to be taken seriously as conversation partners, for they have committed the mortal sin of taking themselves as seriously as we take ourselves; in so doing, they call into question our self-declared right to set the parameters for what gets to count as "decency" and "civility."[35] In response, we withhold the classifications "religion," "faithful," and "spiritual" and excommunicate them from the body of the faithful, giving these people new names, all depending on the degree to which some posited "us" feels estranged from, or threatened by, "them": they can be classified as mildly curious and tolerated as exotic specimens, they can be

[34] As noted in my brief reply to Orsi's review (see Orsi 2004 and McCutcheon 2004), that a hypothetical grieving widower, among others, is used as a trope in an essay meant to score rhetorical points strikes me as begging a series of crucial questions concerning just what type of morality Orsi implies.

[35] See Colas 1997 for an excellent study on the politics of discourses on civility.

understood as deviants and thereby diagnosed and deprogrammed, or portrayed as outrightly dangerous and attacked or jailed as enemies.[36] My suspicion, then, is that scholars in the liberal humanist tradition never have to think twice about whom to include in their list of the faithful, for they are already seated at these Others' kitchen table, swapping stories, and enjoying their no doubt kind hospitality. Only those who are bold enough to involve themselves actively in contesting how the political world works need to be saved from themselves, for their all too apparent interests prevent us from ever being invited into their homes, prompting us to resolve our differences by defining these other Others out of the tradition of the faithful, by saying to them "You're not in the Word." Their subsequent protestations simply confirm the line we have drawn. As for those who pose no threat to our world, they are in no position to challenge our representations; we can therefore speak for them, answering "Amen" to our own other words, without ever fearing reprisals, for we resolve our little differences with them by simply forgetting them.

In both cases, our attempt to resolve conflict and difference, to borrow a few words from Courtright, "is not without its price" (2001: 116).[37] In my estimation, the price we pay when we worry over how scholarship silences the indigenous voice, a concern that prompts us to try to mediate and resolve difference, amounts to (to paraphrase Lincoln's thirteenth thesis [1996: 227]) forfeiting our role of being anything but dedicated disciples to one set of voices, no longer able to be scholars of how the disciplining process happens to take place. It is a forfeiture that comes with far too high a price: the demise of the very institutions in which we carry out our

---

[36] Anyone watching the news these past few years knows that, despite the universalist rhetoric of the humanist position that undergirds the liberal democratic nation-state, the so-called humanity of anyone can easily be defined away, especially those whom we have come to know as "cult fanatics" and "political extremists," those who, despite holding the sort of "deep beliefs" that we are so often told we ought to respect and take seriously, happen to hold the wrong set of deep beliefs.

[37] Courtright is here talking about the resolution of the child/parent conflict as represented in the story of Ganesha.

work. It is therefore rather ironic that fretting over erasing Others ends up in our own demise.[38]

References

Bayart, Jean-François. 2005 (1996). *The Illusions of Cultural Identity.* Trans. Steven Randall et al. Chicago: University of Chicago Press.

Borges, Jorge Louis. 1999 (1989). *Collected Fictions.* Trans. Andrew Hurley. New York: Penguin.

Braverman, Amy M. 2004. "The Interpretation of Gods: Do Leading Religious Scholars Err in their Analysis of Hindu Texts?" *University of Chicago Magazine* 97/2 (December); posted at: http://magazine.uchicago.edu/0412/features/index.shtml, accessed May 29, 2013.

Cabezón, José Ignacio. 2006. "The Discipline and Its Others: The Dialectic of Alterity in the Study of Religion." *Journal of the American Academy of Religion* 74(1): 21–38. http://dx.doi.org/10.1093/jaarel/lfj009.

Cantwell Smith, Wilfred. 1959. "The Comparative Study of Religion: Whither – and Why?" in Mircea Eliade and Joseph Kitagawa, eds., *The History of Religions: Essays in Methodology*, 31–58. Chicago: University of Chicago Press.

Colas, Dominique. 1997 (1992). *Civil Society and Fanaticism: Conjoined Histories.* Trans. Amy Jacobs. Stanford: Stanford University Press.

Courtright, Paul B. 1985. *Ganeśa: Lord of Obstacles, Lord of Beginnings.* New York: Oxford University Press.

Courtright, Paul B. 2001. *Ganeśa: Lord of Obstacles, Lord of Beginnings.* Delhi: Motilal Banarsidass Publishers.

Courtright, Paul B. 2004. "Studying Religion in an Age of Terror." *Religious Studies News* 19(4): 19.

Courtright, Paul B. 2006. "The Self-Serving Humility of Disciplining Liberal Humanist Scholars: A Response to Russell McCutcheon." *Journal of the American Academy of Religion* 74(3): 751–5. http://dx.doi.org/10.1093/jaarel/lfj115.

Covington, Dennis. 1995. *Salvation on Sand Mountain: Snake Handling and Redemption in Southern Appalachia.* New York: Penguin.

---

[38] Although, when first published as a peer-reviewed essay in the *Journal of the American Academy of Religion*, this chapter did not prompt a reply from Robert Orsi, Paul Courtright responded and I replied (see Courtright 2006 and McCutcheon 2006b).

Dalrymple, William. 2005. "India: The War Over History." *The New York Review of Books* 52/6 (April 7): 62–5.

Doniger O'Flaherty, Wendy. 1986. "The Uses and Misuses of Other People's Myths." *Journal of the American Academy of Religion* 54(2): 219–39. http://dx.doi.org/10.1093/jaarel/LIV.2.219.

Eliade, Mircea. 1984 (1969). "A New Humanism." In *The Quest: History and Meaning in Religion*, 1–11. Chicago: University of Chicago Press.

Eliade, Mircea. 1990 (1954). *Yoga: Immortality and Freedom*. Trans. Willard R. Trask. Princeton: Princeton University Press.

Godlove, Terry. 1994. "Religious Discourse and First Person Authority." *Method & Theory in the Study of Religion* 6(1): 147–61. http://dx.doi.org/10.1163/157006894X00073.

Johnson, Bryan Stanley. 1973. *Aren't You Rather Young to Be Writing Your Memoirs?* London: Hutchinson & Co. Publishers.

Juergensmeyer, Mark. 2001 (2000). *Terror in the Mind of God: The Global Rise of Religious Fundamentalism*. Berkeley: University of California Press.

Kripal, Jeffrey. 1995. *Kali's Child: The Mystical and the Erotic in the Life and Teachings of Ramakrishna*. Chicago: University of Chicago Press.

Kripal, Jeffrey. 1998. *Kali's Child: The Mystical and the Erotic in the Life and Teachings of Ramakrishna*. 2nd ed. Chicago: University of Chicago Press.

Kurson, Ken. 2003. "Professor Denies Justifying 9/11 While Doing Exactly the Same." *Chicago Sun-Times* (March 15): Editorial Letters, 13.

Laine, James. 2003. *Shivaji: Hindu King in Islamic India*. New York: Oxford University Press. http://dx.doi.org/10.1093/acprof:oso/9780195141269.001.0001.

Lincoln, Bruce. 1989. *Discourse and the Construction of Society: Comparative Studies of Myth, Ritual, and Classification*. New York: Oxford University Press.

Lincoln, Bruce. 1996. "Theses on Method." *Method & Theory in the Study of Religion* 8(3): 225–7. http://dx.doi.org/10.1163/157006896X00323.

Lincoln, Bruce. 2003. *Holy Terrors: Thinking about Religion after September 11*. Chicago: University of Chicago Press.

Lincoln, Bruce. 2012. *Gods and Demons, Priests and Scholars: Critical Explorations in the History of Religions*. Chicago: University of Chicago Press.

Marty, Martin. 2004. "Scholars of Hinduism Under Attack," posted at *Beliefnet* http://www.beliefnet.com/Faiths/Hinduism/2003/07/Scholars-Of-Hinduism-Under-Attack.aspx?p=1, accessed May 29, 2013; originally published as "Hyper- and Havoc in Hindu Studies," *Sightings* at:

http://divinity.uchicago.edu/sightings/hyper-and-havoc-hindu-studies-%E2%80%94-martin-e-marty, accessed May 29, 2013.

McCutcheon, Russell T. 1997. *Manufacturing Religion: The Discourse on Sui Generis Religion and the Politics of Nostalgia*. New York: Oxford University Press.

McCutcheon, Russell T. 2001. *Critics Not Caretakers: Redescribing the Public Study of Religion*. Albany, NY: State University of New York Press.

McCutcheon, Russell T. 2003. *The Discipline of Religion: Structure, Meaning, Rhetoric*. London: Routledge. http://dx.doi.org/10.4324/9780203451793.

McCutcheon, Russell T. 2004. "A Few Words on the Temptation to Defend the Honor of a Text." *Bulletin of the Council of Societies for the Study of Religion* 33(3&4): 90–1.

McCutcheon, Russell T. 2005a. "Affinities, Benefits, and Costs: The ABCs of Good Scholars Gone Public." *Method & Theory in the Study of Religion* 17(1): 27–43. http://dx.doi.org/10.1163/1570068053429857.

McCutcheon, Russell T. 2005b. *Religion and the Domestication of Dissent, or How to Live in a Less than Perfect Nation*. London: Equinox.

McCutcheon, Russell T. 2006a. "Relating Smith: Review Essay of Jonathan Z. Smith's *Relating Religion*." *Journal of Religion* 86(2): 287–97.http://dx.doi.org/10.1086/499634.

McCutcheon, Russell T. 2006b. "A Response to Paul Courtright." *Journal of the American Academy of Religion* 74(3): 755–6. http://dx.doi.org/10.1093/jaarel/lfj116.

Orsi, Robert A. 1985. *The Madonna of 115th Street: Faith and Community in Italian Harlem, 1880–1950*. New Haven: Yale University Press.

Orsi, Robert A. 2002. *The Madonna of 115th Street: Faith and Community in Italian Harlem, 1880–1950*. 2nd ed. New Haven: Yale University Press.

Orsi, Robert A. 2004. "Fair Game." *Bulletin of the Council of Societies for the Study of Religion* 33(3&4): 87–9.

Orsi, Robert A. 2005. *Between Heaven and Earth: The Religious Worlds People Make and the Scholars Who Study Them*. Princeton: Princeton University Press.

Padoux, André. 1987a. "Hindu Tantrism." In Mircea Eliade, ed., *The Encyclopedia of Religion*, vol. 14, 274–80. New York: Macmillan Publishing Co.

Padoux, André. 1987b. "Tantrism: An Overview." In Mircea Eliade, ed., *The Encyclopedia of Religion*, vol. 14, 272–4. New York: Macmillan Publishing Co.

Proudfoot, Wayne. 1985. *Religious Experience*. Berkeley: University of California Press.

Sharpe, Eric J. 1986. *Comparative Religion: A History.* LaSalle, Illinois: Open Court.

Smith, Jonathan Z. 1982. *Imagining Religion: From Babylon to Jonestown.* Chicago: University of Chicago Press.

Smith, Jonathan Z. 1996. "Why Imagine Religion?" Unpublished manuscript.

Smith, Jonathan Z. 1997. "Are Theological and Religious Studies Compatible?" *Bulletin of the Council of Societies for the Study of Religion* 26(3): 60–1.

Smith, Jonathan Z. 2007. "The Necessary Lie: Duplicity in the Disciplines." In Russell T. McCutcheon, *Studying Religion: An Introduction*, 73–80. London: Equinox Publishers.

Urban, Hugh B. 2001a. *The Economics of Ecstasy: Tantra, Secrecy, and Power in Colonial Bengal.* New York: Oxford University Press. http://dx.doi.org/10.1093/019513902X.001.0001.

Urban, Hugh B. 2001b. *Songs of Ecstasy: Tantric and Devotional Songs from Colonial Bengal.* New York: Oxford University Press. http://dx.doi.org/10.1093/0195139011.001.0001.

Urban, Hugh B. 2003. *Tantra: Sex, Secrecy, Politics and Power in the Study of Religion.* Berkeley: University of California Press. http://dx.doi.org/10.1525/california/9780520230620.001.0001.

Vedantam, Shankar. 2004. "Wrath over a Hindu God: U.S. Scholars' Writings Draw Threats from the Faithful," *The Washington Post* (April 10): A01. Posted at: http://vedantam.com/ganesha04-2004.html, accessed May 29, 2013.

White, David G. 2003. *Kiss of the Yogini: "Tantric Sex" and its South Asian Contexts.* Chicago: University of Chicago Press. http://dx.doi.org/10.7208/chicago/9780226027838.001.0001.

Russell T. McCutcheon is Professor and Chair of the Department of Religious Studies at the University of Alabama. His research focuses on the social and political implications of competing classification systems.

Topic V: Cost-Benefit Analysis

9. Authorizing Identifications, Disciplining Techniques: The Affinities of Public Advocacy

Steven W. Ramey

Affinities for particular interpretations and practices often intersect with a person's identification and the claims to authority that people make based on their identification, which serve to cloak the affinity. For example, a person may present an identification as an academic or a leader in a particular community to authorize their hermeneutical assertions that reflect their affinities. Such connections are present, though often unnoticed and uninterrogated, in much public discourse. One controversial response to Selena Gomez's performance of her song "Come and Get It" at the MTV Movie Awards on April 14, 2013 clearly illustrates such connections. Rajan Zed, who self-identifies as a "Hindu statesman" in the United States, denounced her donning a bindi during her performance. The press release from his organization, the Universal Society of Hinduism, referenced him asserting that the bindi holds religious significance and should not "be thrown around loosely for seductive effects or as fashion accessory aiming at mercantile greed" (full press release quoted in Tiku 2013). He emphasized Gomez's action as disrespecting the ancient Hindu symbol and requested an apology. A month later, when Gomez released the music video of "Come and Get It," with no bindi in sight, Zed's organization expressed gratitude for its absence (Thompson 2013). Interrogating how identifications, claims to authority, and affinities intersect in this example is revealing.

Zed's self-identification as a "Hindu statesman" provided authority to his complaint in two ways. First, his identification as a Hindu and his construction of Gomez as non-Hindu provided grounds for taking offence, as presumably a Hindu has authority to declare what are exclusively the cultural assets of Hindus. Second, his self-proclamation as a (Hindu) statesman suggested that he held an authority beyond that of the average Hindu to speak on behalf of the entire community. These assertions reflect a relatively basic aspect of how identifications function: that is, by differentiating first between those within a group and those outside the group, and then establishing differentiation of authority within the group.

Of course, proclaiming an identification to authorize an assertion does not force others to acknowledge that authority or opinion, as contemporary scholarship often emphasizes conflicts over interpretations. Others, including some who self-identified as Hindu, thus claiming to be within the same group as Zed, referenced examples of the decorative use of bindis in India and their use by those who do not identify as Hindu to contest Zed's assertions. Some also directly dismissed his self-proclaimed authority as a "Hindu statesman" (see, for example, Tiku 2013, including comments).

Such contests of authority and interpretation reveal that this dispute is not simply a critique of Gomez. Others who identify as Hindu contest Zed's assertions, in part because his declarations have implications for them. Implicit within Zed's complaint is the assertion that those who consider the bindi as a part of their heritage should not emulate Gomez's appearance or demeanor. Zed's assertion may be seen as an attempt to define publicly the proper use of the bindi and, subsequently, the acceptable general lifestyle for those females who identify as Hindus. In this disciplining action, the speaker who defines the appropriate practices associated with an identification asserts an ability to authorize who can and cannot claim such an identification. While people can assert any identification that they wish, many want others, particularly those recognized as authorities, to confirm or legitimate that claim.

Acts of interpretation like Zed's involve the selection of which components of the practices and precepts that people identify as their community's can be ignored and which must be defended. As the contestation reveals, Zed's selection of issues and attempt to discipline those identifying as Hindu based on his interpretation reflect his particular interests, background, and assumptions, not a universally accepted conception of the bindi or appropriate practice. Buttressed by his authoritative identification, he is expressing his affinities. Those disagreeing with him also reflect their own affinities drawn from their interests, background, and assumptions. While many of these individuals (both Zed and those opposed to his assertions) use their Hindu identification to authorize their affinity for particular practices, those affinities also contribute to the construction of their identification, leading to debates over who is a "true" Hindu.

Asserting an identification can serve as the basis for asserting authority over assets, information, and membership, but those assertions of authority frequently cloak the promotion of affinities for particular ideas with the illusion that the identification is stable, rather than an ephemeral construction that also reflects some of those affinities. National, ethnic, and ideological identifications, for example, also become avenues for promoting particular behaviors, for which those claiming authority hold an affinity. Anyone who wants those authorities to recognize their inclusion in a community needs to conform to those behaviors. This aspect of identification is fairly easy to recognize when we hold limited affinity for the practices being promoted. Yet, people often fail to see the similar affinities and selectivity in arguments that they already accept as valid and important. Public discourse is filled with selective representations that obscure the complexity of social relations and human practices, so virtually any public argument can be critiqued for leaving out too much in order to promote particular affinities. However, because it is easy to overlook the fallacies and exclusions, and the problematic claims to authority when people like the conclusions of an argument, affinities often determine the application of critiques to the assertions of others.

These same social and rhetorical techniques of asserting authority through an identification, and disciplining others, based on an affinity for particular positions, are also present across academia. The processes of defining group boundaries and establishing a hierarchy within the broad group of scholars obviously proceed within academia. For example, scholars distinguish between those pursuing a terminal graduate degree and those who have such a degree, and both are recognized as different from those who neither have nor are pursuing such a degree. Other distinctions that define academic boundaries include having tenure, serving in a tenure track or contingent position, working outside academia, etc.

Scholars are certainly aware, however, that neither having a degree nor holding a tenure track position guarantees quality scholarship, however that is defined. Like the complex nature of debates over who is "really" a Hindu, which vary depending on the interests and conceptions of those making the distinction, scholars often employ a range of factors and strategies to define who they acknowledge as a "true" or respected scholar or even a scholar at all. This kind of boundary tightening becomes one way to observe the debates about methods in the academic study of religion, such as the proper position of theology in the academy or the sui generis social scientific debate.

For example, as quoted in the following essay, Bruce Lincoln refers to being "a good scholar who addresses serious issues in serious ways," a statement that serves to create a hierarchy of good scholars, as opposed to not-so-good scholars, by enforcing a particular sense of how scholarship ought to be conducted on those who might wish to be seen as good scholars in the eyes of a senior scholar such as Lincoln, or who might already see themselves as such. Many academics, whether they follow Lincoln's specific assertions or not, agree that good scholars, as a starting point, follow a discursive structure that emphasizes adhering to logical arguments with adequate citations and acknowledgment of the works of others. Further, my own preference for nuanced assertions and precision within "serious work" reflects the ways that I see the world around me and, thus, what scholarship I consider more (or less) legitimate.

These discursive structures, however, are not simply a universal good. As Russell McCutcheon emphasizes in the following essay, all communities employ discursive structures that provide authority and discipline within those communities. Zed's assertion of the authority of tradition and an "ancient heritage" to define the proper use of a bindi serves as one example. The non-universal status of academic discursive structures, such as particular forms of citation and rational argument, creates a problematic tension for anyone who stakes authority on being accepted within the club of scholars. Academic discursive structures are superior, rational, and authoritative, if you already accept the premises of academic discourse, thus creating a circular argument at the foundation of rational academic discourse. However, if you see authority solely within a divine revelation or an inviolable cultural heritage, a different discursive structure than academic discursive structures is superior. Thus, the preference for an academic discursive structure simply reflects a pre-existing affinity for that structure, rather than something universally preferable. In essence, the authority of academic discourse, with its notions of logical arguments, citations, precision, and nuance, rests on a circular argument of preference for those elements. Thus, identification as a "good scholar," in Lincoln's terms, comes in part from an affinity for this particular discursive structure.

Similarly, while it is easy to critique Zed's selective interpretation of his sources, ignoring those texts and traditions that he finds less useful, scholars who employ academic discursive structures also tend to rely on their interpretations of a source, ignoring those sources (or passages within the same source) that are less useful for the points that they want to make. Thus, not only is the discursive structure something for which scholars have an affinity, but also their interpretations reflect their particular affinities, a point that people overlook for themselves in ways that they do not for those making assertions that they find less agreeable. Relying on an authority based on identifying with an academic in-group and assuming that some academic discursive structures are more authoritative than others both cloak individual affinities in an aura of authority and miss the complexity of epistemologies and postmodern analyses of the construction of knowledge and its relation to power.

In the following essay, McCutcheon highlights this complicated identity game at work when Lincoln enters public discourse, drawing on his authority as a scholar to give added weight to his public pronouncements that largely opposed certain components of the policies of George Bush as Governor of Texas and President of the United States. Despite McCutcheon's significant affinity for Lincoln's scholarship and many of the opinions presented in his public assertions,

McCutcheon critiques Lincoln's public presentations because they do not adhere to Lincoln's own assertions about academic discursive structures needing precision and nuance, while Lincoln continues to rely on his authoritative identification as a scholar. That point makes this essay critiquing Lincoln particularly unusual, not only in this volume but also within scholarship more broadly. The issue, though, is really not Lincoln's public assertions but the larger questions of the identifying distinctions between a serious scholar and an apologist. Both can reference sources that they consider authoritative as they participate in discourses with different rules.

Thus, the questions that McCutcheon asks probe more deeply the tension between our shared affinity for nuance and complexity, rational argument and careful attribution, and the assumption of scientific objectivity and disinterested scholarship that provide a sense of authority and superiority that many scholars claim through their identification as academics. Moreover, can that authority be separated from other affinities held for particular groups, conceptions, and ideologies? Considering how identification, authority, and discipline interconnect with affinity is central to McCutcheon's assertions here. As these assertions highlight the ways academic claims to authority cloak the uncertainties and selections with an aura of certainty, they should make scholars reflect on the winners and losers that scholarship promotes (to paraphrase Lincoln's theses that McCutcheon uses to conclude this essay).

References

Thompson, Erica. 2013. "Selena Gomez Leaves Bindi out of Music Video after Criticism," Boston.com (May 9). http://www.boston.com/ae/celebrity/blog/popradar/2013/05/selena_gomez_leaves_bindi_out_of_new_music_video.html

Tiku, Nitasha. 2013. "Hindu-in chief Bullies Selena Gomez Out of Copping Forehead Jewelry." Gawker (May 9). http://gawker.com/hindu-in-chief-bullies-selena-gomez-out-of-copping-fore-498754893.

Steven W. Ramey is Associate Professor in the Department of Religious Studies and Director of Asian Studies at the University of Alabama. He has focused his research on the contested nature of identifications in contemporary India and elsewhere.

10. Affinities, Benefits, and Costs: The ABCs of Good Scholars Gone Public[1]

Russell T. McCutcheon

> Those who are seriously interested in understanding the world will adopt the same standards whether they are evaluating their own political and intellectual elites or those of official enemies. One might fairly ask how much would survive this elementary exercise in rationality and honesty. – Noam Chomsky (2003: 49)

Frustrated with the way in which some of our academic peers ventured into writing for wider audiences in hopes of having impact on constituencies beyond the academy, I published in 1997 an essay in which I argued that the scholar of religion qua public intellectual was a troublesome notion. It was troublesome because it was based on the fallacy of misplaced authority: these so-called public intellectuals amounted to people trained in, say, the study of 19th-century American history who, because they happened to study an aspect of the social world commonly classified as religion, were presumed to be legitimate authorities on late 20th-century geopolitics. What's more, in many cases, the politics advocated in their interventions was simply an updated version of the social gospel movement, indicating that there was much at stake in failing to ask *which* of the many publics comprised their influence (largely liberal Protestant) and also their intended audience.

[1] My thanks go to Bill Arnal, Willi Braun, and the late Tim Murphy for our extremely helpful exchanges on these topics and for their comments on early drafts of this paper (a shorter version of which was presented at the regional American Academy of Religion meeting in Atlanta, March 2004, as part of a panel to which Lincoln responded). Small portions of this essay appear in McCutcheon 2005.

I concluded that essay by arguing that scholars of religion who conceived their object of study as an observable (and thus inescapably public) form of human behavior, rather than an ahistorical, private instance of experience, already and always were public intellectuals, insomuch as their work had no alternative but to conform to publicly contestable standards of evidence and argumentation commonly used throughout the modern university. The label "public intellectual" that some adopted was therefore recast as simply a way of legitimizing their specific type of punditry in what is an obviously competitive economy of experts who think they have something to say.[2]

In a letter to me dated July 15, 1997, Bruce Lincoln commented on this essay, agreeing that our field's effort to establish its institutional territory through appeals to the ahistorical and utterly unique nature of its object of study "keeps its practitioners from functioning as intellectuals in any meaningful sense." In arguing this point in my essay, I had already been significantly influenced by Lincoln's own work for, in a piece from 1985 co-written with the late Cristiano Grottanelli, they had concluded that

> [t]here can be no shrinking away from the painful fact: the establishment of an autonomous field has, paradoxically, damaged the study of religion (and of religions) immensely.... The consequences of this situation may be summed up by stating that the discipline of "History of Religions" managed to marginalize itself in the name of autonomy. Its connections with history, anthropology, sociology, political science, and other relevant fields are scarce, while its ties with theology – however much they are denied – remain strong, if implicit, covert, and distorted. (Grottanelli and Lincoln 1985: 8)

Lincoln's letter to me proceeded to put a finer edge on the issue than I had in my essay, questioning what it was that constituted a scholar as

[2] As I revise this essay for publication in this collection I have just written a post on Culture on the Edge's blog (June 7, 2013) addressing this very topic, this time with regard to the inappropriateness of scholars of the Bible informing Christians what their text actually means. See "Biblical Literates" posted at http://edge.ua.edu/russell-mccutcheon/biblical-literate/ (accessed June 7, 2013).

a public intellectual: "Is it simply the kinds of issues s/he addresses," he asked, "or also the way they are addressed, which is itself a function of the kinds of audiences s/he engages?" Elaborating on the distinctive style of their discourse and their intended audience, he added:

> I'm inclined to think that as one seeks a broader audience, one has to modify one's presentation, sometimes radically. The basic move is simplification, not just of language but of analysis. To have an effect on a broad public and/or to (re)shape policy, one is virtually forced to make a compelling case, which involves ironing out complexities and nuance, stripping evidence to a few choice bits, suppressing one's doubts, deploying metaphors, anecdotes, and conventional platitudes to maximum purpose. To my mind, these are all sacrifices in which the "intellectual" component is offered up for the benefit of the "public."

Having suggested some of the costs required of those who "go public," he concluded his letter as follows: "Personally, I don't think it's worth it, and would prefer just to be a good scholar, who addresses serious issues in serious ways and attempts to make the classroom and the pages of academic journals and books a site of moral reflection and political intervention."

Although I could begin my essay by pressing Lincoln on the use his letter made of the rhetoric of "seriousness" and "complexity" – asking him to consider how they function to authorize a particular brand of materialist scholarship by juxtaposing it with those whose work is presumably silly and simplistic – I think it far more important to begin by requesting him to reflect back on the author who wrote his 1997 letter to help us to understand what prompts good scholars to go public.

Now, as Jonathan Z. Smith has told us so many times, all acts of comparison take place in light of an often unarticulated third: the criterion in light of which any two items are being juxtaposed. As Smith has phrased this point:

> a well-formulated comparison must specify the precise mode of relation,...it must recognize the relativity of relations by comparing (where possible) more than two items,...it must identify

> the third element in a proper comparison, the "with respect to"
> that governs the comparison in terms of some conceptual cate-
> gory, and...it [must] make explicit that the comparison is not in
> terms of entities or totalities, but rather in terms of aspects and
> relations. (2003: 8–9)

Although I'm not entirely sure what all characterizes serious scholarship, both Smith and Lincoln have persuaded me that it is at least
the consistent effort to articulate and rationally defend the parameters
in terms of which one is working and the criteria whereby something
gets to stand out as worthy of our collective attention. So, with all this
in mind, and to get us started on this imaginative act of comparison,
I would like to propose that the two Lincolns now before us – letter
writer and, now seven years later, letter reader – can be compared
"with respect to" the events of September 11, 2001. I suggest this
specific comparative basis not simply because I was requested to take
as my point of departure for this essay his 2003 collection of essays
entitled *Holy Terrors: Thinking About Religion after September 11*
– a book which was obviously influenced by the events of that, and
subsequent, days, but which also includes chapters originally written,
delivered orally, or published as long ago as 1981. I also propose it
because, soon after the attacks, Craig Prentiss, a colleague teaching at
Rockhurst University in Kansas City, MO, sent me a link to an op-ed
piece written by Lincoln and that appeared in the October 23, 2001,
edition of the *Kansas City Star* – an approximately 1,200 word article
that marked for me the first appearance of Lincoln's public persona.[3]
Recalling his 1997 letter – which I had kept folded in my copy of
his 1994 book, *Authority: Construction and Corrosion* – I was rather
surprised and a little perplexed to see Lincoln writing op-ed pieces
for mid-western newspapers. After a little digging – and thanks to

---

[3] As an example of his historicist commitment to, as he aptly phrased it
in the epilogue to *Theorizing Myth*, "show his work" (1999: 208), in a footnote in *Holy Terrors* (2003a: 113) Lincoln notes that this brief op-ed piece
– entitled "The Other War: The War of Words" – was part of a larger paper
presented on October 22, 2001, at the University of Chicago and eventually
published as chapter two of *Holy Terrors*.

a some helpful bibliographic suggestions from Lincoln himself – it turned out that his *Kansas City Star* article was but one of several examples of his having left the classroom and the pages of journals and books, to offer his moral reflections and to make tactical, political interventions.[4]

But citing the events of September 11, 2001 as having played a pivotal role in bringing about an apparent change in Lincoln's

---

[4] As communicated to me by Lincoln in a January 21, 2004, email, his public pieces from around this time are the following:

"Mr. Atta's Meditations, Sept. 10, 2001: Close Reading of the Text," available in pdf form at http://divinity.uchicago.edu/sites/default/files/imce/pdfs/webforum/122002/Lincoln_Commentary2.pdf (accessed June 7, 2013; apart from several unsolicited responses to this web posting, Bruce B. Lawrence's and Mark Jurgensmeyer's solicited replies are also posted at this site).

"Yankee, Dannati due volte," *Il Sole-24 Ore: Domenica* 8 (September 2002): 27.

"The Rhetoric of Bush and bin Laden," posted at http://fathom.lib.uchicago.edu/1/777777190152/ (accessed June 7, 2013).

"The Other War: The One of Words," *Kansas City Star*, October 23, 2001. Originally posted at http://www.kcstar.com/item/pages/opinion.pat,opinion/3acd143c.a23,.html (no longer available; reprinted in *Bulletin of the Council of Societies for the Study of Religion* 31/1 [2002]: 9–10 and included in Lincoln 2003a in a revised form as chapter 2. A preview of this chapter is available online at http://www.press.uchicago.edu/Misc/Chicago/481921.html [accessed June 7, 2013]).

"The New Crusade: New Rounds in an Endless String of Reprisals," originally posted at http://www.tompaine.com/features/2001/09/28/index.html (no longer available).

"Jesus Done Wrong: Bush's Proclamation of Jesus Day," posted at http://tompaine.com/Archive/scontent/3520.html (accessed June 7, 2013; reprinted in *Creative Loafing* [Atlanta] 29/15 [August 26, 2000]: 40).

"Dubya, Defender of the Faith," posted at http://tompaine.com/Archive/scontent/4025.html (accessed June 7, 2013).

In addition to these articles, Lincoln noted in his email that he has been interviewed for National Public Radio (NPR) and was also interviewed for BBC TV.

work[5] turns out not to be the whole story, for some of these popular articles appeared prior to that date, such as his web op-ed piece entitled, "Jesus Done Wrong: Bush's Proclamation of Jesus Day" (an article on then Texas Governor Bush's declaration that June 10 was to be "Jesus Day" in Texas), which appeared on August 16, 2000, or another web essay entitled, "Dubya, Defender of the Faith" (concerned with the manner in which the Bush administration's "faith-based initiatives" undermined the First Amendment), which appeared on February 5, 2001. So, despite his stated interest in *Holy Terrors* "to react in an intellectually responsible fashion to the immediate events and the broader, more complex issues that day [i.e., September 11] raised" (Lincoln 2003a: ix), my hunch is that sometime prior to the events of September 11, 2001, Lincoln had made the decision that the gains of simplification and going public far outweighed the sacrifices to be made by those who understood themselves to be serious scholars.

Because the first of his public pieces (of which I am aware, that is) appeared just two weeks after Bush was declared the Republican candidate for President (the convention being held in Philadelphia between July 29 and August 3, 2000), it strikes me that the decision to "go public" with his critiques of – among other topics – the past US administration's rhetoric and practices seems to have been made in light of the possibility, and eventually, the actuality, of George W. Bush's movement from the confines of the lone star state to the centre stage of this country's federal political dramas. I therefore suggest that the conceptual category we employ in considering Lincoln's pre-

[5] The postscript to Lincoln 2007 (in which links are evident from his research on ancient Persia to events at the US military prison in Abu Gharib, Iraq) makes evident that these issues persist as important in Lincoln's scholarship. "I am persuaded," he writes there, "that the minidramas staged at Abu Gharib were not designed to degrade the Iraqi prisoners. Rather, like the treatment of Mithridates by Artaxerxes' soldiers, they were designed to confirm the captors' worst suspicions concerning the Iraqis, whom they had been trained to regard as 'terrorists,' as 'fanatics,' as 'diehard Baathists,' or, simply, as Arabs and Muslims, but, in any event, as *always already* degraded. The point was to establish that such people got what they deserved and deserved what they got, being exactly what 'we' always knew them to be" (103).

Dubya and post-Dubya writings is what I choose to call *disaffection*, or, thinking back to the opening pages to his influential 1989 book, *Discourse and the Construction of Society*, what we might also call the *sentiment of estrangement* (1989: 10).

I suggest that we employ this particular mode of relation to govern our comparison of his works not to play a coy game of "Gotcha" with Lincoln (a point I also made in a previous essay concerned with addressing "crucial ambiguities" in the sort of autobiographical disclosures that appear in his 1999 book, *Theorizing Myth* [see McCutcheon 2003: 225]); moreover, I am curious about the change in his work not because I presume an author's texts must all be consistent, as if an author is a uniform subjectivity which, like Hegel's *Geist*, gradually unfolds in history – Michel Foucault's often quoted quip in the opening to *The Archaeology of Knowledge* about leaving "it to our bureaucrats and police to see that our papers are in order" comes to mind at this point (1989: 17). Instead, I draw attention to this shift in genre and in intended audience, in relation to this change in federal political leadership, because given how clearly his 1997 letter articulated the unacceptably high cost to be paid by serious scholars who address publics wider than those whom they teach and those reading their journals and their books, I am curious about whether he has in fact paid any of these costs.

Assuming that the sacrifices of going public remain the same now as when he assessed them, then, why have they become worth making? More importantly, perhaps, what standard of worth and value are we employing in making these cost/benefit calculations? Furthermore, has Lincoln joined the ranks of those scholars who gamble that their audiences will not detect that they are trading if not on misplaced then at least on creatively embellished authority when commenting outside their usual domains of expertise? Or could the entire world of current events be fair game to the scholar trained in discourse analysis – or what some might generally refer to as culture studies – in much the same way that some of our predecessors once thought that the comparative study of religion provided them with expertise so deeply human(e) as to be applicable to virtually everything? Or, are his more public writings far more humble than this, comprising an example of a scholar using his well honed, critical tools closer to home than the sites from which he has drawn his data in the past (everywhere from ancient Vedic texts to the Spanish revolution). If the latter, then Lincoln seeks not to persuade the writers whose words he scrutinizes; instead, he aims simply to describe and explain the mechanisms whereby cultural contests take place – those in our back-yard as well as those far from home both in time and space. But if he enters the public square in order to contest the claims made by those whose texts he tackles – something I do not find him doing when the data he selects is more strange than it is familiar – then is he, like so many public intellectuals before him, possibly trading on an authority that perhaps is not rightly his?

For instance, consider the remarks of a reader such as Alain Epp Weaver, responding to Lincoln's web article on the instructions found in Mohammed Atta's luggage (this web article is excerpted from *Holy Terrors*; see 2003a: 8–18). Weaver asks: "On what grounds does Lincoln expect religious persons to accept his definition of religion as construction?" No doubt Lincoln had little expectation that so-called religious people would accept his definition of religion, suggesting that Weaver has failed to understand Lincoln's public pronounce-ments as being those of the scholar applying a technical discourse to an item of local significance. On first glance, it appears that, just as with many scholars of religion, Weaver seems to confuse religious persons with scholars *of* religious persons, assuming that the studies of the latter group must somehow accord with the self-reports of the former. But perhaps Weaver is not as mistaken as it might at first appear; for when scholars transgress their usual domain of expertise and write for a wider audience (i.e., making their object of study the intended audience of their texts), is it not inevitable that their work enters a contest over local conceptions of which their readers might reasonably understand themselves to exercise some degree of own-ership and thus control? If so, then as Weaver asks, on what grounds does Lincoln's intervention take place?

In posing these questions I am interested in determining the reason for and the implications of Lincoln's periodic departures from the dis-cursive conventions of Chicago's Swift Hall. Is it merely to apply his detailed socio-rhetorical analysis to the speeches of such rhetors as Bush and the late bin Laden, and to the words of the late Jerry Falwell and Pat Robertson? I think here of the US sociologist, Rodney Stark, and his 1996 book, *The Rise of Christianity*, in which he acknowledges that his foray into the literature of antiquity is simply a test of his theory of religious conversion (1996: xii). Or is Lincoln's choice of just these targets evidence of a specific sort of politics being worked out, much as in the case of Stark's own work, in fact – in which a different sort of politics ensures that his rational choice theory of Christianity's rise ends up being a thinly veiled vindication of Christianity's moral superiority (see especially Stark 1996: 209–215). To rephrase: are Lincoln's public writings merely *descriptive* and *explanatory* – as in his *Kansas City Star* article that draws the reader's attention to the manner in which any speakers' authority is the result of their gaining, as he phrased it, "control over a specific, culturally bound discourse" – or, as in the case of many public intellectuals who debate the common good, does his choice of targets carry *prescriptive* baggage often unwelcome in our field? If prescriptive, then because I have criticized in print the manner in which some no doubt well-meaning colleagues have argued that scholars of religion "should be able to make certain normative distinctions that reflect our commitment to discriminating analysis and critical intelligence" (Raschke 1986: 136), what do I make of someone with whom I agree both theoretically and, perhaps, politically, who serves up a hearty dish of normative judgments for popular consumption? Apart from sheer appetite and desire, on what grounds is it being served? Come to think of it, is anything other than appetite required to justify the shift?

Because I too have many difficulties with the simplistic yet enviably efficacious rhetoric of Federal administrations – as if all social interests can be neatly divided by means of the "with us or against us" mentality that seemingly drove the Wild West view of the world that characterized some of President George W. Bush's foreign policies – I admit that I welcome Lincoln's popular critiques of the artful manner in which the Bush government used certain rhetorical techniques to promote its political program. However, given my own interest in the manner in which *all* liberal democratic nation-states manage dissent and produce conformity by means of their citizens positing distinctive sites of discourse – Church vs State, private vs public, belief vs practice, etc. (see McCutcheon 2005 and Arnal and McCutcheon

2013) – I am wary of his rather robust support for deploying the very binary distinctions that, at least in my analysis, function to produce specific sorts of social worlds to the exclusion of their competitors (as background to this position, see McCutcheon 2003: chapter 12). As this chapter's epigraph from Chomsky makes clear – or as phrased by my late colleague in Alabama, Tim Murphy, "[t]he scientist *qua* scientist must be willing to abandon or overturn *any* belief at any time" (Murphy 2000: 191) – must scholars of social classification also take Lincoln to task for seemingly dividing scholarship between that which is good and that which is, I presume, bad, and for hauling out that old "separation of Church and State" chestnut, as the means for derailing a specific type of social formation currently steaming out of Washington?

Moreover, given the sometimes obscurantist manner in which the trope of "complexity" can often function to pull the rug out from under those analyses with which we disagree – because, after all, they are not complex enough, i.e., they do not take into account factors *we* wish to examine – must I then also question the rhetorical utility of labeling scholarship with which one disagrees as "simplistic"? Even if I grant that some analyses take into account more social factors than others (if this is what we mean by "complex" – although I admit that I'm unsure just why more *is* better), thereby allowing me to distinguish insufficient mono-causal theories from more nuanced analyses, then what am I to make of the cost of simplification that comes with the benefit of going public and reaching a wider audience? If the practical limit of concision that governs all media that have the capacity to reach audiences far wider than the limits of those that govern a semester's worth of lectures ensures that every appearance in the public sphere must necessarily iron out complexities and nuance (as accurately phrased by Lincoln in his letter), then which of the many simplifications that circulate in the popular media will strike me as persuasive and thus acceptable? In other words, what extra-discursive criterion do I, as a newspaper reader or talk-radio listener, use to distinguish between the various competing and compelling simplifications of talking heads from across the political spectrum who appear anywhere from CNN and the *Rush Limbaugh Show* to the pages of *The Nation* and *The National Enquirer*?

Although I fear I've already placed far too much emphasis on a lone letter written to me seven years ago, let me rephrase the issue as follows: if we all know that "fair and balanced" is a thinly veiled rhetorical ploy used to authorize the particular interests of groups who see themselves reflected in the Fox News show *The O'Reilly Factor* – a show whose content, style, and structure is hardly either fair or balanced – what are we to make of the work being done by such phrases as "a good scholar who addresses serious issues in serious ways"? If, as a scholar, I don't cut Bill O'Reilly any slack, what do I do with a friend who seems to be playing the same game, but for the other team?

As evidence of the implications of committing the sin of omission when selecting details while writing for the wider public – let alone any readership, of course – consider the following. As mentioned briefly above, on February 5, 2001, Lincoln published a web article on the Constitutionality (or better, lack of) of Bush's faith-based initiative. Although I am also troubled by what these programs might entail for the kind of social world I wish to inhabit, what am I to make of Lincoln's claim that: "The First Amendment mandates separation of Church and State *in no uncertain terms*" (emphasis added)? That those who are sympathetic with the motives and outcomes of faith-based initiatives certainly disagree with Lincoln's claim is obvious. The Bush administration's own opinion on the Constitutionality of this initiative strikes me as a pretty obvious example. But consider instead a letter to the editor in response to Lincoln's article that was written by J.R. Webber,[6] pointing out that the phrase, "wall of separation," that was used by Lincoln in making his argument does not actually appear in the US Constitution. Webber is correct, of course; this well known phrase comes from a January 1, 1802 letter written by President Thomas Jefferson to Connecticut's Danbury Baptist Association (in response to their letter of October 7, 1801) as part of

---

[6] Originally posted at www.tompaine.com/feature2.cfm/ID/5056 (no longer available).

a defense of his decision not to proclaim national days of fasting and thanksgiving, as had his predecessors in office.[7]

Of course, whether or not this particular phrasing is found in the Constitution might strike some as irrelevant, since – as so many of my students have been instructed in their civics classes – the First Amendment clearly *intends* this separation to be the case. However, since the recovery of intention, as well as the recovery of the meaning and thus authority of the Constitution are – as Lincoln persuaded me in his study of authority – based on a group of like-minded (or better yet, like-interested) people prepared consensually to overlook the interpretive sleight of hand required to make such a definitive statement as, "the First Amendment mandates separation of Church and State *in no uncertain terms*" (italics added), it seems quite sensible that readers such as Webber trump Lincoln's use of the Constitution as a self-evidently authoritative document by taking the text's self-evidently authoritative status *even more seriously* in pointing out that Jefferson's clever turn of phrase, despite coming from the quill of a so-called Constitutional framer, *does not in fact appear in the document*. Instead, it is but one person's interpretation of the intentions of a document that was, in fact, written by many different social actors, ensuring that it is the product of a variety of intentions, thereby resulting from concessions and compromises; the "wall of separation" is therefore a paraphrase, a translation, a simplification that uses an architectural metaphor that, in practice, turns out to omit a great deal – such as the need to develop and artfully apply what has come to be known as the Lemon Test (developed by the US Supreme Court in 1971), a set of criteria devised to figure out the extent to which this so-called wall is, in day-to-day practice, terribly (and necessarily) porous.[8]

---

[7] The text of Jefferson's letter is posted at the Library of Congress's site: http://www.loc.gov/loc/lcib/9806/danpre.html (accessed June 7, 2013).

[8] I add "necessarily" because, if we presume (as I do) that the distinction between the sacred and the secular is itself a historical, rhetorical distinction, i.e., the distinction does not name a difference in substance or in kind, then virtually anything can be labeled as one or the other, all depending on one's point of view and social interests. Taking into account the variety of interests that comprise any social group – and thus the variety of ways "religion"

Of course the clever scholar can come back with "Yes, but all we have are paraphrases and there's no proverbial source of the Nile when it comes to reading texts and making meaning!" But, as I read Lincoln's claim concerning the settled meaning of the First Amendment, there is no place for playful paraphrases in public discourse – which leads me to wonder if building a persuasive public case where something material seems to be at stake requires us to drop our usual rhetorical pretense of being good scholars addressing serious issues in serious ways.

Recalling what I am grateful to have learned from Lincoln's own work – for instance, that authority "operates in similar fashion whether it is legitimated through a religious ideology or through mystificatory claims of other sorts" (1994: 117) – as a scholar qua scholar am I prepared to identify the means by which Lincoln and Webber, like the users of all texts, are both translating and paraphrasing in scripts other than the supposed intentions of this text's set of disparate authors, all of which means that both are doing significant work to make sense of, for example, such odd things as the role to be played by the present participle "respecting" in the Establishment Clause's "respecting an establishment of religion" phrase? If so, then we have here an instance of two social actors on the same stage, using the same text, but for dramatically different ends, which means both must rhetorically harness their text's inherent semantic uncertainties and ambiguities (e.g., by elevating but one agent's interpretation – Jefferson's – to the level of certain truth) to sanction social worlds in which they more than likely intend to have no ambiguity whatsoever. But what happens when readers wish to live in just one of those social worlds yet continue to desire to play the role of serious scholar? Do they then no longer see one side's simplifications as the result of a concision that misportrays complex worlds as simple for political effect? Or, like walking and chewing gum at the same time, is it all

---

will or won't be used to name the seemingly same item – there are bound to be a variety of boundary skirmishes over whether something is or is not religion, and thus whether it is or is not Constitutional for the government to be involved with it. The so-called wall of separation is therefore not porous because of the essentially spiritual or amorphous nature of religion but, instead, because we can call anything we like religious.

but impossible to be both scholar and citizen, both serious and silly, at one and the same moment, leading us to conclude that choosing which we'll be, and when, is merely a strategic act of convenience?

That those who disagree with pundits and politicians certainly jump at the opportunity to express their estrangement is obvious – and here I think not only of Lincoln's apparent post-Dubya change in rhetorical styles but also of Ken Kurson's angry letter to the editor of the *Chicago Sun-Times* (2003) in which he notes that, because Lincoln stated on NPR (in early March 2003) that "Bush and bin Laden are one and the same" (as Kurson phrased Lincoln's thesis) Kurson is now ashamed to have attended the University of Chicago.[9] That Lincoln had indeed compared both Bush's and bin Laden's rhetorical styles, and found significant similarities (as made clear in Lincoln 2003a: 19–32), rather than finding similarities in the truth of their words, was a point either willfully or inadvertently overlooked by Kurson in his rush to assert that the US's foreign policy "is on the right side of the battle for the world's soul." Lincoln made clear in the published letter (2003b) in which he replied to Kurson that, contrary to Kurson's portrait, his analysis did not treat Bush and bin Laden as moral equivalents. "Rather," Lincoln writes, "I stress important differences between the two, while also identifying some less obvious commonalities in their rhetoric."

I assume that we have here but one example of what might be at stake when serious scholars get busy "ironing out complexities and nuance" – though we should not forget that this happens all the time when scholars read each other's works as well.[10] A perhaps less significant, but still useful, example of the price to be paid occurred when

[9] Kurson, a finance writer who is also known for his appearances on CNBC's and ABC's investment shows, assisted Rudolph Giuliani in writing his 2002 book, *Leadership* (New York: Miramax). In 2003 he ran an unsuccessful campaign as the Republican candidate for State Assembly for New Jersey's 34th District.

[10] I think here of the reception of some of my own work on the use of the classification "religion," in which some scholars suggest their incredulity by quoting, without commentary, background, or elaboration, my claim that religion does not exist. Their application of this taxon strikes them as so self-evident that it seems impossible for them to shift their attention to an analysis of the taxon itself.

Lincoln was once identified in a *New York Review of Books* article as a "Biblical scholar" (Krugman 2004: 5) – along with being classified simply as a "professor of divinity," he was also mistakenly identified as such in the book under review, Kevin Phillips's analysis of the Bush family's history and political influence, *American Dynasty* (2004: 225, 236). But what other prices are being paid, not simply by a serious scholar gone public but when those who normally understand contingent and thus contestable social worlds to exist in utterly uncertain terms – hence their interest in the roles played by ideologies in normalizing and rationalizing social worlds – come across a peer who speaks not of being on the right side in the battle for the world's soul but of certain, and thus incontestable, meanings?

Because I happen to be persuaded that scholarly discourse and practice ought to be probed by means of critical inquiry as much as any other form of practice – to borrow some of the words from the ninth of Lincoln's own "Theses on Method" – I therefore wish to pose these questions about a colleague for whose work I happen to have tremendous affinity. But, as indicated above, it is precisely the tactical, ad hoc, ultimately self-interested nature of all affinity/ estrangement dynamics that causes me to pause, for it is my hope that it is not merely sentiments of affinity and estrangement – what Lincoln has also termed "sociogravitational forces of attraction and repulsion"(1989: 176, n. 9) – that drive our conceptions of good and serious scholarship, not to mention the manner in which we choose among the simplifications that attend all acts of signification. For, such sentiments are self-serving, transitory, happenstance, and therefore unpredictable; must we conclude that so too are our academic standards and the seriousness by means of which we attend our labors? If so, then what warrant have we for investing significant energy in developing "a rigorously historical discourse analysis," as phrased by Tomoko Masuzawa (2000: 164)? Because – to borrow from the fifth of Lincoln's "Theses" – reverence is a religious and not a scholarly virtue, my hope is that my sense of debt and respect for Lincoln's work will not undermine this opportunity that we have today to offer some critical analysis of a good scholar gone public. For regardless the affinity or estrangement that we happen to feel towards our object of study, such sentiments ought not to prevent us from offering critiques of the manner in which all social actors negotiate issues of identity and meaning by routinely universalizing and dehistoricizing their inevitably provincial and strategic interests. Of course, the questions I pose of Lincoln are not new; in an ill-formed way I now realize that they arose for me as far back as his 1994 book *Authority*, in which he attempted to distinguish types of authority despite recognizing their basic similarities (see McCutcheon 2000 for my review of this book). They go back also to his 1999 book *Theorizing Myth*, in which he reflected on changes in his personal and theoretical interests that have taken place over the past 30 years – changes that revolved around his increasing awareness of scholarship's political context (1999: xii–xiv). But in posing the questions that I have in this essay, concerning his most apparent change of heart, I invite readers to reflect on the benefits, costs, and most importantly the warrants for not just going public but also for considering scholarly discourse as somehow set apart by a seriousness that must be suspended if we are to enter the fray, in a more detailed manner than that which occupied Lincoln in the epilogue to *Theorizing Myth*.

I have in mind two sets of often quoted words from the close of that book, sets of words that I've approvingly quoted before:

"show your work" (1999: 208)

"scholarship is myth with footnotes" (1999: 209)

As I read him, Lincoln offers these words in an effort to distinguish his discourse on discourse from the discourse itself. His response was aimed at a persistent question that, as he tells the story, greeted some of the public presentations of the essays that became the chapters of this award-winning book,[11] essays that each apply a rigorously historical discourse analysis to the history of scholarship on myth – an analysis astutely concerned with the practical implications of using

---

[11] *Theorizing Myth* was awarded both the American Academy of Religion's Award for Excellence in the Study of Religion (2000) as well as the University of Chicago Press's Gordon J. Laing Prize (2002). Regarding the latter, which "is given to the Chicago faculty member

the category myth itself and not concerned simply with analyzing the narratives we commonly call myths, whatever definition of myth you happen to use. As he narrates it on the opening page of the epilogue, in reply to his conclusion that "myth is ideology in narrative form," he would sometimes receive a question from, as he describes it, "an undergraduate whose seat toward the rear of the room signals her alienation, not just from the lecture but also from the institutions that, with equal pomposity and pathos, gamely try to make lectures interesting and important" (1999: 207). As he phrases it, the student would say:

> But isn't that true of all scholarship as well?... Isn't scholarship just another instance of ideology in narrative form? Don't scholars tell stories to recalibrate a pecking order, putting themselves, their favorite theories, and their favorite people on top? (207)

Or, as I might phrase it, is not a discursive analysis of discourse itself but a deployment of discourse that, if we are equal opportunity critics, ought to be studied by means of the same set of tools?

Although I was once persuaded that the historicity of our discourse – with its feet planted firmly in "the social" and "the historical," thus making it distinguishable from the ahistorical discourses we as scholars of religion take as our objects of study[12] – was signaled by such things as the way in which our footnotes allow readers to trace the paths down which we went in building our persuasive arguments, I am no longer satisfied by this reply to the disaffected student's astute

---

whose book has brought the greatest distinction to the Press' list," see the article posted at: http://www.uchicago.edu/about/accolades/34/ (accessed June 7, 2013).

[12] See the second of Lincoln's "Theses on Method": "Religion, I submit, is that discourse whose defining characteristic is its desire to speak of things eternal and transcendent with an authority equally transcendent and eternal. History, in the sharpest possible contrast, is that discourse which speaks of things temporal and terrestrial in a human and fallible voice, while staking its claim to authority on rigorous critical practice" (1996: 225; see also 2003a: 5). See also Lincoln 2012: chapter 1 for these Theses. (See McCutcheon 2013 for a review of this 2012 book by Lincoln.)

question. I am no longer persuaded because conventions of citation, let alone the constraints that determine such things as who counts as an authorized speaker, what counts as a legitimate source, what counts as credible evidence, and what comprises a persuasive argument worth citing or making, are characteristics of a specific type of discourse and *not* criteria that operate free of discourse and by means of which we can adjudicate among the discourses. Showing your work in this or that particular manner, therefore, merely marks one as a competent user of a specific set of conventions and tells you nothing whatsoever about the conventions themselves; because all discourses conform to conventions, and since all discourse-users are more than likely capable of making apparent the manner in which they are following their particular conventions, the ability to use and recognize one's conventions tells us nothing about which set of constraints we ought to be following or which ought to win our allegiance. Here, I think of the tremendous number of detailed citations to the Bible that were contained in the Alamo Christian Ministries' *World Newsletter* that I once found tucked under my car's window wiper as I left my office for home. The work behind this text was more than apparent – most impressively and elaborately, in line after line of tiny footnotes. Yet while the conventions were not mine, Tony Alamo, of the Holy Alamo Christian Church in Alma, Arkansas, was nonetheless showing his readers that he had done his homework.

Despite my earlier affinity for the way in which Lincoln once distinguished one discourse from another, I therefore find "scholarship is myth with footnotes" insufficient, for anyone with even a passing acquaintance with discourse theory will see that showing one's work – or what Lincoln refers to elsewhere as "rigorous critical practice" (1996: 225, Thesis 2) – does not bring us any closer to "meaning" or "intentions" let alone "the past." While I certainly *wish* not to equate all authorizing conventions – as if citations as part of a rational discourse were nothing but equivalents to the "Once upon a time" that opens bedtime stories – for the life of me I cannot come up with an intellectually satisfying way to distinguish among them other than to say that each operates by means of its own discourse-specific sets of rules, each of which in turn operates within its own institutional setting. For while "showing your work" indicates that you've played by the rules, it certainly does not mean that your work is somehow *true*, merely *valid* given this or that set of constraints. And it certainly does not mean it is *persuasive*, for one must already be playing by the rules in order to be persuaded. Case in point: having looked through Tony Alamo's 24-page newsletter I am no more enlightened than I was before wading through his 328 footnotes, each containing numerous Bible citations without commentary or elaboration. This problem is, of course, not new. It has long been known to many scholars, by reflexive anthropologists who realized that they could never obtain authentic, indigenous meanings that existed apart from their own preconceptions, vocabularies, etc., and by historians who realized that, despite their best efforts, the accumulation of ancient artifacts does not result in time travel. For, regardless how yellowed, shattered, or provenanced the artifact – say, a nation-state's Constitution or a letter by one of its Founding Fathers – it is always in the present, in front of the eyes of modern observers who try to conjure up a past (that, as past, is necessarily irretrievably gone) by means of some imaginative act that is regulated only by contemporary disciplinary rules and *not* by the ability to stand outside history and judge whether our accounts actually correspond to some bygone fact that still hovers in the air somehow – say, what a Constitution actually says *in no uncertain terms*. Commenting on the role the science of bibliography once played in efforts to reconstruct the original Shakespearean text (and hence the original Shakespearean intention), the Princeton historian, Robert Darnton, has recently phrased it as follows:

> Textual conundrums...inspired generations of scholars to feats of ever-greater virtuosity. By poring over early editions, they have traced typographical clues over every variety – inconsistent spelling, irregularities in spacing, chipped type, anything that could help them reconstruct the production processes of Elizabethan printing shops and therefore get closer to Shakespeare's missing copy. Many learned to set type themselves and turned into amateur letterpress printers. In their imaginations, Ph.D.s became companions of the workers who first turned Shakespeare's words into books. It was an intoxicating idea, and it did not last. (2003: 43)

That scholars still try to bridge discursive gaps and anchor just some selections in the firm soil of "history," "the social," "biology," or, as in our case today, "certainty," should not go unnoticed; we should also not overlook the fact that the conundrums yet persist – as when another of my astute (former) colleagues in Alabama, Kurtis Schaeffer, once asked my friend, Willi Braun, after a lecture in which Braun had advocated a social theory of Christian origins, "But where *is* 'the social'?" Schaeffer was not being coy; if we do not grant the existence of Tony Alamo's repeated references to "heaven," then what do we make of our own references to "history" and "the social"?

I have no doubt that Lincoln is more than aware of all this, something signaled by the fact that it appears that he was not satisfied by his answer to the disaffected student in the back row, for he characterized it as "a variant of the lame formula, 'Well, yes and no....'" (1999: 207). Although he goes on to elaborate how it could be both/ and – how scholarship and myth are and are not the same – my guess is that we cannot have it both ways when we strip our scholarship of its footnotes. So, to conclude, when we read good scholars going public (to borrow one last time, from the fourth of Lincoln's "Theses on Method") there are a few questions that need asking:

> The first of these is "Who speaks here?," i.e., what person, group, or institution is responsible for a text, whatever its putative or apparent author. Beyond that, "To what audience? In what immediate and broader context? Through what system of mediations? With what interests?" And further, "Of what would the speaker(s) persuade the audience? What are the consequences if this project of persuasion should it happen to succeed? Who wins what, and how much? Who, conversely, loses?" (1996: 225–6)

References

Alamo, Tony. 2003. *World Newsletter* (January–March). Alma, Arkansas: Holy Alamo Christian Church.

Arnal, William E., and Russell T. McCutcheon. 2013. *The Sacred is the Profane: The Political Nature of "Religion."* New York: Oxford University Press.

Chomsky, Noam. 2003. *Hegemony or Survival: America's Quest for Global Dominance.* New York: Metropolitan Books.

Darnton, Robert. 2003. "The Heresies of Bibliography." *The New York Review of Books* 50/9 (May 29): 43–5.

Foucault, Michel. 1989 (1969). *The Archaeology of Knowledge.* Trans. A.M. Sheridan. London, New York: Routledge.

Grottanelli, Cristiano, and Bruce Lincoln. 1985. "A Brief Note on (Future) Research in the History of Religions." *Center for Humanistic Studies Occasional Papers.* Center for Humanistic Studies, University of Minnesota, 4: 1–15. Reprinted in *Method & Theory in the Study of Religion* 10/3 (1998): 311–25.

Krugman, Paul R. 2004. "The Wars of the Texas Succession." *The New York Review of Books* 51/3 (February 26): 4–6.

Kurson, Ken. 2003. "Professor Denies Justifying 9/11 While Doing Exactly the Same." *Chicago Sun-Times* (March 15): Editorial Letters, 13.

Lincoln, Bruce. 1989. *Discourse and the Construction of Society: Comparative Studies of Myth, Ritual, and Classification.* New York: Oxford University Press.

Lincoln, Bruce. 1994. *Authority: Construction and Corrosion.* Chicago: University of Chicago Press.

Lincoln, Bruce. 1996. "Theses on Method." *Method & Theory in the Study of Religion* 8(3): 225–7. http://dx.doi.org/10.1163/157006896X00323.

Lincoln, Bruce. 1997. Private Correspondence. July 15 (quoted with the permission of the author).

Lincoln, Bruce. 1999. *Theorizing Myth: Narrative, Ideology, and Scholarship.* Chicago: University of Chicago Press.

Lincoln, Bruce. 2003a. *Holy Terrors: Thinking About Religion after September 11.* Chicago: University of Chicago Press.

Lincoln, Bruce. 2003b. "Letter to the Editor." *Chicago Sun-Times* (March 20): Editorial Letters, 34.

Lincoln, Bruce. 2007. *Religion, Empire & Torture: The Case of Achaemednian Persia, with a Postscript on Abu Gharib.* Chicago: University of Chicago Press. http://dx.doi.org/10.7208/chicago/9780226481913.001.0001.

Lincoln, Bruce. 2012. *Gods and Demons, Priests and Scholars: Critical Explorations in the History of Religions.* Chicago: University of Chicago Press.

Masuzawa, Tomoko. 2000. "From Theology to World Religions: Ernst Troeltsch and the Making of *Religionsgeschichte.*" In Tim Jensen and Mikael Rothstein, eds., *Secular Theories on Religion*, 149–66. Copenhagen: Museum Tusculanum Press.

McCutcheon, Russell. 1997. "A Default of Critical Intelligence? The Scholar of Religion as Public Intellectual." *Journal of the American Academy of Religion* 65(2): 443–68. http://dx.doi.org/10.1093/jaarel/65.2.443.

McCutcheon, Russell. 2000. "Review of Bruce Lincoln, *Authority: Construction and Corrosion*." *Religion* 30(1): 82–5. http://dx.doi.org/10.1006/reli.1999.0212.

McCutcheon, Russell. 2003. *The Discipline of Religion: Structure, Meaning, Rhetoric*. London: Routledge. http://dx.doi.org/10.4324/9780203451793.

McCutcheon, Russell. 2005. *Religion and the Domestication of Dissent, or How to Live in a Less than Perfect Nation*. London: Equinox Publishers.

McCutcheon, Russell. 2013. "Review of Bruce Lincoln, *Gods and Demons, Priests and Scholars* (University of Chicago Press)." *History of Religions* 53(2): 212–15.

Murphy, Tim. 2000. "Speaking Different Languages: Religion and the Study of Religion." In Tim Jensen and Mikael Rothstein, eds., *Secular Theories on Religion*, 183–92. Copenhagen: Museum Tusculanum Press.

Phillips, Kevin. 2004. *American Dynasty: Aristocracy, Fortune, and the Politics of Deceit in the House of Bush*. New York: Viking.

Raschke, Carl. 1986. "Religious Studies and the Default of Critical Intelligence." *Journal of the American Academy of Religion* 54(1): 131–8. http://dx.doi.org/10.1093/jaarel/LIV.1.131.

Smith, Jonathan Z. (2003). "Why Compare Religions?" Unpublished paper presented at a conference in honor of John F. Wilson, Princeton University (October).

Stark, Rodney. 1996. *The Rise of Christianity: A Sociologist Reconsiders History*. Princeton: Princeton University Press.

Russell T. McCutcheon is Professor and Chair of the Department of Religious Studies at the University of Alabama. His research focuses on the social and political implications of competing classification systems.

Topic VI: Limiting Engagements

11. What's New Is Old Again: The Αναπαλαίωση[1] of Tradition

Vaia Touna

The words tradition or traditional are often thought to name something that possesses an essence that is transmitted or handed down like a material object from generation to generation. In contrast to this common understanding, I am less interested in maintaining the conventions of such terms and more curious about who holds the power to define something as a "tradition" or "traditional," by what means, and what modern interests drive that very definition. In other words, I am more interested in the anachronism within the discourse on "tradition." But before I go into more details, and finally suggest how this brief introduction opens the way into McCutcheon's essay, let me take you first to a village that is located in Pieria, a regional unit in Central Macedonia, Greece.

The name Pieria may not be very familiar to many outside Greece but it is an area of significant historical importance, not only to Greeks but also to anyone who visits the northern part of Greece, since this is where Mt Olympus is located, there's the nearby ancient city of Dion, an archaeological site from the 5th century BCE dedicated to the cult of Zeus, and the area is said to be the home of Orpheus and the Muses, daughters of Zeus. In the southern part of Pieria, on the

---

[1] Αναπαλαίωση (*anapalaiosi*) is a technical term, a noun, which derives from the Greek verb *anapalaiono* (αναπαλαιώνω) meaning again (*ana*) to make old (*palaiono*), used for the restoration of buildings to their original form.

lower slopes of Mt Olympus, there is a mountain village called Old St Panteleimonas, a village that, when you visit it, gives you the sense that it has been trapped in time ever since its settlement about 200 years ago. It is, in a word, *a traditional village.*

Old St Panteleimonas is surrounded by forests of chestnut, oak, and arbutus trees, and as you approach it, driving up the mountain, the only thing that you can discern are red-tiled rooftops on a sliding scale looking out over the Aegean Sea and the Thermaic Gulf of Thessaloniki. As you walk into the village – since cars are not allowed to enter – you will likely be impressed by the harmony of the buildings' architecture – known to locals as Epeirotiko or Macedonian style – that is, two-story buildings built tightly together against one another, with white and green or grey tiled walls, wooden doors and windows, and red-tiled roofs. Although some of those buildings bear the marks of time, others seem very well preserved. Walking through the narrow, cobbled alleys you eventually find yourself in the village's central square, common to all Greek villages, where the inhabitants along with tourists socialize under the shade of a big oak tree. Prominent in the square is a church dedicated to St Panteleimonas – the village's namesake – along with taverns serving excellent food, cafés providing homemade or traditional pastries and Greek coffee, little stores selling all sorts of memorabilia, all of which make the village a favorite destination for a weekend away from the noisy cities.

According to the people in Old St Panteleimonas, the village was built in 1803, during the Ottoman period, by people trying to find a safer settlement as a deadly disease was threatening their community. It is said – again according to locals – that a man came to them with an icon of St Panteleimonas (a saint and martyr said to have lived in the 3rd century CE in Nicomedia, whose name means charitable [eleimon] to all [panton], and who according to his life story, studied medicine and was known for his healing abilities), which miraculously saved the inhabitants and who in return built a church dedicated to the saint and named their settlement after him. Although this older church doesn't exist anymore, a new church was built in 1914 at a nearby location, which has been restored many times over the years following various natural destructions including a fire.

Old St Panteleimonas is a village that has been characterized, since 1978, as "traditional" by a Greek Presidential enactment (to which I shall come back later) and also a place that is protected by UNESCO (United Nations Educational, Scientific and Cultural Organization) as a world heritage site. "Tradition" and "traditional" are therefore commonly used to describe not only its architecture but also the way of life that, it is believed, has not changed too much – a belief shared not only among the residents living there, on that small mountain, but also by those who visit the village.

My interest in how people use the discourse of tradition brought me again to the mountain in September of 2013 to do some research, knowing that the village – as I've been there many times, taking friends who would want to experience a different Greece (different from that of the city, that is) – was famous for its traditional architecture and lifestyle. Since I was there on a weekday and finding a place to stay would be easy – given also that the tourist season was almost over – I decided to spend the night in one of those quaint traditional houses located at the heart of the village square, where the owner has turned the second floor's three rooms (the first floor is used as a tavern) into very comfortable accommodations with private bathrooms. After browsing around the narrow streets filled with taverns, cafés, and small souvenir stores, I went to ask the owner of the hotel what time breakfast would be the next morning. I found myself a little surprised to learn that even 8 a.m. might be a little bit early for him to open the café – surprised only because of my previous assumptions of what it means to live in a village, where life (again according to many who dwell in the cities, such as myself) is supposed to start very early. Soon those assumptions completely faded away, for I was told that most owners and employees leave Old Panteleimonas after closing their stores each day. Later that night I could gradually hear silence falling as the tourists were leaving and the owners, closing their stores, taverns, and cafés, began commuting back down to their homes, located about 6 kilometers south, near the base of the mountain, in the village of New Panteleimonas.

This daily movement of people up and down that mountain is something that, most likely, goes unnoticed if we travel like visitors and not as analytical scholars, if we visit as people who *simply* want to experience the beauty and uniqueness of the traditional village of Old Panteleimonas which has survived for 200 years holding onto its traditions and traditional aura. For if this is how we visit then what goes unnoticed is the work done by anachronism in the discourse of tradition, a discourse which manages and bridges the distance between the top and the bottom of the mountain, between past and present, traditional and modern. For, as will become evident, despite its governmental classification as traditional, Old Panteleimonas is, in many ways, *far newer than New Panteleimonas*. To better understand not only this irony but also this process of strategic anachronism we need to look at the history of these two villages within the wider social world in which they are situated.

After WWII St Panteleimonas (what is now known as Old Panteleimonas), like most villages, was affected as Greece was gradually transformed from an agricultural economy to an industrial-based economy. During the 1940s, large parts of the population moved away from Greece's many small, rural villages in search of better working opportunities and thus better living conditions in big city centers. Despite the population increase in most areas during the 1950s due to the post-war baby boom, amid economic and political instability, many rural areas continued to decline in population, especially in the 1960s. The main reason for the decline in population was emigration to Western Europe, North America and Australia, as well as to the major Greek urban centers such as Athens and Thessaloniki. Between 1951 and 1971, these two urban centers were the only areas to record high increases in population while mountainous areas (villages) and islands were losing population. As a result, most villages in Greece were not only abandoned but the way of living in villages then, especially evident through Greek films and theatrical plays of the time, was portrayed as rough, with no household comforts and with no indoor plumbing (i.e., in some cases people would have to go and get water from a nearby fountain or a fountain that was usually located in the yard). Furthermore, villages in most cases did not have hospitals and sometimes even doctors were a luxury, so it was common to find some people turning into charlatans. High rates of superstition were common, as depicted in the popular 1958 film entitled *Our Midwife*, in which a practitioner from Athens having retired decides to go with

his family to his wife's village to practice medicine only to be faced
with the superstitions of the villagers who trust the charlatan practices
of the Midwife more than the scientific knowledge of the Doctor. The
film is a characteristic representation of village life, which at the
time was not viewed as ideal by the people who lived in the cities.
Of course, the village that we today call Old Panteleimonas was no
exception and, in 1965, suffering from the same economic challenges
that faced all rural life in Greece, its remaining inhabitants petitioned
the government to allow them to relocate further south, down the hill,
to a newly established village to be called New Pantaleimonas – with
the excuse that rainfall had caused many landslides that were affect-
ing the village. The new location, far closer to the sea, it was also
hoped, would attract tourism and provide new job opportunities. A
number of modern hotels, restaurants, and cafés along the coast were
then created, offering an ideal vacation destination for tourists.

And what was now known as Old Panteleimonas was, understandably, left to deteriorate – prompting one to wonder how that quaint
traditional house came to be my home for the night in September of
2013. Such a query necessitates more context.

In 1972 the General Conference of UNESCO, which met in Paris,
decided on a convention concerning the Protection of World Cultural
and Natural Heritage. The first article of the convention defines "cultural heritage" as:

> ***monuments:*** architectural works, works of monumental sculp-
> ture and painting, elements or structures of an archaeological
> nature, inscriptions, cave dwellings and combinations of fea-
> tures, which are of outstanding universal value from the point of
> view of history, art or science; ***groups of buildings:*** groups of
> separate or connected buildings which, because of their archi-
> tecture, their homogeneity or their place in the landscape, are of
> outstanding universal value from the point of view of history,
> art or science; ***sites:*** works of man or the combined works of
> nature and man, and areas including archaeological sites which
> are of outstanding universal value from the historical, aesthetic,
> ethnological or anthropological point of view.

UNESCO also set criteria for countries to apply for funds under this act. Criteria for naming something as Heritage or Traditional were set both by the UNESCO program and the EU, but also by the various countries, including Greece.

At the same time, Greece was trying to acquire a distinct sense of its own identity within what was then the newly emerging commonality of the EU, doing so with reference to its glorious past and its collective continuity with it. People who had left their villages during the 1950s and '60s, seeking a better life in the urban centers began – mainly after the fall of the Greek dictatorship in 1973 – to develop a romanticized view of their families' past in the village (to this day many metropolitan Greeks retain close ties with their familial village, traveling there for holidays, burials, etc.). And it was mainly the emigrants from the villages who then started to form groups and societies in order to "preserve" the history and traditions of their homeland's (i.e., village's) music, dances, cooking – that is, their traditions. So, in 1978 (as mentioned at the outset) a Presidential Enactment (after which followed others in 1985 and 1989, and the list is ever-growing) was issued which was the first to provide a list of villages that were characterized as "traditional," but also and more interestingly for our purposes, giving detailed instructions on what could be restored – and how – always under the supervision and approval of the "Commission Exercising Architectural Verification" (*Επιτροπή Ενασκήσεως Αρχιτεκτονικού Ελέγχου*). This was the first time in Greece that "traditional" was used to distinguish between various types (and statuses) of villages, at least in official government documents – for although two villages might no doubt be of comparable age, only one might be classed as traditional.

In addition, towards the end of the 1970s, the Greek state supported this movement through the establishment of folklore museums that served "to teach the urban public about the indigenous folk sources of their culture and to generate support (financial or otherwise) for folklore research" (Handler and Linnekin 1984: 279). During the same period, a variety of economic benefits (funded both by the EU and the Greek state) were given to people whose villages or houses could be characterized as "traditional," such as low-interest loans to fund authorized renovations. Thus, an archival quest was started by people, for there was now a need to find evidence of the historical significance of a village or a house. At the same time, and in distinction from the decades prior, people in the cities had started to romanticize the old, simpler way of living and to look for touristic resorts in old villages. Accordingly, villages that were closer to the set of assumptions city people had about what was traditional, or to what for the European community would count as traditional, as well as those fitting the criteria set by the state, saw a growth in population and in their economy as people began to restore their village houses in the now appropriate architectural styles in order to attract more tourists.

Old Panteleimonas was one among 300 villages that made it to the 1978 Presidential Enactment's list of "Characterization of Housing Estates as Traditional," and its entire area, as indicated above, is now under the protection of UNESCO. However, the effort by its current residents to restore and renovate their parents' village (for a generation had by now passed) was not immediate, for only as recently as 1990, during and especially after the nearby Yugoslavian war (which negatively affected their hopes for seaside tourism), did the people of New Panteleimonas start to show interest in their ancestors' decaying village at the top of their hill, seeing it now as an alternative tourist destination, this time mainly for Greek vacationers. And so, the residents of New Panteleimonas began applying for funding to restore (*anapalaiono* = to make old again) their long-abandoned houses along the slope of the mountain, in many cases turning them into quaint hotels or stores, restaurants, and cafés that would offer visitors a taste of authentic Greek "tradition." And it was in one of these that I found myself that evening in September 2013, when I learnt that the village did not reopen until sometime after 8 o'clock each morning.

What we may now begin to understand about claims of tradition from this tale of these two villages – one that closes at night and where pretty much no one really lives – is how strategic social actors construct their representations of the past to suit their present social, economic, political needs, and how they authorize their present by linking it to a past *that suits these practical interests*. When it comes to studying people's traditions and the stuff of which they are made, though, we should not simply reproduce their claims about tradition – that is, as something handed down to them from the past – and this is exactly what Russell McCutcheon, in the following essay, cautions about when he critiques the anachronistic use of "religion" and "the West" in the work of scholars. That is, McCutcheon argues for a different approach that should not simply repeat that very anachronism but rather, as I have tried to do above, look at the historical processes and situations so as to understand how it is that those claims about the past and the present come to make sense to people, to "us." For as was evident from the above example, the construction of "traditional villages" is far more complicated than asserting, as do the people we study, that traditions are static and handed down to them from the past. Instead, what one might call tradition was and is the continuous working result of various social sites and institutions within and outside Greece setting their all too modern criteria of what gets to count as "traditional," as well as active social actors who try to fit into their new re-creation of the "old" village (i.e., in their *anapalaiosi* of the village) the assumptions and expectations of tourists. A re-creation that not only has to provide a certain *imaginaire* of the past based on the criteria set by the state but also provide for the comforts and safety regulations of modern living.

Words such as "traditional," much like "authentic" or "original" and the like are, therefore, social constructions, always invented in the present. The discourse on tradition then is a technique people use in order to gain benefits, whether social, economic, or otherwise. For the residents of New Panteleimonas, "tradition" became a useful anachronistic tool that enabled them to revive their local economy, within an ever-changing and in many ways uncontrollable world. As evident in the following essay, unless we want to be merely descriptive, our analysis of historical processes ought to be something different than simply repeating the anachronisms social actors use to anchor their present. We should, instead, look at all the other variants (e.g., political and economic changes in Greece, the role of EU and its relation to Greece, UNESCO, etc.) that were in place, prompting these people to turn their attention – and travel up the mountain – this time to their new "traditional" village.

It is time, though, now to open the ground to McCutcheon's essay in which it will be evident that this anachronistic strategy, which is useful for authorizing specific and contemporary social arrangements, is not unique or limited either to Greek villages or to the discourse on tradition, and can be accomplished with words, and in scholarship, and not just with government-approved building materials. His essay offers a caution for analytical scholars to be self-reflexive, and aware of the limits of *their* conceptual tools and the manner in which they are themselves the makers of what is old (i.e., of a certain type of *anapalaiosi*), when despite using modern concepts such as "religion" or "the West" they project them backwards in time as if they have always been there, as if those concepts have come to us unchanged; in other words failing to recognize that the discourse on "religion" or "the West" (and I would add to that the discourse on "tradition") is, as McCutcheon phrases it, "part of *our* cosmographic formation," an anachronistic strategy that makes possible a certain identification in the present.

Reference

Handler, Richard, and Jocelyn Linnekin. 1984. "Tradition, Genuine or Spurious?" *Journal of American Folklore* 97(385): 273–90. http://dx.doi.org/10.2307/540610.

Vaia Touna is Assistant Professor in the Department of Religious Studies at the University of Alabama, Tuscaloosa. Her research focuses on the sociology of religion, acts of identification and social formation, and uses of the Greco-Roman past.

12. The Resiliency of Conceptual Anachronisms: On Knowing the Limits of "the West" and "Religion"

Russell T. McCutcheon

> We are bound to employ novel terms to denote novel ideas.
> – Cicero, *De Natura Deorum*

In the second chapter of Anthony Grafton's *Bring Out Your Dead* (2001), we learn of the case of Lorenzo Valla (1407–57), the Italian humanist now remembered for his early enthusiasm for using the comparative and historical methods when studying documents from antiquity. According to Grafton, in studying the historicity of the *Donation of Constantine* – a legal text in use since the Middle Ages which was once believed to date from the 4th century, documenting Constantine's transfer of the governance of Italy and the western Roman provinces to Pope Sylvester I (d. 335), in appreciation for having been cured of his leprosy – Valla

> quoted lavishly from texts of several kinds, and proved that the document represented the Romans as using words that had not yet been coined to describe institutions that they would not have recognized. A text that contained such anachronisms could not have been written in the time it claims to come from. Unfortunately, Valla's demonstration threatened not only cherished beliefs but the political and economic powers of the popes. (Grafton 2001: 52)

With typical irony, Grafton concludes his story of Valla by noting that "[s]ince he could not be convinced of his error, he was offered a good job in Rome." In the words of Michael Corleone, recalling one of the lessons his father taught him, "keep your friends close, but your enemies closer" (*The Godfather, Part II* [1974]).[1]

Given the manner in which the *Donation* functioned as part of a system that – until scholars such as Valla got their hands on it, that is – legitimized papal control by seamlessly linking the present with what was then seen to be an authoritative past, it is understandable that the historicization of such documents – i.e., identifying the gaps between present and past – does not normally win scholars friends in high places. For example, consider that in its article on Valla, the *New Catholic Encyclopedia*'s entry informs its readers that he was arrogant and quarrelsome (Montano 2002: 377), and that in its very brief article on Valla, the *Dictionnaire de Théologie Catholique* concludes that, although he certainly wrote a lot, he leaves behind a deplorable, or at least a regrettable, reputation (*"une fâcheuse réputation"*) (Vacant et al.: vol. 15, 2526). To be fair, such minimalizations are no more significant than the popular *Christian History* magazine's sensationalist portrait of Valla as a proto-Reformer and hero who uncovered "Church history's biggest hoax" by means of his quest for the "authenticity" of historical documents (Prosser 2001: 35).

The case of Valla, along with both the jabs at his character and praise concerning his role in blowing the lid off of the supposed Catholic hoax, nicely sets the table for current efforts to historicize the primary taxon of our field, the classification "religion" itself – what I shall refer to as a resilient conceptual anachronism, adapting a phrase from H.A. Drake's impressive study of Constantine

---

[1] Of course this line is believed to be derived from Sun Tzu: "...when we are near, we must make the enemy believe we are far away; when far away, we must make him believe we are near" (*The Art of War*, I.19 [11 of Clavell's edition]). It should be noted that Valla was tried for heresy by the Curia at Naples, a trial cut short by King Alfonso's intervention. That Alfonso, King of Aragon, Sicily, and Naples, was intent on extending his control over what were then papal lands, should not go unnoticed when trying to understand his interest in Valla's case, whose study of the *Donation* was written under Alfonso's protection. However, Valla eventually wrote *"Apologia ad Eugenio IV"* in which he asked to be excused for his shortcomings, and under Pope Nicholas V was appointed as *scriptor*, and ended his days as the canon of St John Lateran (the Pope's own church).

(2000: 17),[2] but one equally at home in the work under consideration here (e.g., Dubuisson 2003: 67). In the case of Valla we have an early modern episode in the clash between systems of authority, or what others might simply call "regimes of truth" (e.g., Lincoln 1996: 227, Thesis 13), a clash that had something to do not only with contesting the perceived continuities between the present and the past, the local and the universal, but also between the presumed inner essence of persons, texts, and institutions, on the one hand, and their material worth, social status, and thus continued legitimacy, on the other. Moreover, the tale of Valla's attempt to contest the Rome of his day, by tackling the historicity, and thus authority, of one of its central legal texts, only to end up acting as the canon of the pope's own church, provides a sobering example of what can happen when one tries to pull the rug out from under some cherished assumptions. For, all too predictably, perhaps, "[e]ven those who set out with the most honorable of intentions," concludes Grafton, "could easily take wrong turnings in this rebarbative intellectual country" (2001: 53).

Although he was here speaking about 15th-century Italy, Grafton might as well have been talking about contemporary scholarship, for despite the critiques of a number of scholars – and Daniel Dubuisson's *The Western Construction of Religion* is one of the most thorough – "religion" has proved itself to be an example of one of those surprisingly resilient holdovers from a previous era ("world religions" is one as well; on its history, see Masuzawa 2005). Its resiliency, Dubuisson argues, is linked to the fact that (much like "meaning" or "intention") it is a signifier that is believed by its users to refer not to anything in the observable world of mere appearances but, instead, either to unseen beings or inner feelings and dispositions – both of which are thought to exist wholly apart from the causality of the contingent world of mundane human existence. By definition, then,

[2] Drake uses this phrase to characterize the manner in which modern scholars of Constantine seem incapable of distinguishing their own viewpoint from that of people in ancient times, such as Jacob Burckhardt who, in writing his influential *Die Zeit Konstantins des Grossen* (published in 1853, and translated as *The Age of Constantine the Great*), assumed that "the disdain for established institutions which he [Burckhardt] saw all around him prevailed in the fourth century as well" (Drake 2000: 17).

religion – both the signifier and that which it apparently signifies – defies definition. Yet it is precisely in this defiance that its legitimacy is supposedly found, insomuch as one's inability to define it somehow validates the presumption that the term refers to some stable yet unseen world, either within the human heart or somewhere out there in the great beyond. Although it is hardly news to many scholars that all signifiers are empty, arbitrary signs that derive meaning from their circulation within a series of relationships with other equally empty signifiers, this playfulness of meaning-making apparently stops at the door of "religion."

An "empty core" (Dubuisson 2003: 68) that is said to be in-step with an ever-changing reality is a pretty handy rhetorical device to have in one's toolbox (whatever the toolbox), for it allows us to weather the sorts of storms regularly thrown at us by history (e.g., those inconvenient gaps that go by the names of chance, accident, forgetfulness, ambiguity, etc.). For example, consider a 2004 conference that I attended, devoted to "Conflicts at the Border of Religions and the Secular,"[3] at which I drew attention to the manner in which writers – despite acknowledging that the term "religion" has a specific yet sadly vague etymology – nonetheless assert that all human beings are religious.[4] (This is none other than an instance of having one's cake and eating it too, for the influence of history is acknowledged amidst holding onto a transcendent element that successfully rides the unpredictable waves of historical happenstance, i.e., although the names change, Led Zeppelin was right: the song remains the same [see McCutcheon 2005a]). In the animated conversation that followed, a scholar *asserted* (I use this word purposefully, for I cannot imagine what an argument for this point might look like) that the Arabic term *dīn* "*means* religion" – not just today, not just for contemporary,

[3] The one-day conference, held on April 23, 2004, was sponsored by the Center for the Study of Religion and Conflict, Arizona State University. My thanks to Linell Cady, for the kind invitation to speak to this interdisciplinary faculty/grad student group, and to Carolyn Forbes, for making the arrangements.

[4] For an example of this, see the textbook by Esposito et al. (2002: 5; the text appears unchanged in the 2006 edition). For a critique, see McCutcheon 2005b: 40–1.

trans-national Arabic-language users thoroughly acquainted with the Euro-North American semantic world of "religion," but that it has *always* meant "religion." Despite the fact that even for ancient Romans *religio* (along with its variations) did not *mean* "religion" as we have come to use it today, this scholar employed the concept/ word distinction much the same as the traditional essence/manifestation distinction was once wielded by phenomenologists, relying on the connector "means" (as in *"dīn* means religion") to be doing some pretty heavy metaphysical lifting.[5]

Despite this asserted correspondence between word/concept, a rather different story is told by more historically nuanced studies such as Dubuisson's, suggesting that what is at stake in this debate are, as in Valla's day, different philosophies of history and thus systems of authority.[6] Case in point, consider the *Encyclopedia of Islam*'s persuasive case for understanding *dīn* to have developed from the notion of a debt that must be settled on a specific date, which in turn leads to such successive usages as: the idea of properly following an established custom of settling debts; the act of guiding one in a prescribed direction; the act of judging whether such a prescription has in fact been followed; and visiting retribution upon one who has failed to follow the required path (see Lewis et al. 1965: 293–6). As such, *yawm al-dīn*, or what we might translate as "Day of Judgment," therefore comes to signify the day when Allah gives direction to all human beings. So, much as with the relation between the geographic and prescriptive senses of such English words as "direction" and "directive," we see here a gradual mingling of social exchange with geographic movement and, eventually, with rules of propriety. Accordingly, *dīn* eventually moves from the more narrow sense of a debt to be discharged to being a term that stands in for "the body of obligatory prescriptions to which one must submit" (Lewis et al. 1965: 293).

[5] Anyone who studied literature in high school, and who has since come to see the study of meaning and intentionality as a rather thorny problem, is more than familiar with the ahistorical work being done by this sort of meaning-talk, as in the proverbial question: "What did Shakespeare mean by...."

[6] The following analysis of *dīn* derives from McCutcheon 2005b, chapter 3.

Therefore, it is rather misleading to suggest, as does one reference resource which agrees with the colleague cited above, that *dīn* is "*employed to mean* a religion together with its practices in general" (Glassé 1989: 99; emphasis added). Although italicizing this intimation of intentionality may put too fine an edge on the issue, *dīn* is not "employed to mean a religion" or even some sense of worship or religiosity – as if early Arabic writers were hunting for a local equivalent for what some of us *now* take to be the obviously universal concept that lurks deep within the word "religion." Instead, as Dubuisson might observe, an ancient Arabic term is translated *by contemporary English speakers* intent on finding a universal phenomenon to confirm their particular way of organizing the world.

If the above etymology is persuasive, then there is a great deal lost in this translation, for "the concept indicated by *dīn* does not exactly coincide with the ordinary concept of 'religion' precisely because of the semantic conception of the word" (Lewis et al. 1965: 293). Just what is lost is significant. For instance, consider a recent translation of the Qur'an's famous *surā* 5.3:

> Today I have perfected your system of belief
> and bestowed My favours upon you in full,
> and have chosen submission (al-Islam) as the creed for you.
> (Ali 1988: 98)

Or, as phrased in a popular translation of the Qur'an:

> The day I have perfected your religion for you and completed My favour to you. I have chosen Islam to be your faith. (Dawood 1983: 387)

Just as Dubuisson might have predicted, both "system of belief" and "creed" in the first instance, and "religion" and "faith" in the second, are English renderings of *dīn* – translations that nicely lock the Arabic term within a discourse on inner sentiment and individual choice concerning a series of systematically related propositions (i.e., a creed that expresses a deep faith and meaning with which one either does or does not agree). Nothing could be further from the complex social, transactional history of the ancient Arabic concept.

Although "[t]hese few remarks...perhaps oversimplify the diffi-culties encountered in translations the *dīn* of Kur'anic [sic] verses into Western languages" (Lewis et al. 1965: 293–4), we see that a concept that once marked one's changeable status within an historical world of differing ranks and competing interests and entitlements has even-tually come to be sentimentalized as a matter of inner faith, belief, opinion, and judgment, all of which are what we today commonly *mean* by "religion." The history of *dīn* could therefore be the topic of a chapter in what we might call the modernist sentimentalization of classical piety (e.g., see Smith 1998: 271). But this is a book that can only be written by one who, along with writers such as Dubuisson, presumes that both words *and* concepts, essences *and* manifesta-tions, are all malleable historical products that change over time and place, in light of differing interests and preferences. This is clearly *not* the presumption of those historians of religion whom Dubuisson rightly critiques, especially in the first part of his book, "The West and Religion" (chapters 1–3) – those who seek "to preserve an essen-tial (timeless?) tie between the current, living acceptance of a word and its hypothetical first reception, raised to the status of original, founding datum" (2003: 22). For such scholars, "religion," much like the unsinkable Molly Brown, is a wonderfully resilient signifier that bounces back no matter what one throws at it. However, much like the wishful tale of Molly Brown taking charge of the *Titanic*'s famed lifeboat number six, "religion" as we have it today may be nothing more or less than a product of the Victorian imagination.

It is just this presumption of universal signification – what Dubuisson (2003) calls the "learned confusion between etymological signification and essences" (22), as well as "the old Platonic nostal-gia" (23) – along with the related "propensity of Western thought to discover the religious everywhere (from the caves of Lascaux to the coast of California)" (43), that he subjects to repeated and hard-hit-ting critique. Although "religion" came to prominence in modernity, during which time it came to be used to name an inner disposition rather than an outer social status, Dubuisson is particularly interested in that set of preconditions, which he traces to early Christianity, that helped to set the stage for the modern rise of "religion." Using the writings of Paul as an early example, Dubuisson draws attention to the utility of "the circumcision of the heart" rhetoric (Romans 2:29); this handy little device helps us out with the pesky fact that the empirical thing we call the letter of the law sometimes (well, let's be honest, and just say most of the time) is incapable of matching, and therefore, furthering our context-specific, practical interests; it's therefore pretty tempting to think up a spirit of the law (call it the law's essence, its intention, or meaning, etc.).[7] This crafty piece of metaphysics nicely enables us to side-step a basic tenet of historically-based scholarship: that our rules, curiosities, and tools are just that – *ours*; neither are we to expect them to be everyone else's nor are we to assume that they will always be ours.

It is the mark of a certain kind of hubris when one fails to see this, when one fails to understand that the utility of one's tools (i.e., conceptual categories) is linked to questions and interests and not to their ability to fit reality in a seamless manner. With this hubris in mind – one that often attends our use of such signifiers as "religion" and "human nature" – I cannot help but recall Clint Eastwood's second "Dirty Harry" film, *Magnum Force* (1973), in which his corrupt superior, Lieutenant Briggs (played by Hal Holbrook), drives away from the crime scene at the film's end, in Harry's car, prepared to indict Harry for his own crimes. Unbeknownst to Briggs, of course, the bomb intended for Harry is still in the car and, in Eastwood's typically detached style, Harry passively watches his Lieutenant's car blow up as it drives away. "A man's got to know his limitations," Harry says dryly. Those who make their categories do far too much work fail to recognize their limitations and the limitations of their tools.

Of course there are those, like Dubuisson, who think "religion" can do no heavy lifting whatsoever, thus recommending that we

---

[7] See Arnal (2008) for a novel argument that draws on Pierre Bourdieu's work on *doxa* to argue that, contrary to popular scholarly conceptions, Paul was not a critic of the Judaism of his day but was, instead, intent on making what Arnal terms "artificial Jews" – that is, in disengaging the preferential status of turn-of-the-era Jews from any biological or ethnic sense and, instead, redeploying this identity as an immaterial (or, as Paul might have written, "spiritual") identity, thereby extending this social identity (and privileges that come with it, e.g., God's promise to Abraham) to a new group.

throw it out altogether when doing anything but description. For such writers, there is likely no "sound principle of economy" that, as Dubuisson suggests, "obliges us to use it [i.e., religion]" (2003: 102). Although the work of Tim Fitzgerald (2000; 2003a; see also his edited volume [2007]) certainly comes to mind as one of the better known recent critics of "religion," the work of Ronald Inden provides another example, one worth considering here because it may not be as familiar to general theorists as that of Fitzgerald.[8]

In an understatement worthy of Grafton, Inden – the author of *Imagining India* (2001) – comments in a footnote to the introduction to his co-written book, *Querying the Medieval*, that the "various ideas of religion that scholars have used have a complicated and contested history, which we will bypass here" (2000: 22, n. 50). This bypass consists of dropping the term completely, and replacing it with "way of life." "Ritual" goes out the door as well, being replaced by "life-transforming practices"; "disciplinary order" replaces such notions as "school" or "sect"; and as for such favorites as "myth," "ideology," and, for many in our field, the much coveted "worldview," well, they all get replaced by such terms as "life-wish," "royal wish," "imperial wish," "world wish," "life-account," "world account," and "world vision" (22–23) – all in an effort to indicate the often overlooked social sites and effects of these idea systems.

Although writers long accustomed to finding only "religion" to have scholarly merit will likely see such terminological revisions to embody a "barbarism of remarkable infelicity" (as Strenski [1998: 124] once described my own suggestion [McCutcheon 2001: chapter 2] of re-describing "religion" as "social formation"),[9] those who are suspicious of the manner in which "religion" is used within social systems in which doctrine is presumed to take priority over social practice, belief over behavior, private experience over public behavior, and authoritative tradition over the contingent present, will more

[8] For an example of how heated these debates can get, readers are recommended to see Fitzgerald's recent exchange with Ian Reader (Fitzgerald 2003b; 2004; Reader 2004).

[9] For a reply to some of Strenski's recent critiques of scholarship on "religion," see McCutcheon 2004.

than likely welcome the attempt to introduce a greater degree of theory into our technical terminology, as is evident with Dubuisson's preferred re-description: "cosmographic formation" (2003: 17, 69, and 199 ff.). But bringing social theory to bear on the texts, behaviors, and self-reports of so-called religious people irritates quite a few of our peers – an irritation that stymies the creation of new knowledge, for the application of theories that are separate from the data inevitably leads to a systematic renaming and reconsideration (i.e., part of what we mean by re-description) of that which participants take for granted. For, as Cicero had his Epicurean philosopher, Velleius, tell his readers, "we are bound to employ novel terms to denote novel ideas, just as Epicurus himself employed the word *prolepsis* in a sense in which no one had ever used it before" (*De Natura Deorum*, I: xvii, 44). Accordingly, criticism of new words is, in fact, criticism of new ideas and their new institutions by other means.

Dubuisson's new technical term is connected to the idea that, instead of presuming "an objectively constant thing, a 'religion'" (as phrased by Inden et al. [2000: 23]), we ought to take seriously that the study of human practices must consider the complex world of intention and structure, of agency and accident, where textual and doctrinal artifacts are tips of competitive social economies, each concocting a habitable semantic world. With just this presumption in mind, Dubuisson's work has much in common with a writer such as Inden; for instance, consider how the latter's "disciplinary order" – much like cosmographic formation – makes eminent sense if we problematize the manner in which "school" presumes a static homogeneity and uniform opinion and procedure. Instead, "disciplinary order" draws attention to the many techniques that are up and running when any social world is perceived/portrayed by its participants – or by scholars – as a consensual arrangement that endures over time. In the words of one of Inden's reviewers, the things many of us call religions are therefore "significant competing articulations of knowledge about the world and proper action in it, with the power to fashion and order the lives of those who accept them" (Davis 2002: 1410). This also strikes me as a rather useful definition for Dubuisson's notion of cosmographic formation.

The advantage of this theory-based approach, in the words of Davis once again, is that it "represents a significant and challenging revision" to indigenous self-reports, insomuch as it places those groups who are self-described religious elites (as well as those who are described in this way by scholars who merely paraphrase a specific subgroup of participant self-reports – after all, not all Jews or Muslims can be included in such statements as "Jews believe…" or "Muslims practice…") "in their broader sphere of action [i.e., social world] and envision[s] them as seriously engaged in projects of constructing polities" (2002: 1410) – it was just such a revision that got Valla into a fair bit of trouble back in 15th-century Italy! If we're willing to risk a little bit of trouble today, then we'll see that there's nothing particularly religious about so-called religious elites for they, like us all, are working within a competitive context and drawing on useful discursive conventions to fashion a socially habitable world that accords with their interests and expectations.

Swimming against the anti-historicist presumption that at the root of a text there lies some coherent and uniform meaning – a presumption that fueled the development of textual criticism and philosophy alike – Inden is equally suspicious of alternative approaches that emphasize context (e.g., class, gender, etc.) as the non-agential setting that determines what gets to count as meaningful. Instead, he attempts to steer a middle course between text and context, agency and structure:

> If we give up the notion of a universal truth grounded either in theology or scientific knowledge, if we no longer think of the state of affairs in the world as God's plan or nature's design, then the object of our inquiry shifts. We no longer concern ourselves with trying to know God or one of his reborn substitutes – human nature, reason, creative genius, modes of production, and the like – but turn to the causes of the human world; transitory human agents and their actions. Of special importance are the practices, persistent and consciously ordered activities, in which people engage because these, more than other activities, have to do with ordering the world and disrupting orders. (2000: 4)

To those who welcome the appearance of Foucault in the Department of Religious Studies (though in a manner somewhat different from Carrette's attempt [2000] to use his work to recover a politically oppositional spirituality), this all makes great sense. To those intent on doing God's work or finding either the religion gene or the religious genius, these are dangerous words for they, as the old proverb says, throw the baby out with the bath water.

Keeping in mind Inden's critique of the type of agency that haunts much work in our field, I realize that, despite my support for Dubuisson's effort to start emptying this murky tub, I do not think that we have yet arrived at the point of putting forward a fully re-described approach to the study of human behavior bereft of that pesky little conceptual anachronism from which the journal (*Religion*) in which an earlier version of this essay first appeared gains its name and identity.[10] If all we're interested in is description, and more specifically, descriptions of the self-reports of just those people who use a specific linguistic device to classify features of their lives, then by all means, let's keep "religion." But our failure to elevate other indigenous concepts to the level of theory (i.e., people around the globe use a lot of local concepts to organize their lives, so where is our journal entitled *Mana*, *Dīn*, or *Bhakti* with "religion" faintly appearing in the background?)[11] suggests that those who are interested in doing

---

[10] Note that this journal's redesigned cover, which presents a collection of what are presumably various languages' synonyms for "religion," provides surprisingly useful grist for Dubuisson's critical mill.

[11] Despite the late Ninian Smart's recommendation that we internationalize the field by using concepts such as *bhakti*, *li*, *marga*, and *shariah* in our scholarly studies (Smart 1994: 902–3; see McCutcheon 1997: 148–9), as Dubuisson notes, we would likely feel odd having other scholars arrive on our shores searching for the dharmic nature to our social institutions, informing us that, whether we knew it or not, we all had dharmic experiences. As he observes, "India has never been tempted or never been able to impose its concept of dharma on anthropological thought as an absolute system of reference. Nor did it ever claim that there was a universal essence of dharma present in all cultures, that every person carried within him or her a *homo dharmicus*" (2003: 101).

something more than repeat self-reports that regularly distinguish religion from politics, for example, will have to go looking for other conceptual helpers to make sense of such talk. But the advantage of the helper Dubuisson offers – cosmographic formation – is *not*, as he argues, that it is "freed from all religious concern and all Western prejudice" (2003: 69). If, for the moment, I can be granted the right to talk about such an unwieldy thing as "the West," it occurs to me that the level of material affluence necessary to be able to sit back and discuss the cognitive/political systems humans devise to classify and negotiate their worlds is something that only exists in certain historical periods and specific contemporary national regions. In other words, the very distinction between "participation in" and "study of" – a distinction that forms the basis of our field – is itself evidence of a particular social world, call it "the West" if you like but more accurately, it might be specified in terms of the economic privilege required for developing the appearance of intellectual distance and emotional detachment necessary for such scholarly pursuits.

Although I certainly prefer his theory-based term to "religion" – since it helps us to see so-called religious behaviors as but one ordinary instance of human efforts to create seemingly meaningful and totalized environments in which to live – I would argue that the preference for "cosmographic formation" is *not* based on the fact that it is either freed of Western prejudice or that it is *more* intelligible (as Dubuisson also does [2003: 69]). Instead, the term has utility for those of us working in the human sciences because its intelligibility is based on a social theory concerning the variety of ways in which people go about establishing and contesting their systems of habitability (recalling Inden as well as the work of William Paden [e.g., 2000]). Although "religion," along with its many uses, is certainly intelligible to vast numbers of people (hence, few are perplexed when they find a religion section in their newspaper, as pointed out by Strenski [1998: 113]), it is precisely this intelligibility – the common, taken-for-grantedness of intertwined discourses (what Dubuisson likens to a hypertext [32]) on invisible beings, morality, endtimes, origins, ritual specialists, textualization, experience, and the supposedly distinct nature of the institutions in which these discourses routinely circulate – that ought to occupy the attention of scholars. Just how is it that this grouping appears to so many people *as* intelligible? If these things, taken together, count as religion, then the problem of why it is that just these things are so commonly grouped together by certain societies, in clear distinction from other parts of their social worlds, will only be answered by a theory from outside the discourse on religion. Because religion cannot levitate itself, concepts such as cosmographic formation, relying on the muscle provided by a social theory that is interested in all instances of world-making activity, therefore step in to do some of the work.

The point is that scholarly terms are not neutral or more intelligible than folk concepts; despite my own difficulties with the rhetorics of good and evil that populate international relations post September 11, 2001, I do not fail to recognize that these rhetorics are extremely *useful* for large numbers of people – all of whom are intelligent, creative, human beings – who are trying to make sense of their worlds, and in so doing, create worlds that are conducive to their interests. Instead, the advantage for scholars of using concepts such as cosmographic formation is that our tools are placed within a discourse *other than the one that is under study*, ensuring that the interests advanced by our work are ours, and not those of the people we study.

But having said all this, I admit that I have a nagging hunch that, despite replacing "religion," the old philosophical idealism yet seeps back in to many of our efforts to rethink our field. For instance, *The Western Construction of Religion* is, in the final analysis, an intellectual history in which actual human beings do not appear all that often; it is a critique of ideas, paradigms, and "intellectual hegemony" (Dubuisson 2003: 94) and not, for example, a book about economics and material interests. Examining "cosmographical schemas deeply buried in our ways of thinking" (ibid.) therefore seems strangely reminiscent of the one-time emphasis on studying beliefs, ideas, and doctrines, or studying such observable things as behaviors and texts as if they were the merely outward expressions of inner sentiments, intentions, or mentalities – the very type of scholarship that Dubuisson critiques so masterfully in the first half of the book. Had he prioritized the study of the structures and institutions that make ideas possible, rather than the study of ideas that animate institutions (and civilizations, such as "the West"), had his critique of "religion" not been premised on the historic influence of specifically Christian thinkers,[12] then perhaps he would have arrived at different conclusions; for then, instead of concluding that "the West" "espouse[s a] bad epistemology …that in the last analysis simply does not work" (94–5), he might have seen that our (scholars included!) continued success at thinking this thing so many of us know as "the West," or the ease with which we today look back on two millennia and pick out the specifically "early Christian" writers from among a host of other people in antiquity, and then posit them/their artifacts as having a causal impact on contemporary modes of thought, is all evidence of the tremendous success of the institutions represented by this epistemology. For if, along with Dubuisson, we are going to say that the West created religion and that "the concept of religion eventually came to be the core of the Western worldview" (94) then, whether we like it or not, we might have to conclude that it *works extremely well* for it is only by using "the West" that a book such as this can be written, for central to its thesis is the posited direct link between a turn-of-the-era Mediterranean text (i.e., the letters of Paul) and current European/ North American scholarship. Therefore, his critique of the manner in which "the West continuously speaks of itself to itself, even when it speaks of others" might, ironically, be but one more piece of evidence concerning just how well these mechanisms continue to work. Or, to phrase it another way, it might not be due to "intellectual laziness" (102, 107), or even the inevitable inertia that attends all social existence,[13] that such anachronisms continue to be employed in the early 21st century; instead, it may be because they work so well in helping a host of agents to address the inevitable gaps of historical existence,

---

[12] That is, there is the nagging problem of writers who throw out "religion" but end up studying Christians, Muslims, Hindus, etc. – in a word, the things we already (and somehow) seem to know to be religions.

[13] As my late colleague, Tim Murphy, once phrased it, plain old inertia might explain more than we realize. The prominence of "world religions" as a concept, despite some devastating recent critiques, provides one possible example. Attending the American Academy of Religion's 2006 Southeast Commission on the Study of Religion's regional meeting in Atlanta (March 10–12), it was as if no one had ever offered a critique of the concept/term.

and thereby further their various (and more than likely competing) interests. Laziness might be better re-described as an efficacious social strategy. As well, I admit to having some ambivalence towards Dubuisson's critique of idealist notions of subjectivity (2003: 107–12). For despite my enthusiasm for the manner in which he argues that modernity's increasing preoccupation with "the torments of the interior life" (107), as evidenced by the rise of discourses on faith and experience, can be linked to the rise and dominance of mass movements (on this topic, see Perkins 1995), I am left slightly unsatisfied concerning the thoroughness of this critique. Case in point: although it may seem a small quibble, consider Dubuisson's use of Saint Paul.[14] Concerning the Stoic ideal of a universal civilization, we read: "Here one cannot but recall Saint Paul's bold, inspired decision to turn away from the Jewish world (which he saw as too sectarian and ungrateful), evangelize the heathen, and finally, go to Rome, the heart of the pagan empire" (103). Citing Acts 13: 46–49 (which details the divine mandate for Paul to establish a mission to the gentiles), Dubuisson elaborates on what he describes as "Saint Paul's choice": "Without doubt this decision, which inaugurated what in its further propagation would be transformed into a veritable world conquest, must be seen as one of the founding acts of the West, one of those of which we can say with certainty that it influenced the fate of humanity" (103).

My difficulty with this passage concerns the manner in which social change in particular, and history in general, are presumed uniformly to develop from the choices of long past individual social actors – choices seamlessly communicated to us by means of texts that later generations of readers can employ to understand the intentions of

---

[14] As an aside, let me say that I am curious as to why Paul is always referred to as "Saint Paul" in his text for, to my mind, the theological honorific common in French discourse places this figure within a specific setting – one Dubuisson works to historicize throughout the book. Unless, of course, his intention is merely to refer to this figure in a descriptively accurate manner, at least as particular contemporary Christian insiders might (i.e., Roman Catholics). However, if this was the case, then would he also follow any reference to Muhammad by adding "peace be on him"?

their predecessors. This view of social and historical change – what we once might have termed a great man view of history – seems at odds with much of Dubuisson's own critique. In fact, a view of history more in keeping with his very useful analysis of representation – one in which we presume from the outset that "the world is mute about itself" (2003: 127) – would find the signifier "Saint Paul," along with such things as "the book of Acts" and the "Pauline epistles," to be discursive constructs that resulted from the social activities and collective interests of subsequent generations working with a host of raw materials from various of their many pasts. (For instance, many scholars of Christian origins are rather suspicious of treating Luke/ Acts as a resource for understanding the earliest Jesus movements, given both the suspiciously uniform portrait it offers of their early intentions and effects as well as the later period to which it can be dated.) I use the adjectives "social" and "collective" in the previous sentence to underscore that the institutions that enable artifacts from prior social worlds to be preserved, collected, archived, and continually reinterpreted and applied to new and previously unforeseen situations are not, in fact, coterminous with the activities or interests of any one agent; they are, instead, the non-intentional results from the commingling of large numbers of intentional actors, collaborating, disagreeing, forming, and undermining coalitions, and remaining silent at opportune times.[15]

If this view of history informed our reading of "the past," then neither does the Book of Acts necessarily tell us anything about an intentional agent's choices nor is the present the direct result of any such choices. In addition, adopting this view of history as a continual, hindsight concoction of the continually changing present makes it increasingly difficult to speak of "the West" as a coherent historical formation, for if the world is mute about itself, then so too are those things we call civilizations, making all claims about "the West" or "the western mind" (Dubuisson 2003: 128), let alone claims concerning their originary point and their lines of historical development, techniques that a specific "we" in the present use to organize the

---

[15] This view of archiving the past is influenced by Trouillot 1995; my thanks to Willi Braun for bringing this book to my attention.

unwieldy world of competing interests and sensations – which is none other than the way that otherwise disparate people *become* a we. So, perhaps it is the case that the discourse on "the West," along with our penchant for tracing significant historical developments to origins in the ancient Mediterranean world, is part of *our* cosmographic formation! If so, then much of what Dubuisson says about the strategic uses for "religion" is equally applicable to our own work as scholars, for just as the essentialists who yet cling to "experience," the individual, intentional subject we find at places in his text, as well as his sense of "the West," seems yet to presume the existence of an "unchanging transcendence" (130–1). Although his notion of transcendence is hardly the "benevolent divine providence intervening in the universe" (131) that we find in the work of so many scholars of religion, it nonetheless shares in a number of the assumptions that seem to drive those whom Dubuisson critiques so well. For if Dubuisson is correct, if all human beings set about the work of building a comprehensive world by drawing on a similar set of techniques, then it should be no surprise to find ourselves in our own data set. So, despite some authors' best intentions, their historicizations of the category religion, along with their critiques of the interrelated faith/institution, apolitical/political, and private/public classifications, risk reproducing the very conditions they thought they were criticizing. For, as Grafton phrases it: "When any discipline takes a new shape, antitraditionalist rhetoric becomes the standard mode of framing one's work as virtuous and innovative, and several *Hindenburgs* are produced for every *Spirit of St. Louis*" (2001: 75).

If my above assessment is persuasive, then we must be on the lookout for critiques of "religion" that, knowingly or not, re-admit through the side door that which was kicked out the front. Case in point: consider Jeremy Carrette and Richard King's *Selling Spirituality* (2005); though both authors are known for their suspicion of what they characterize as the imperial and oppressive foundations of the imported category religion (notably King 1999), their co-authored work nonetheless advocates for an "engaged spirituality," lamenting the commodification of what they characterize as "the world's religious traditions [which] provide the richest intellectual examples we have of humanity's collective effort to make sense of life, community, and ethics" (2005: 182). Or consider Aaron Ketchell's analysis of tourist attractions in the Ozarks region of the US state of Missouri (Peterson and Walhof 2001: 156–75). Despite appearing in a book entitled *The Invention of Religion* – a book in which contributors seek to historicize the category religion – Ketchell's chapter seems only to critique the manner in which such prior, internal things as "pious impulses" (160) and "religious sentiments" (172) are commonly manifested (i.e., as Carrette and King might say, commodified) in tacky, popular culture. Or perhaps we could even cite David Chidester, whose collection of essays on religion and American popular culture, entitled *Authentic Fakes* (2005), aims to recover this thing he calls "human authenticity." Despite being known for his earlier historical work on the colonial impact of early comparative religion in southern Africa (1996), his effort to contextualize religion nonetheless uncovers the pan-human kernel that might otherwise go unnoticed. For instance, in the opening to his new book he writes:

> At work and at play, human authenticity is at stake in American religion and popular culture. Religion is the real thing but, as we already know from the world of advertising, Coca-Cola is also the real thing. Baseball, rock 'n' roll, McDonald's and Disney, Tupperware and Nike, along with all the other permutations of the popular, have artificially produced a real world. Religion, *mediated* through popular culture as ordinary leisure and entertainment but also as human possibility and experimentation, has appeared in the traces of transcendence, the sacred, and the ultimate in these cultural formations. (2005: 9–10)

Apparently, there is a really real and an artificial, and, or so Chidester argues, the latter is capable of *mediating* – a key word that tells us much – the former, thereby providing us with glimpses of the ultimate in the most unlikely of places (i.e., sports, food storage systems, etc.). How this differs from van der Leeuw's work on manifestations or Eliade's work on hierophanies popping up in unexpected sites, I am not sure.

All of which brings me back to Grafton and his description of Pope Sixtus V's (1521–90) efforts to resurrect the relics of Egypt – architectural anachronisms in desperate need of retooling if they were to prove of use in their transplanted setting in the piazza out front of the Vatican. "In elaborate ceremonies," writes Grafton, "the obelisk was exorcised and rededicated to the service of the true God; a cross was set on its top, replacing the ball which had once been thought to contain the ashes of Caesar Augustus" (2001: 59). With Sixtus V's exorcisms in mind, we find an important lesson that can be applied to our efforts to exorcize the imperialism of "religion." For by means of our scholarly ceremonials we sometimes replace a ball said to contain one hero's ashes (i.e., studies intent on divining the deeply held religious experience) with a cross thought to have carried another's corpse (i.e., studies that, instead, work to uncover the enduring human spirit or the deep ideas that drive history). For, as the old saying goes, the more things change....

So, despite not yet being the retooled field's equivalent to the *Spirit of St. Louis* that touched down at La Bourget field, just outside Paris, in 1927, unlike many other critiques of "religion" Dubuisson's book is certainly no *Hindenburg* either; I therefore fear that some of the above criticisms might be mistaken by the hasty reader for something other than disagreements between colleagues with shared interests. For those willing to take seriously that human behavior, and its scholarship, are all historical products of a happenstance world of competing agents, *The Western Construction of Religion* points them in the right direction by helping to lay to rest some nagging assumptions and troublesome categories. Its shortcomings simply make all the more evident the importance of its thesis concerning the tenacious hold these ideas have had on our minds – not to mention the grip these institutions have had on our bodies.

References

Ali, Ahmed. 1988 (1984). *Al-Qur'ān: A Contemporary Translation.* Princeton, NJ: Princeton University Press.
Arnal, William. 2008. "Doxa, Heresy, and Self-Construction: The Pauline *Ekklesiai* and the Boundaries of Urban Identities." In Eduard Iricinschi and Holger Zellentin, eds., *Heresy and Identity in Late Antiquity*, 50–101. Tübingen: Mohr Siebeck.

Carrette, Jeremy. 2000. *Foucault and Religion: Spiritual Corporality and Political Spirituality*. London, New York: Routledge. http://dx.doi.org/10.4324/9780203457818.

Carrette, Jeremy, and Richard King. 2005. *Selling Spirituality: The Silent Takeover of Religion*. Oxfordshire, UK: Routledge.

Chidester, David. 1996. *Savage Systems: Colonialism and Comparative Religion in Southern Africa*. Charlottesville: University Press of Virginia.

Chidester, David. 2005. *Authentic Fakes: Religion and American Popular Culture*. Berkeley: University of California Press.

Cicero. 1933. *De Natura Deorum, Academica*. Trans. H. Rackham. The Loeb Classical Library. London: William Heinemann, Ltd.

Davis, Richard H. 2002. "Review of Ronald Inden, Jonathan Walters, and Daud Ali, *Querying the Medieval*." *Journal of Asian Studies* 61(4): 1408–11. http://dx.doi.org/10.2307/3096503.

Dawood, N.J. 1983. *The Koran*. 1956 ed. London, New York: Penguin Books.

Drake, H.A. 2000. *Constantine and the Bishops: The Politics of Intolerance*. Baltimore, MD: The Johns Hopkins University Press.

Dubuisson, Daniel. 2003 (1998). *The Western Construction of Religion: Myths, Knowledge, and Ideology*. Trans. William Sayers. Baltimore: The Johns Hopkins University Press.

Esposito, John L., Darrell J. Fasching, and Todd Lewis. 2002. *World Religions Today*. New York: Oxford University Press.

Esposito, John L., Darrell J. Fasching, and Todd Lewis. 2006. *World Religions Today*. 2nd ed. New York: Oxford University Press.

Fitzgerald, Tim. 2000. *The Ideology of Religious Studies*. New York: Oxford University Press.

Fitzgerald, Tim. 2003a. "Playing Language Games and Performing Rituals: Religious Studies as Ideological State Apparatus." *Method & Theory in the Study of Religion* 15(3): 209–54. http://dx.doi.org/10.1163/157006803322393378.

Fitzgerald, Tim. 2003b. "'Religion' and 'the Secular' in Japan: Problems of History, Social Anthropology, and the Study of Religion." *electronic journal of contemporary japanese studies*. Posted at http://www.japanese-studies.org.uk/discussionpapers/Fitzgerald.html, accessed May 29, 2013.

Fitzgerald, Tim. 2004. "The Religion-Secular Dichotomy: A Response to Responses." *electronic journal of contemporary japanese studies*. Posted at http://www.japanesestudies.org.uk/discussionpapers/Fitzgerald2.html, accessed May 29, 2013.

Fitzgerald, Tim, ed. 2007. *Religion and the Secular: Historical and Colonial Formations*. London: Equinox.

Foucault, Michel. 1985 (1st ed. 1984). *The Use of Pleasure, Vol. 2 of the History of Sexuality*. Trans. Robert Hurley. New York: Random House.

Glassé, Cyril. 1989. *The Concise Encyclopedia of Islam*. Intro. Huston Smith. San Francisco: Harper & Row.

Grafton, Anthony. 2001. *Bring Out Your Dead: The Past as Revelation*. Cambridge, MA: Harvard University Press.

Inden, Ronald. 2001. *Imagining India*. 1990 ed. Princeton: Princeton University Press.

Inden, Ronald, Jonathan Walters, and Daud Ali. 2000. *Querying the Medieval: Texts and the History of Practices in South Asia*. New York: Oxford University Press.

King, Richard. 1999. *Orientalism and Religion: Postcolonial Theory, India, and "The Mystic East"*. London, New York: Routledge.

Lewis, B., Ch. Pellat, and J. Schacht, eds. 1965. *The Encyclopaedia of Islam*. New ed. Vol. II, C-G. Leiden: E.J. Brill.

Lincoln, Bruce. 1996. "Theses on Method." *Method & Theory in the Study of Religion* 8(3): 225–7. http://dx.doi.org/10.1163/157006896X00323.

Masuzawa, Tomoko. 2005. *The Invention of World Religions, Or, How European Universalism Was Preserved in the Language of Pluralism*. Chicago: University of Chicago Press. http://dx.doi.org/10.7208/chicago/9780226922621.001.0001.

McCutcheon, Russell T. 1997. *Manufacturing Religion*. New York: Oxford University Press.

McCutcheon, Russell T. 2001. *Critics Not Caretakers: Redescribing the Public Study of Religion*. Albany, NY: State University of New York Press.

McCutcheon, Russell T. 2004. "Religion, Ire, and Dangerous Things." *Journal of the American Academy of Religion* 72(1): 173–93. http://dx.doi.org/10.1093/jaarel/lfh008.

McCutcheon, Russell T. 2005a. "The Perils of Having One's Cake and Eating it Too: Some Thoughts in Response." *Religious Studies Review* 31: 32–6.

McCutcheon, Russell T. 2005b. *Religion and the Domestication of Dissent, or, How to Live in a Less than Perfect Nation*. London: Equinox Publishers.

Montano, R. 2002. "Valla, Lorenzo." In *New Catholic Encyclopedia*, 2nd ed., exec. ed. Bernard L. Marthaler, Vol. 15, 376–7. Detroit: Thomson Gale.

Paden, William. 2000. "World." In Willi Braun and Russell T. McCutcheon, eds., *Guide to the Study of Religion*, 334–47. London: Continuum.

Perkins, Judith. 1995. *The Suffering Self: Pain and Narrative Representation in the Early Christian Era*. London, New York: Routledge. http://dx.doi.org/10.4324/9780203210062.

222   *Claiming Identity*

Peterson, Derek, and Darren Walhof, eds. 2001. *The Invention of Religion: Rethinking Belief in Politics and History*. New Brunswick, NJ: Rutgers University Press.

Prosser, Peter E. 2001. "Church History's Biggest Hoax." *Christian History & Biography* 72: 35.

Reader, Ian. 2004. "Ideology, Academic Inventions, and Mystical Anthropology: Responding to Fitzgerald's Errors and Misguided Polemics." *electronic journal of contemporary japanese studies*. Posted at http://www.japanesestudies.org.uk/discussionpapers/Reader.html, accessed May 29, 2013.

Smart, Ninian. 1994. "Retrospect and Prospect: The History of Religions." In Ugo Bianch, ed., *The Notion of "Religion" in Comparative Research: Selected Proceedings of the XVI IAHR Congress*, 901–3. Rome: "L'Erma" di Bretschneider.

Smith, Jonathan Z. 1998. "Religion, Religions, Religious." In Mark C. Taylor, ed., *Critical Terms for Religious Studies*, 269–84. Chicago: University of Chicago Press.

Strenski, Ivan. 1998. "On 'Religion' and its Despisers." In Thomas A. Idinopolus and Brian C. Wilson, eds., *What is Religion? Origins, Definitions, and Explanations*, 113–32. Leiden: E.J. Brill.

Trouillot, Michel-Rolph. 1995. *Silencing the Past: Power and the Production of History*. Boston: Beacon.

Tzu, Sun. 1983. *The Art of War*. Ed. and foreword James Clavell, trans. Lionel Giles. New York: Delacorte Press.

Vacant, A. et al. 1908–50. *Dictionnaire de Théologie Catholique*, 15 vols. Paris: Libraire Letouzey et Ané.

Russell T. McCutcheon is Professor and Chair of the Department of Religious Studies at the University of Alabama. His research focuses on the social and political implications of competing classification systems.

Afterword

Accidental Favorites: The Implicit in the Study of Religion

Steven W. Ramey

So, what can scholars do within the academic study of religion in light of critiques surrounding processes of classification and identification, both in their teaching and research? As the essays in this volume illustrate, any discourse, including discourse within the academic study of religion, reflects a range of assumptions and interventions, often disguised as objective description. This concluding essay addresses one aspect of these issues by considering the implications of how people employ identifying labels (for themselves, others, and objects) and the ways in which labels invariably take sides, often unintentionally and even unknowingly, in contested fields.[1] Of particular interest are the broader, more generalizing labels (e.g., Hindu, Sikh, Indian, American, religion, orthodox) that generate significant contestation. The result of an awareness of these implications becomes a shift in the focus of research away from finding the best general labels to analyzing how others use such labels. To enable such a shift, however, scholars must alter the ways that they describe and analyze to avoid directly applying identifying labels that enter such contested terrain.

---

[1] The essay is a modified version of the Presidential Plenary address that I presented at the 2013 meeting of the Southeast Region of the American Academy of Religion. While the ideas are my own, I am indebted to my colleagues in Culture on the Edge, whose discussions and insights have helped me to extend these ideas.

The phrase culture wars, that evokes communities wrestling over competing interests and visions of morality and society in the American political context, generates significant academic reflection. My focus in this essay is the way the discourse that religious studies scholars often employ tends to play favorites in such contests within and between communities around the globe. Rather than focusing on the role of normative and theological assertions in the discipline that have been, and will be, debated for a considerable time, the primary context of playing favorites that I am addressing is the one of "accidental favorites," that is, when academic discourse, the set of terms that scholars choose, implicitly supports a position within a contested landscape, a position that those scholars have not necessarily analyzed and may not intend to support. For those scholars who choose to make prescriptive statements concerning the ways people who adopt a particular identification should live, whether couched as theology, hermeneutics, or ethnography, they should acknowledge that they are taking sides in a contested field and argue persuasively for the side(s) that they take. However, even those scholars explicitly taking sides often reinforce implicitly one side of other contested terrains when they intend only to describe aspects of human experience, as the language of labels and identities has prescriptive implications. Even more so, for scholars and others who understand their task to be analyzing human activity in a descriptive or social scientific sense, the implicit, though often unintentional, prescriptions within the current discourse on religion and religions makes it too problematic to continue to use. Avoiding the labels (Hindu/Sikh, religious/secular, orthodox/heterodox) that dominate the current discourse creates space for scholars to focus consistently on the more important issues surrounding the ways people use those labels, such as the interests that particular classifications serve, rather than debating into which classification an action or idea fits.

Consider the following examples. A recent court case in California (a prime example of the culture wars), involves a yoga program in a public school system, funded by a private foundation. The opposition to the program hinges on the question of the "religious" nature of the program, which would then place it in opposition to the freedom of religion guaranteed in the constitution of California. A scholar of religious studies at Indiana University appeared as an expert witness in the case, arguing in her declaration that the yoga program "promotes and advances religion" and "incorporates and endorses religious concepts" (Brown 2013: 4, 9). That assertion is certainly not an accidental favorite. A full analysis of her arguments and their implications would be worthwhile, though it moves far beyond my focus here. Rather, looking at one of her opening assertions about the religious nature of the yoga program illustrates more specifically how accidental favorites develop and function through the uses of labels like "religion." In the declaration, she quotes from the mission statement of the American Academy of Religion (AAR) Yoga in Theory and Practice Group, which includes an assertion that the group "examines the relative pervasiveness of spiritual and religious ideologies in manifest or latent forms within the contemporary yoga scene" (quoted in Brown 2013: 5). In the context of the construction of an AAR group, such an assertion served the interest of connecting the study of "the contemporary yoga scene" to the broader study of religion through the AAR. I suspect that at least some of those promoting the AAR group never intended to make a declaration about the religious nature of a yoga program in a school and its relation to the principle of the separation of church and state. While it is possible to argue that the legal declaration misinterprets the mission statement and the declaration does not rely on this statement solely, the application of the labels "spiritual" and "religious" in the mission statement (along with the implications of the term "latent") implies a categorization that supports one side of this legal debate. My concern, then, is the broader implications of the use of language and how academic discourse has not kept up with the critical examination of the category "religion" and the various labels for "religions."

Some other examples will further illustrate the difficulties that the implicit normative assertions create in relation to academic discourse. When Robert de Nobili as a Jesuit priest in India adopted marks of high caste status, including the saffron robe and sacred thread, vegetarian diet, and avoidance of pollution by avoiding contact with those identified as untouchable, he distinguished between cultural elements he adopted and religious elements he rejected in his effort to convert members of the upper castes. However, other Jesuits considered these practices that de Nobili identified as cultural to be religious, so that following them accepted aspects of another religion, in part (Cronin 1959; Forrester 1980: 15–18). When scholars identify practices of food, social relations, and dress, and in the context of India the maintenance of caste distinctions, as either "religious" or "not religious," they are entering theological/philosophical disputes that have practical implications. Some who identify themselves as Hindus label caste as religious, thus inscribing these social relations with the presumed authority of texts such as the Vedas. Others reject the connection of caste to religion and specifically "Hinduism," which preserves within parts of contemporary society a more palatable image of Hinduism and a positive notion of religion generally.[2] Describing caste as religious or based on Vedic passages within a course or text, as many scholars do (Dumont 1980: 201, 270; Fisher 2014: 98–9), enters these debates that few have analyzed carefully.

Making distinctions between labels that scholars readily accept and those that scholars leave in doubt also implicitly reinforces marginal statuses. The 2012 US Presidential Election raised questions of the religious identification of Mormons as Christian or non-Christian. Sometimes in my own teaching I have implicitly inserted a distinction, asserting that "Mormons claim to be Christian," a phrase I have not commonly used in relation to those who identify as Protestants, Catholics, or Eastern Orthodox. Thus my statement creates an accidental favorite on an issue I have not researched intensively. Similarly, textbooks that describe particular religions implicitly take sides in contested fields with selections of what receives unqualified inclusion. The Ahmadiyya, who identify as Muslim but whose identification others who also identify as Muslim often contest, seldom appear as unqualified Muslims in texts or courses, while particular

[2] For example, the tension between Gandhi's view of caste as an aspect of Hinduism that needs revision and Ambedkar's rejection of a Hindu identification because of its connection to caste discrimination illustrates one side of this divide (Jabbar 2011). Other opponents of caste, such as Raja Ram Mohan Roy, separated the practice from an idealized Hinduism. For more discussion of these debates, see Susan Bayly's descriptions of caste debates (1999: 146–60).

communities such as Wahabbis or Sufis, are given a central, legitimated position.

The Guru Granth Sahib, the text that many who identify as Sikh typically recognize as their living guru, is often described as "the Sikh text." A common way of expressing reverence to the "Sikh text" includes placing it in the centre of an institution under a canopy with brocaded cloths covering it. Some who revere the Guru Granth Sahib and install it in their institution, though, do not recognize the text, or themselves, as Sikh. Many who identify as Sindhi Hindus, for example, express devotion to the Guru Granth Sahib along with Durga, Rama, Krishna, and other deities commonly identified as Hindu. They understand themselves and the Guru Granth Sahib to be Hindu and present multiple historical arguments for that identification. Glossing the Guru Granth Sahib as "the Sikh text" reinforces the assertion that Sikhism represents an entirely distinct religion, an episteme that became dominant in the early 20th century, and marginalizes groups, like Sindhi Hindus, who identify different relations between these varied conceptions and practices (Oberoi 1997; Ramey 2008). While referring to the Guru Granth Sahib as Sikh may seem to be an appropriate application of the label to facilitate communication with people unfamiliar with the text, even such simplistic assertions of the labels create accidental favorites that cloak the contested nature of these labels.

And these seemingly obvious labels have consequences. Multiple cases exist where people who identify as Sikhs in India and Pakistan have claimed a legal right to take control of an institution or have forcibly removed the Guru Granth Sahib from an institution that Sindhi Hindus have founded.[3] These legal and physical actions develop

---

[3] In 2010, a group who identified themselves as Khalsa Sikhs entered several centers in Delhi that housed the Guru Granth Sahib, mostly centers identified with Sindhi Hindu communities, and removed the copies of the Guru Granth Sahib, claiming that these centers were disrespecting their living guru by having images of deities and other gurus in honored positions beside, and even higher than, the Guru Granth Sahib (*Global Sikh News* 2010; Khalsa Press 2010). Similarly, a court case in Karachi, Pakistan, centered on an institution that a community who self-identified as Sindhi Hindus had constructed in Pakistan after Partition, placing the Guru Granth Sahib in

from a notion that the Guru Granth Sahib is "their" text, which Sindhi Hindus disrespect by placing images of Rama, Durga, and Krishna or particular gurus alongside it. A simplistic assertion of labels within academic work has reinforced the conception of the Guru Granth Sahib as exclusively Sikh.

Ignoring Theory

Within the academic study of religion over the past several decades, the understanding of the contested and constructed nature of various labels that scholars use has become more recognized. After analyzing the historically shifting use of the terms religion, religions, and religious in a frequently cited essay, Jonathan Z. Smith asserts, "'Religion' is not a native term; it is a term created by scholars for their intellectual purposes and therefore is theirs to define. It is a second-order, generic concept." Religion, thus, is not a natural or obvious object but a product of scholarly constructions (Smith 1998: 281). Therefore, declaring what is and is not "religion," as Brown does in the yoga case, is not an objective description. Even accepting another's declaration that something is "religion" and repeating it as fact, rather than interrogating the interests and assumptions behind the declaration, enters contested debates that have significant consequences. Several decades ago, Talal Asad similarly highlighted the connection between the dominant conceptions of religion, most notably Geertz's classic definition, and particular European and Protestant conceptions of Christianity (Asad 1993). These connections illustrated how the construction of the category religion reflected a range of interests of European cultures and attributes of European Christianity rather than reflecting a natural object that Europeans merely described.

Other scholars, such as Daniel Dubuisson, carry this point further, arguing that the term "religion" reflects the interests and assumptions

---

its center. One person, who identified as Sikh, entered the court case arguing that the site, as it contains the Guru Granth Sahib, is a gurdwara and should be placed under the management of Sikhs, such as himself (*Dawn* 2005).

of Europeans and Americans so much that it is not useful in analyzing the world more broadly and should be replaced, in Dubuisson's construction, with "cosmographic formations" (2003). Similarly, Timothy Fitzgerald argues that some apply the category so broadly that it becomes analytically meaningless. Therefore, he, like Dubuisson, asserts that scholars should avoid it completely (Fitzgerald 2000).

These ideological concerns are apparent in the ways that groups employ the separation of the categories religion and politics. Labeling protest as an illegitimate application of religion, in some cases, or as political and not religious, in other cases, depends on the context, as those in power often employ whatever provides the easiest means to suppress dissent, depending on what type of activity is more legally protected in that particular context. Fitzgerald sees these various assertions as forms of "epistemic violence" (Fitzgerald 2010:192).

Beyond the deconstruction of the category "religion," other scholars have pointed out similar assumptions and problematic definitions related to particular religions. Tomoko Masuzawa has argued that the World Religions paradigm was invented as a part of the colonial endeavor, and that the understanding of what constituted different religions has shifted over time (2005). More specifically, Richard King has argued that the British constructed both Hinduism and Buddhism, in interaction with particular informants, according to their colonial conceptions and interests (1999).

Despite all of the pages focusing on the critique of these labels and their relation to the interests of the powerful and the producers of knowledge, these categories have persisted. Little has changed in the World Religions textbooks. Little has changed in the willingness of scholars to apply these terms in research. In fact, the tenacity of these labels is apparent even in the work of those deconstructing them. Richard King, in *Orientalism and Religion*, still employs the labels at times, referring, for example, to "Buddhist doctrine" and the "Westernization of Buddhism," implying that Buddhism has a specific trans-historical content that can be distinguished from other categories, points which he contests in his overall analysis (King 1999: 144, 152).

These theoretical reflections on the construction of categories and labels correlate with the recognition that the application of these labels is contested in societies, a contestation that develops out of a range of emphases and interpretations. The dominant language and conceptions of the field cloak both the constructed and contested nature of what people commonly label "religious." Rather than providing access to a trans-historical reality, academic descriptions enter into a competition between a variety of both current and historical negotiations of interests, often entering those competitions unintentionally to create "accidental favorites."

Avoid Applying the Labels Directly

Taking seriously these theoretical reflections, it becomes imperative to approach the application of these terms differently. Because of the connotations and assumptions that adhere to the terms "religion/religious," "sacred," and "transcendent" and the various labels marking individual religions, ethnic groups, and other markers of difference, scholars should avoid applying those terms directly, whether used as nouns or adjectives. When a scholar declares that yoga or caste is religious, Mormons are Christian, or the Guru Granth Sahib is the Sikh text, they enter the contested fields of what counts as belonging to that label, and what does not. Moreover, they reinforce the assumption that these labels reflect definitively bounded, stable categories rather than shifting and contested constructions. Avoiding the direct application of the labels helps avoid both entering specific competitions about the content and boundaries that these labels generate and reinforcing the dominant discourse about religion and religions that serve the interests of some over others. Instead of applying the labels directly, scholars should analyze the ways others apply those labels for particular ends, thus shifting the focus away from constructing a better description of religion or Hinduism.

Excising the labels is not only something to be done with care when communicating in verbal presentations or in writing but also must be done within thought processes and research. Just as it is not sufficient to cite these scholars and continue to describe things in the same fashion, it is not sufficient simply to replace a few words with a few other words, like the effort of some practitioners to replace "religious" with "spiritual." It calls for a disciplined effort to alter the questions asked and the assumptions made when scholars observe aspects of human existence. For example, avoiding the application of the category "religion" shifts the debate from what makes "religious" elements distinct or exceptional to the different ways groups identify particular elements as having a special status, either protected and authentic or problematic and questionable. Similarly, resisting the labels of individual religions can shift the questions from delineating syncretism and the original form of each religion, which remain in a state of change or development, to analyzing the interests that encourage people to bring varied activities together and to label some things original and other elements syncretic and/or out of bounds. So, avoiding the application of the labels facilitates a focus on different questions concerning processes of identification. This effort provides a freedom to see the world differently, recognize other connections, and construct different classifications, yet the dominant discourse and its related labels are not something easily resisted, as the structures in which scholars function create an almost automatic reliance on many of these labels, which requires effort to avoid.

So, how can scholars communicate without directly applying labels, since language relies on arbitrary signs to transmit knowledge? This shift in language at times requires lengthier descriptions that avoid the more problematic and highly contested general terms. Generic categories like "Hindu deities" should be replaced with specific examples, e.g., "images of deities such as Radha-Krishna, Lakshmi and Vishnu." Such a shift reduces the broader contestations surrounding the more generic label, as labels such as Hindu or Sikh that various communities use for themselves have significant potential to marginalize or legitimize normative constructions, whereas the more specific names of deities, while sometimes also contested, do not carry the same broad implications. Such specificity also enhances the description by providing additional information. In other contexts, simply avoiding a label completely provides a description of a group while removing one layer of preconceptions that come with the broader label. For example, the label Orthodox Jew, for example, reinforces a normative vision of practice and marginalizes the non-orthodox, which a description of people following their under-standing of appropriate practice in dress and food avoids.

Of course, communities apply the labels to themselves. This prohibition against using labels applies exclusively to the scholar's act of categorization. The analysis of the discursive strategies and contestations that I advocate depends on the acknowledgment of how others apply these labels that the scholars avoid applying themselves. Referencing the common association of particular practices with Orthodox Judaism, for example, is useful if the reference acknowledges whose construction of boundaries the labeling reflects. Questioning, in both writing and research, why communities apply (or reject) identity labels for themselves, for others, and for specific activities and objects should be central in the analysis. Therefore, it is imperative to repeat these labels, but only if acknowledging whose constructions are being repeated. Doing so highlights the political nature of such categorizations and denaturalizes the broader labels that have often served the interests of some groups to marginalize their opponents. In other words, avoiding a direct application of labels helps scholars avoid creating accidental favorites and opens research to another level of analysis.

Analysis of Labels

The recognition of the constructed and contested nature of these terms, which necessitates the refusal to apply particular labels, calls for a different analysis. Rather than developing a better description of what people do or analyzing the content of a social formation as a trans-historical object, scholars need to analyze how people employ these terms, the discourses surrounding these terms, and the interests that applications of those terms serve. In other words, the focus shifts to an analysis of the categorizations that people employ, which seems especially important in discussing contemporary society. Categories such as "religion," "tradition," "heritage," and "culture" often serve to legitimize a practice or social formation in a particular context.

In this I differ from some of the characterizations of critical theory. For example, Timothy Fitzgerald and Daniel Dubuisson, among others, advocate avoiding the term "religion" because it has little analytical value as a category (Dubuisson 2003; Fitzgerald 2000). While I appreciate their arguments, their prescription, generally, fails to account adequately for the continued use of the terms, even within communities where the presence of the term "religion" represents a relatively recent colonial intervention. The term is a significant social element that various individuals and groups employ in relation to particular discourses to promote a range of interests and receive particular institutional benefits. The analysis of those interests and the varied applications of the term are important for the analysis of society more generally. Scholars should use the label "religion," not to categorize the world, but to talk about how others use the term to categorize the world. Similarly, labels such as Hinduism and Buddhism, however they came about, have been adopted by many groups to label themselves and their practices. It is impossible to take these terms back and destroy them. However, scholars can avoid adding their application of the term to the cacophony and, instead, analyze the different ways these communities apply these terms for various interests.

The plaintiffs in the court case concerning the yoga program describe the program as "religious" because that label serves to disallow the activity in this legal context. In other circumstances, the label functions differently. A successful claim that a practice is a part of one's religion can produce particular results in the United States in relation to tax benefits and some exemptions from particular regulations (e.g., dress code, non-discrimination hiring practices, etc.).

Labeling conflicts, such as the Israeli-Palestinian conflict and the question of Jerusalem, as religious has several potential effects. It emphasizes a sacred quality or divine designation for the material resources, thus justifying extreme sacrifices to control and protect them. An emphasis on irreconcilable differences based on religious identification also suggests an unresolvable conflict, at least until the enemy is completely vanquished. Thus, those who profit from ongoing conflict (politically, financially, ideologically) have an incentive to put the conflict in the language of religion or other differences that some presume to be trans-historical.

Beyond external policies and regulations, labels also serve to distinguish one group from another and to discipline those who claim a label, as some distinguish "true" Muslims, "real" Americans, "committed" socialists, or, as has become popular recently, "Republican in name only," thus demonstrating what people must do to have their self-identification accepted as valid. Avoiding the application of such labels not only avoids implicitly reinforcing particular positions but also enables the analysis of the interests that those labels may serve.

Therefore, acknowledging who categorizes the particular social formation is central to facilitate consideration of the interests that such categorizations promote and the ways others might categorize the same elements differently. Recognizing the complexity of processes of identification, rather than assuming that accepting a particular label presumes particular practices or conceptions, facilitates the analysis of the powers and interests informing those identifications. The image established, then, is a complicated one that undermines the simplistic assertions of the division of human activities between religion and the secular and the division of communities into different ethnicities, nationalities, and religions.

This analysis of the discourses supporting these categories does not necessarily mean that participants are consciously identifying a practice with a particular category to gain a direct benefit. Many people employ a general sense of the categories, a conventional wisdom, without necessarily reflecting on the access to resources or prestige that may arise from these identifications. However, restating conventional wisdom reinforces the hegemony of particular definitions that are, in a broader view, contested and serves the interests of some more than even those employing the terms, at times.

Ideally, altering academic language improves research, serving to uncover these discursive histories and their social influences instead of reinforcing those histories and influences. Scholars should also be willing, though, to turn that critical gaze towards the analysis of the interests within scholarly production. Academic research frequently reflects traditional categorizations and the power relations that those categorizations serve. At times, the analysis also becomes directly self-serving. An emphasis on the importance of religion within communities who have experienced migration often comes from scholars who happen to specialize in religious studies. This point is not to demonstrate malfeasance in that scholarship but that the categories that relate to a scholar's specialization are what the scholar observes most closely, and the assertions of others who also emphasize a scholar's specialization are more quickly accepted than those of scholars who implicitly question the significance of another scholar's specialization.

A Different Goal, A Different Approach

In conjunction with the various critiques and analyses of scholarship outlined throughout this volume, analyzing the application of these labels – what they enable, for whom, for what interests, and so on – rather than applying them directly to each scholar's own chosen data, can realign much of what occurs in religious studies. The shifts in goal and approach towards identification outlined in this volume reflect how the critical study of religions pushes scholars to do more than avoid particular terms or replace one term with a more specific phrase. If "religion" is a European construct applied to other societies, and if "religion" has a diverse and shifting history of meanings, then continuing to operate as if "religion" referred to something existing outside of human formations is untenable. Similarly, if scholars consider the constructed nature of categories like "Hinduism," "Buddhism," or "Christianity," then those terms do not correspond to some trans-historical reality. While the constructed nature of specific religions is debated, the ways these labels are applied has not been static. Selecting one application of the label as correct, whether explicitly or implicitly, is not something easily defended, even if you question the assertion that these labels are social constructions. Similarly, the selection of approach and goal, as outlined throughout this volume, reflects the interests of particular scholars, including the authors included in this volume. Acknowledging that and avoiding the assumption that applying these labels is simply an act of description of something that exists outside the researcher is a significant step forward.

The question arises, then, what is the role of scholars of religion? Too often, academics act as if they are called on to present better descriptions of the ideal form, the reality, of this category called "religion" or of a collection of elements commonly defined as a specific religion. Describing what is the true content, scholars implicitly correct those who identify as Hindu, for example, as to what their religion is. Such an approach reflects paternalistic and neo-colonialist assumptions. Moreover, considering the interpretability of texts and notions of tradition, what becomes the standard by which to judge scholarly descriptions and the assertions of others? Scholars are not disinterested observers who provide an objective analysis; they are like the British colonizers in India who could not escape their interests and cultural assumptions. In advocating for approaches that acknowledge the diverse interests informing acts of identification, the scholars in this volume too are not disinterested descriptivists but have selected approaches that highlight dynamics of power that are of interest to us.

Instead of striving for a better description of a trans-historical object labeled religion, scholars should strive to analyze critically the various representations – from politicians to community leaders, laypeople, and the media – to see how different groups employ these various labels and the assumptions and interests that might inform their application of the labels. In this, scholars do not treat those applying the labels as ignorant children who do not understand their own traditions as clearly as scholars do, as some colonizers referred to the people of India, but they treat others as capable agents who have the power to construct their own representations according to a variety of interests.

This approach presents a significant change that challenges many preconceived notions. Rather than picking favorites accidentally, in pedagogy, public presentations, and writing, the approach that I am advocating, like the approaches that various contributors to this volume present, has another significant benefit. Analyzing particular contestations of power and access to resources and social capital within the workings of the identifications that make contemporary society possible provides an avenue for those engaged in the academic study of religion to address a range of contemporary issues in society, not as objective descriptivists but as participants in those processes of identification and subsequent contestations. Focusing on how groups employ terms that inform a significant aspect of contemporary public discourse, and in that process avoiding the application of particular labels that our analyses emphasize, opens up for scholars additional questions that help us analyze a range of discourses in a more complex fashion that can generate a renewed relevance of religious studies in today's world.

References

Asad, Talal. 1993. *Genealogies of Religion: Discipline and Reasons of Power in Christianity and Islam*. Baltimore, MD: Johns Hopkins University Press.

Bayly, Susan. 1999. *Caste, Society, and Politics in India from the Eighteenth Century to the Modern Age*. Cambridge, UK: Cambridge University Press. http://dx.doi.org/10.1017/CHOL9780521264341.

Brown, Candy Gunter. 2013. "Declaration of Candy Gunther Brown."*Motion For The Issuance Of An Alternative Writ Of Mandamus; Memorandum Of Points And Authorities; Declarations of Jennifer Sedlock, Candy Gunther Brown, Ph.D., and Dean R. Broyles, Esq.* http://www.nclplaw.org/wp-content/uploads/2011/12/DECLARATION-OF-CANDY-BROWN-FINAL.pdf, accessed February 23, 2013.

Cronin, Vincent. 1959. *Pearl to India: The Life of Robert de Nobili*. New York, NY: E.P. Dutton.

Dawn. 2005. "Goods Taken Away From Disputed Temple" (June 29). http://www.dawn.com/2005/06/29/local14.htm, accessed July 13, 2007.

Dubuisson, Daniel. 2003. *The Western Construction of Religion: Myths, Knowledge, and Ideology*. Trans. William Sayers. Baltimore, MD: Johns Hopkins University Press.

Dumont, Louis. 1980. *Homo Hierarchicus: The Caste System and Its Implications*. Complete Revised English Edition. Trans. Mark Sainsbury, Louis Dumont, and Basia Gulati. Chicago, IL; London, UK: University of Chicago Press.

Fisher, Mary Pat. 2014. *Living Religions*. 9th ed. Upper Saddle River, NJ: Pearson.

Fitzgerald, Timothy. 2000. *The Ideology of Religious Studies*. New York, NY; Oxford, UK: Oxford University Press.

Fitzgerald, Timothy. 2010. "The Deployment of "Religion" and Other Categories as an Act of Epistemic Violence." *Religious of South Asia* 4(2): 189–98.

Forrester, Duncan B. 1980. *Caste and Christianity: Attitudes and Policies on Caste of Anglo-Saxon Protestant Missions in India.* Atlantic Highlands, NJ: Humanities Press.

Global Sikh News. 2010. "Beadbi of 2500 Saroops of Guru Granth Sahib Ji" (August 12, 2010). http://www.sikhsangat.com/index.php?/topic/56724-beadbi-of-2500-saroop-of-guru-granth-sahib-ji/, accessed September 7, 2010.

Jabbar, Naheem. 2011. "B.R. Ambedkar's Challenge to the Puranic Past." *Postcolonial Studies* 14(1): 23–43. http://dx.doi.org/10.1080/13688790.2011.542116.

Khalsa Press. 2010. "Controversy Erupts at Chellaram's Sindhi Mandar." Panthic.org (March 25, 2010). http://www.panthic.org/articles/5234, accessed March 29, 2010.

King, Richard. 1999. *Orientalism and Religion: Postcolonial Theory, India and "The Mystic East."* New York, NY: Routledge.

Masuzawa, Tomoko. 2005. *The Invention of World Religions, or, How European Universalism Was Preserved in the Language of Pluralism.* Chicago, IL: University of Chicago Press. http://dx.doi.org/10.7208/chicago/9780226922621.001.0001.

Oberoi, Harjot. 1997. *The Construction of Religious Boundaries: Culture, Identity and Diversity in the Sikh Tradition.* Oxford, UK; New York, NY: Oxford University Press, 1994. Reprint Delhi, India: Oxford India Paperbacks.

Ramey, Steven. 2008. *Hindu Sufi or Sikh: Contested Practices and Identifications of Sindhi Hindus in India and Beyond.* New York, NY: Palgrave. http://dx.doi.org/10.1057/9780230616226.

Smith, Jonathan Z. 1998. "Religion, Religions, Religious." In Mark C. Taylor, ed., *Critical Terms for Religious Studies*, 269–84. Chicago, IL; London, UK: University of Chicago Press.

Steven W. Ramey is Associate Professor in the Department of Religious Studies and Director of Asian Studies at the University of Alabama. He has focused his research on the contested nature of identifications in contemporary India and elsewhere.

Index

240   *Claiming Identity*

culturalism, 5, 8, 10
culture, 2–11, 15, 16, 48–50, 68, 88,
   89, 106, 107, 218
Culture on the Edge collaborative,
   8–13, 17, 170, 223
culture studies, 175
culture wars, contemporary, 16, 224

death, 46, 47, 55, 56, 62, 84, 138,
   153
debates, 89, 92, 164, 165, 208, 226
Deen, Paula, 87–95
difference, irreducibility of, 2, 4, 11
discursive structures, academic,
   165–7
domains, 7, 9, 10, 12, 13, 16, 22, 175,
   176
Drake, H.A., 201, 202
Dubuisson, Daniel, 10, 34, 202–17,
   229, 232–3
      cosmographic formation, 199,
         209, 210, 212, 213, 217, 229
      *Western Construction of
         Religion*, 202, 213, 219

Eliade, Mircea, 50, 52–71, 76–85,
   106, 107, 115, 116, 131, 144, 145,
   158–60
      Comparative Religion, 54
      early years and Romanian
         fascism, 54, 57, 60, 61, 63,
         68, 75
      Encyclopedia of Religion, 81
      terror of history, 64–9, 84
      trip to India, 56–61
      University of Chicago, 54, 55,
         57, 62, 69, 71, 81
      young generation and, 68–9, 80
emotions, 47, 48, 50, 54, 73
erotic, 104, 117, 127, 159
estrangement (category of), 139, 142,
   156, 175, 182, 183
Europe, 33, 36, 54, 59, 61
experience (category of), 6, 7, 20–6,
   35–9, 52, 89, 90, 114–16, 193, 215,
   217

faith, 37, 68, 73, 99, 102, 103, 107,
   140, 174, 205, 215
Fausto-Sterling, Anne, 120–1
First Amendment (US Constitution),
   174, 179–81
Fitzgerald, Tim, 208, 229, 232–3

gays, 30, 90, 98, 118–20, *see also*
   homosexuality
gender, 9, 15, 18, 21, 26, 27, 51, 96,
   111, 210
Gettysburg, Pennsylvania, 46–51,
   see also Civil War
gift, 94, 98, 113, 115, 117
God, 5, 55, 74, 105, 121, 122, 148,
   150, 207, 210, 211, 219
Godlove, Terry, 136, 147
Grafton, Anthony, 200, 202, 208,
   218–19
Greece, 47, 97, 191, 193–6, 198
Guru Granth Sahib, 227–8, 230

Hindu, 2, 4, 5, 8–10, 16, 163–5, 223,
   224, 231, 236
      Sindhi Hindus, 227–8
Hinduism, 2, 3, 60, 128, 129, 142,
   162, 226, 229, 230, 233, 235
historic mission, 68–70, *see also*
   messianic movements
history, 5–6, 39, 43, 47, 49–50, 79,
   82, 85, 108, 175, 185–8, 195–6,
   203, 216, 234
      terror of history, 64–9, 84
history of religions, 53, 57, 62, 78, 81,
   99, 106, 170
homosexuality, 118–21
      in ancient Greece, 118–21
human experience, 102, 103, 107,
   112, 224

identification, 8–20, 162–4, 166–7,
   199, 223, 226, 234–6, *see also*
   identity
      authoritative, 164, 167
      operational acts of, 7, 9, 11,
         17, 20